Celebrity Tantrums!

THE OFFICIAL DIRT

Celebrity Tantrums!

THE OFFICIAL DIRT

Lisa Brandt

ECW PRESS

Published by ECW PRESS
2120 Queen Street East, Suite 200, Toronto, Ontario, Canada M4E 1E2

NATIONAL LIBRARY OF CANADA CATALOGUING IN PUBLICATION DATA

Brandt, Lisa
Celebrity tantrums: the official dirt / Lisa Brandt.
ISBN 1-55022-566-9
1. Celebrities—Anecdotes. 2. Temper tantrums—Anecdotes. I. Title.
CT105.B72 2003   920.02   C2002-905427-3

Acquisition editor: Emma McKay
Copy editor: Jodi Lewchuk
Design & typesetting: Guylaine Régimbald—Solo Design
Production: Emma McKay
Printing: Transcontinental
Cover illustrations: Aislin

This book is set in RedFive and Profile

The publication of *Celebrity Tantrums: The Official Dirt* has been generously supported by the Canada Council, by the Government of Ontario through the Ontario Media Development Corporation's Ontario Book Initiative, by the Ontario Arts Council, and by the Government of Canada through the Book Publishing Industry Development Program.
Canadä

DISTRIBUTION

CANADA: Jaguar Book Group, 100 Armstrong Avenue, Georgetown, Ontario L7G 5S4

UNITED STATES: Independent Publishers Group, 814 North Franklin Street, Chicago, Illinois 60610

EUROPE: Turnaround Publisher Services, Unit 3, Olympia Trading Estate, Coburg Road, Wood Green, London N2Z 6T2

AUSTRALIA AND NEW ZEALAND: Wakefield Press, 1 The Parade West (Box 2266), Kent Town, South Australia 5071

PRINTED AND BOUND IN CANADA

ECW PRESS

For **WRAY**, my first editor

CONTENTS

My thanks go to the following wonderful people for their support and enthusiasm over this project.

The most creative person I know, my husband, Wray Ellis.

Everyone at ECW Press, especially Robert Lecker, Emma McKay, Jodi Lewchuk, Lisa Jorgensen, James Bassil, and Aislin, for his terrific cover illustrations.

My friends and colleagues at Rogers Radio Toronto, especially Erin Davis, Karen Parsons, Paul Cook, Stephanie Smyth, John Hinnen, and Thomas D'Monte. Also, my cheerleaders Helen, Jack, Kevin, Lisa Joyce, Elsie, Ellis, and Tabitha. And the editors who gave me my first professional breaks: Cheryl Homan and Jill Davis.

My inspirations in the world of entertainment: Brian Linehan, Denise Donlon, Liz Smith, Mary Hart, and Dave Barry.

And my gratitude to the stars themselves for being unpredictable, and above all, human.

INTRODUCTION

It has been said that fame doesn't change a person, it just makes them *more* so. In other words, the media's fierce stare has a way of distilling a complex personality down to its core elements. If, pre-fame, an individual is paranoid, smart, impatient, angry, abusive, angelic, or insane, the intrusive lens of celebrity worship—according to the theory—only intensifies that quality. In the glare of stardom, the former playground bully becomes a tyrant on the film set; the once impossibly self-centered teenager becomes a demanding diva on the concert stage.

In twenty years of conducting celebrity interviews I have learned that we like our icons served to us in these small, neat, easily digested packages. Consider how often we whittle the personality of an actor or musician down to just one word or phrase: "She's a flake," or "He loves 'em and leaves 'em." And more often than not, those labels are earned in the moments when a celebrity is caught behaving badly. It is those defining moments, whether accidental or predictable, that are chronicled on these pages.

Allow me to tell you what this book is not. It is not a collection of biographies. I am well aware that Frank Sinatra was a generous softie who had a weakness for children's charities; that Hugh Grant, in person, is a lovable, self-deprecating cutup; and that Woody Allen is an accomplished musician. Do not expect complete portraits of the stars here. Instead, I offer you snapshots from their lives. Many of the celebrities profiled in this volume are good and decent souls who briefly lost their cool. Some are victims of bad advice. Others are truly mean and nasty. It's for you to decide who's who.

As for the question of who did and did not qualify for inclusion in this "official guide," I offer you my three top criteria in the selection process.

First, the person must have already been a celebrity and not gained their fame because of their bad act. Monica Lewinsky, for example, is included only in the Bill Clinton story because she is crucial to the facts. She was an unknown who came to fame solely because of the 1998 White House scandal, and therefore did not merit a separate entry of her own. However, if a legitimate star behaved badly enough to be included in this collection, their previous, pre-fame bad acts were also fair game. I've watched enough legal dramas to know how a person's priors can come into evidence. (Thank you, David E. Kelley.)

The bad behavior must also have been substantiated in some recognized form by journalistic standards; it either was published in a reputable paper or stood as public record. Nothing unconfirmed, whispered to me, or revealed thirdhand made the grade, although plenty of incidents were offered, believe me. The episodes themselves were subjected to a bit of scrutiny as well. Lots of celebrities have waved guns and a few have shot their televisions, but only one name comes to mind—Elvis, of course—when you think of bullet-riddled TVs. I had to use a wee bit of discrimination in choosing the sorriest of a sorry lot.

Finally, the celebrity's name had to be virtually instantly recognizable, or at least identifiable within the context of his or her work. Robert Iler may not be a household name, but when you learn that he plays the son on *The Sopranos*, his face immediately springs to mind. Anyone too obscure or whose name was associated with a very narrow field of notoriety didn't rate. Represented here are the top celebrity tantrum-throwers and there was no room for a fringe element. If your favorite star didn't make it past my selection process, well, they're just not trying hard enough.

Having separated the wheat from the chaff, what you are about to read is the best of the best—or rather, the best of the worst. So come along for the ride and experience the most memorable days in the lives of your favorite celebrities, the days they're hoping against hope the world will forget.

TIM ALLEN

Turning the spotlight on his own hardships and spinning them into comic fodder is de rigueur for *Home Improvement* star Tim Allen.

It started in his childhood when he spent his time constantly defending his surname, Dick, against the many ways cruel classmates found to distort and hyphenate it. The situation was torturous enough that he eventually decided to drop "Dick" and make a stage name from his first and middle names —but he still managed to poke fun at his plight. It would prove good practice for the more serious issues he'd have to grin and bear later.

Unlike many of his fellow celebrities, Allen's descent into the realm of drugs didn't accompany the excesses of fame and fortune. His greatest transgression came early and nearly prevented him from achieving the tremendous success he now enjoys.

It was Allen's 1978 prison sentence for attempting to deal drugs to an undercover cop that actually launched his career in stand-up comedy. He served two and a half years of what could have been a life sentence had he not turned state's evidence. In his 1994 autobiography *Don't Stand Too Close to a Naked Man*, the former "Tool Time" host wrote that his sense of humor about jail began in the holding cell. Being funny was how he survived in prison's general population, a frightening environment where everyone is either desperately pleading innocence or aggressively staking territory.

Allen kept his Ferrari mostly on the straight and narrow for several years after serving his time. He had a thriving comedy career that propelled him into becoming—at one point—the highest paid sitcom actor in history. The rest of his energy was consumed by family concerns (splits and reconciliations with wife Laura; they're now legally separated) and attempts at movie star status. He had scored a silver screen hit with 1994's *The Santa Claus*. But his run came to a halt with a May 1997 arrest for drunk driving near his home in a Detroit, Michigan, suburb. Police in Bloomfield County claimed they clocked the actor traveling 70 mph in a 40 mph zone in addition to finding him unsteady on his feet and smelling of liquor. Tests showed his blood alcohol level was .15, well above the .10 limit. A humiliated Allen later claimed he learned from the experience—and the court-ordered visit to rehab—but it's amazing he needed any enlightenment at all. Young Tim Allen Dick lost his own father to a drunk driver more than thirty years earlier. ✪

WOODY **ALLEN**

The heart wants what the heart wants.

That's the classic lame excuse often offered in response to criticism for acting on inappropriate feelings when all rules of decency say *Stop!* Like, for instance, when you become physically involved with your longtime girlfriend's daughter. And this after said daughter has been in your life long enough to consider you a father figure.

Woody Allen shunned the limelight for years after his affair with Soon-Yi Previn, daughter of his ex-partner Mia Farrow, was revealed. But lately, the wizened little moviemaker has been forced to emerge from his burrow even as his truest fans have begun to realize that this emperor of New York independent films isn't wearing any clothes. And his nakedness is not a pretty sight.

The sometimes-brilliant mind behind *Annie Hall* used to refuse to take part in the celebrity dog and pony shows. His obvious absences at awards ceremonies and other movie star gatherings didn't hurt the bottom line of his modestly successful movies. Rather, they added to his mystique, making the wee saxophone-playing actor and director seem above it all. But all that has changed and Allen has decided to play the game. If he used to lay low because of "The Scandal," he's now lighting up like a neon sign for business reasons: considering that even his most staunch supporters, the faithful who flocked to his films despite his being frontpage news, have abandoned him, he needs to boost ticket sales. Critics accuse him of repeating himself creatively and continuing to cast himself opposite beautiful starlets beyond reason. His films, once called little gems, are now just little seen. So Allen is risking the wrath of those who call him a pervert to drum up dollars from the moviegoing public.

ALLEN SHUNNED THE LIMELIGHT FOR YEARS AFTER HIS AFFAIR WITH SOON-YI

The writer, producer, director, star (and probably caterer!) behind dozens of so-called small films fell out of favor with previously devoted fans and a large segment of the movie industry when his affair with Soon-Yi Previn first came to light. Soon-Yi was a Korean orphan, adopted by Mia Farrow and her former boyfriend, conductor André Previn. During Allen's twelve-year love affair with Farrow, he became a virtual father to Soon-Yi, being thirty years her senior and Farrow's mate. As Farrow tells it, it wasn't until she accidentally discovered naked photos of then twenty-two-year-old Soon-Yi in Woody's apartment that she learned her lover was also loving her daughter. Hell hath no fury, as the saying goes, and fueled by pain and disgrace, Farrow launched a bitter attack in the media and the courts, which stretched to include allegations that Allen had abused the couple's jointly adopted daughter, Dylan. He was also stripped of almost all contact with their biological son, Satchel. Woody staunchly defended himself in court and in the press, but Soon-Yi's presence served as a constant reminder of his transgression. The unusual couple married in Venice, Italy, in 1997 and are now the proud parents of two adopted daughters. (Insert tasteless jokes here.) Allen continues to maintain that he did nothing wrong with any of his children, or mates ... or children-mates.

ALLEN CONTINUES TO MAINTAIN THAT HE DID NOTHING WRONG WITH ANY OF HIS CHILDREN, OR MATES ... OR CHILDREN-MATES

In 2002, "no show" Allen made his first trip down the red carpet at the Oscars, despite having won several statues in absentia over the years. He basked in a standing ovation at the ceremony as the star-studded crowd was overcome by patriotism and emotion. Allen's presence as a symbol of New York City moviemaking was orchestrated as part of a show of solidarity against the perpetrators of the September 11 terrorist attacks. He also braved the heat at Cannes, allowing his grinning self to be photographed among mainstream stars like Sharon Stone and Melanie Griffith. His wife was safely tucked away as he waved to the puzzled crowds and gave witty interviews about his latest projects. Soon-Yi's is a face seen only in full panic mode, whenever she is caught by surprise by a tabloid photog's lens.

In mid-2002, the *New York Post* reported that Allen was musing about a permanent move to Europe, à la fellow cradle-robbing directors Charlie Chaplin and Roman Polanski. It seems his bride prefers life in Paris to the mean streets of New York. But it may be money that is making Woody opt for a change of venue and a cheaper lifestyle.

It was not until he tried to buy a house, Allen claimed, that he realized his finances were in disarray. The director blamed his longtime production partner Jean Doumanean for the fiscal mess and sued her, claiming she skimmed $12 million in profits from many of the movies they worked on together, including *Mighty Aphrodite*, *Deconstructing Harry*, and *Everyone Says I Love You*. After days of tearful testimony from the former friends, the lawsuit was settled under confidential terms. The most surprising aspect of the case? That there was $12 million available to be skimmed from the profits of Allen's films! ✪

ADAM ANT

"Goody Two-Shoes" was the title of Adam Ant's biggest hit, but it wasn't an autobiographical number. Ant became somewhat of a pop idol in the early 1980s thanks to that bouncy song and others, including "Stand and Deliver" and "Friend or Foe." He fashioned a unique look that was part David Bowie, part KISS. Dressed as a pirate or an American Indian, he would appear on album covers and on stage with a white stripe painted across his face. Some pub-goers from Kentish Town, North London, think that stripe should be painted on Ant's back due to his skunk-like behavior in January 2002.

The then forty-seven-year-old, whose real name is Stuart Leslie Goddard, is alleged to have pulled out a pistol — which may have been a fake—and waved it menacingly at fellow patrons at the Prince of Wales Pub. Witnesses say Ant was shouting obscenities at a man he believed had made threats against his four-year-old daughter. He was immediately committed to a mental hospital for evaluation. In a telephone interview from the psych ward, Ant told Britain's *Sun* newspaper, "I'm not mad. The whole thing's a conspiracy and they're just out to get me."

> **"I'M NOT MAD. THE WHOLE THING'S A CONSPIRACY AND THEY'RE JUST OUT TO GET ME"**

The self-admitted sufferer of manic depression faced charges of criminal damage, assault, and possession of a firearm, and was ordered to stay at least 100 meters from the pub. He recently pleaded guilty to the charge of affray, with sentencing pending. The brouhaha prompted Ant to pull his band out of a 1980s revival concert tour of the UK, where he was headlining alongside other pop stars of the era, including Howard Jones and Belinda Carlisle of the Go-Gos. Sadly, the tour might have been the tonic Ant needed to stop the downward slide he's reported to be on, thanks in part to his sagging career. A 1995 comeback CD went mostly unnoticed, making his most recent chart hits twenty years old. ✪

MARC **ANTHONY**

This Latin heartthrob was pushed over the edge in July 2000. A combination of stress on the home front and pressure on the job shattered his calm and classy demeanor—if only for a moment—and prompted a regrettable altercation.

The incident came just weeks after Anthony wed former Miss Universe Dayanara Torres. Fresh from his first and monstrous English-language hit "I Need to Know," Anthony was in high demand in both the Spanish- and English-speaking worlds. At an airport press conference in San Juan, Puerto Rico, local talk show host Leo Fernandez III quizzed the salsa singer about rumors that his new bride was already pregnant. In his lawsuit, Fernandez alleged Anthony roughed him up instead of simply refusing to answer. It later came to light that Torres was indeed expecting the couple's first child but was also suffering from complications, forcing

IN HIS LAWSUIT, FERNANDEZ ALLEGED ANTHONY ROUGHED HIM UP INSTEAD OF SIMPLY REFUSING TO ANSWER

Anthony to cancel several appearances to be by her side. (Christian Anthony Muniz—the child has been given his pop star father's real surname—was born during a trouble-free birth on February 5, 2001. The tot's parents separated a year and a half into their marriage but reconciled after five months. In December 2002 they renewed their vows in Puerto Rico's San Juan Cathedral.) The lawsuit was settled in rare form, with a mea culpa from the proud new papa. Anthony apologized to Fernandez in open court in exchange for the reporter agreeing to drop the lawsuit. Said Anthony's lawyer, "It was an incident that never should have happened." ✪

ALEC BALDWIN

The eldest of the Massapequa, New York, band of Baldwin brothers-actors sports a wicked combination of devastating good looks and an explosive temper. That spicy recipe likely cooked up the demise one of the most enduring modern love stories in Hollywood: Baldwin's apparent wedded bliss with actress Kim Basinger. His loose cannon was even sometimes fired on the public, leading a reporter from the *New York Post* to dub Baldwin "The Bloviator," a nickname quickly adopted by tabloids everywhere.

As the news of Baldwin and Basinger's seven-year marriage hitting the skids broke in December 2000, the Academy Award–winning actress refused at first to launch a he said, she said media war despite being on the receiving end of calls from nearly every reporter and gossip columnist in the free world.

> **BALDWIN WENT "BALLISTIC" WHEN LINSON ASKED HIM TO SHAVE**

Her father, however, had no qualms about going public in a January 2001 edition of *People* magazine, claiming the sole reason for the split was Baldwin's uncontrollable anger. "This has happened publicly," said Don Basinger. Indeed, one tabloid ran a photo of the couple engaged in a screaming match outside a Los Angeles restaurant just months before Kim filed divorce papers. Her father explained, "When it started happening in front of [their daughter] Ireland, Kim said, 'I'm not going to put up with that.'"

The public record confirms his father-in-law's accusation. Baldwin, star of several films, including *The Hunt for Red October*, *Pearl Harbor*, and *Ghosts of Mississippi*, flew off the handle when a videographer ambushed Kim and the newly born Ireland as they came home from the hospital to their Woodland Hills mansion in March 1996. Baldwin admittedly kicked and punched the shutterbug, later claiming it had been in self-defense. The resulting court case wrapped nearly two years later and resulted in Baldwin paying a small fine for negligence. The photographer, also found partly to blame for the fracas, was on the receiving end of a similar verdict.

Don Basinger further claimed that Baldwin enrolled in an anger management course to learn to control his short fuse, but quit after a couple of classes. Too bad; if he had finished, the life of an innocent piece of technology may have been spared. Early in 2002, witnesses told New York media they saw Baldwin strolling a city street, engaged in a heated cell phone discussion. The conversation came to an abrupt end when the actor smashed the phone to bits against a brick wall. One wonders who was on the receiving end of such a violent hang-up.

Not surprisingly, the Baldwin-Basinger split turned ugly after having gotten off to a civil start. Kim finally broke her silence in April 2002 and gave an exclusive interview to the *National Enquirer* in which she accused her estranged husband of physical abuse during their marriage. An enraged Billy Baldwin lashed out a week later in defense of his big brother, calling Basinger a "nut case" and "a black widow." He claimed her mood swings were out of control and the real reason behind the breakup. Billy said it was time the Baldwins jumped down from the high road and defended their brother, who was being drawn and quartered in the press, even if it annoyed or embarrassed him. (Alec wasn't rushing to defend himself.)

As an interview subject, Alec Baldwin is alternately charming and aloof. He often refuses to meet with small groups of journalists while promoting one of his movies, preferring instead to attend press conferences. You know, safety in numbers and all.

The broody star reportedly turned up for work on the set of 1997's *The Edge* bloated by twenty extra pounds and hidden under several weeks' worth of beard, much to the dismay of director Lee Tamahori and producer Art Linson. Studio executives and others had apparently tried to talk the duo out of hiring Baldwin, claiming he wasn't able to carry a picture and was too much trouble for his $5 million salary. Although the film's story centers on two men lost in the wilderness, Baldwin was supposed to start out as a hunky leading man, a slick fashion photographer, who evolves into a sort of Grizzly Adams as the story progresses. Instead, he looked older than Anthony Hopkins, his elder costar. The *New York Post* reported Baldwin went "ballistic" when Linson asked him to shave. Linson later learned why Baldwin was so attached to his facial forestry: he felt it camouflaged a double chin.

SHE ACCUSED HER ESTRANGED HUSBAND OF PHYSICAL ABUSE DURING THEIR MARRIAGE

It appears the man *Entertainment Weekly* named one of the 25 Greatest Actors of the 1990s is currently attempting to channel his energy into activism, using his influence in support of causes ranging from politics to pets. A staunch advocate of former President Bill Clinton and supporter of Hillary Clinton's bid for a seat in the Senate, the actor is also a champion of animal rights and the environment. His involvement with those endeavors has cured the quick-tempered Baldwin of any ambition to run for public office himself. It is, after all, a place where anger erupts more often than even he could imagine. "Things are so nasty now in Washington," he said, "it's unspeakable to me." ✪

HALLE BERRY

This beautiful actress and model knows we find it very hard to believe she doesn't remember the February 2000 hit-and-run crash she was involved in—and fled—a stone's throw from her West Hollywood home. That's because she can hardly believe it herself.

Halle Berry, the first African-American woman ever to win a Best Actress Academy Award (in 2002 for *Monster's Ball*), claims to have no recollection of slamming her rented SUV into a Pontiac Sunbird on a rain-slicked road and leaving the woman she hit to be pried from the wrecked car with the jaws of life. Fortunately, Hetal Raythatha suffered only minor injuries: a broken wrist and an aching back. Berry's people initially claimed their client, who costarred with John Travolta in *Swordfish*, dashed off to seek medical treatment and informed hospital officials and police all about the mishap that left her with a gash in her flawless forehead big enough to require stitches. The actress denied intoxication, an angle of the ensuing investigation later dropped due to lack of evidence.

SHE EVENTUALLY SURRENDERED HERSELF TO THE LOS ANGELES COUNTY SHERIFF'S DEPARTMENT

Berry's initial silence regarding the accident spoke volumes, and the late-night talk shows feasted on her shapely carcass. She eventually surrendered herself to the Los Angeles County Sheriff's Department. That action resulted in one measly misdemeanor charge of leaving the scene of an accident, a tremendous reduction from felony hit-and-run, which prompted Raythatha's lawyer to cry preferential treatment. His client filed a civil lawsuit against the *Die Another Day* star, who later admitted the first few months following the crash were "a living hell." Wracked with guilt and unable to satisfy even herself with a valid explanation for dashing from the scene, she developed insomnia and stopped eating—a dangerous prospect for a diabetic, which she has been since 1989.

The famous face of Revlon cosmetics pleaded no contest to the minor infraction and took her lumps: two years on probation, $14,000 in fines, and 200 hours of community service. Had she fought the charge and lost, her next performance would likely have been booked in a prison for women, where she could have spent up to a year. The civil suit with Raythatha was settled out of court; the terms were not revealed.

Although not nearly as severe, widely covered, or the butt of as many jokes, Berry was involved in a similar incident three years earlier when the Range Rover she was piloting plowed into a Volkswagen. The VW's driver, Kevin Ackerman, also took legal action and received an undisclosed settlement to ease his pain and suffering. Hopefully hell-on-wheels Halle is now giving up her keys to husband Eric Benet or, better yet, a chauffeur.

ROBERT BLAKE

Based solely on the evidence of his résumé, Robert Blake should be a beloved star. Fame came into his life twice, professionally speaking. As a young child, he was a member of TV's adorable *The Little Rascals*. Then, in the 1970s, he starred as the tough, cockatoo-owning maverick NYPD Detective Baretta, in the show of the same name.

Blake's hot temper created chaos on the *Baretta* set. Producers loathed his constant minor complaints; name it and Blake thought he could do it better. The diminutive actor was extremely difficult to work with, but his show was a hit and that was enough to motivate the crew into building a high threshold of tolerance for the irritating star.

Blake nearly went three for three as a TV star with the 1985 series *Hell Town*. Despite its good reception, the newly divorced celebrity bailed on the project when his personal life became too much to bear. His erratic real-life behavior and blatant anger over a childhood he felt was misspent in front of the camera lens severed the emotional attachment fans had to him. The self-imposed exile from show business that followed lasted nearly a decade. He returned to take critically acclaimed roles in films and on TV, but never quite reclaimed his blinking dot on entertainment radar screens. Now, of course, he's more of

THE DIMINUTIVE ACTOR WAS EXTREMELY DIFFICULT TO WORK WITH

a curiosity, as if he were living in a fourth grade science class's petri dish. Since Blake has become a murder suspect, the public has been rubbing its hands together in anticipation of peeking into the (hopefully) seedy side of his troubled life.

Blake's late second wife was no saint. Bonny Lee Bakely made finding and marrying famous people her life's work. A modestly attractive woman, she allegedly ran a mail-order business that involved suckering lonely older men into sending her money in exchange for nude photos and the promise of a rendezvous, neither of which would ever materialize. All the while, she sought to bed celebrities. And she succeeded, to the degree that a paternity test was required to prove her daughter Rose was fathered by Blake and not her other lover, Christian Brando. Bakely is reported to have considered the merits of marrying each man, and weighed Blake's temper favorably against Brando's murder conviction (*see* Marlon Brando).

> **MISERABLE BLAKE TRIED SEVERAL TIMES TO HIRE HIT MEN TO DO IN HIS BRIDE**

For his part, Blake seemed caught between respect for old-fashioned values and disgust for this woman he apparently felt forced him into a marriage. According to a report in the *National Enquirer*, Bakely and Blake met at a nightclub as he and friends celebrated his sixty-sixth birthday. Their physical affair began almost immediately and the actor asked repeatedly for assurance that she was on the Pill. Though Bakely said she was, in actual fact she was reportedly taking fertility drugs. She became pregnant the first time they had sex, which was in a Holiday Inn hotel room. The *Enquirer* claims Blake pushed for an abortion, but Bakely refused. Instead she demanded a diamond ring—one carat minimum—if Blake wanted to see his youngest child. The actor agreed to marry Bonny after DNA test results showed he was the little girl's father. Robert Blake became Bakely's tenth husband on November 19, 2000. His lawyer would later explain that Blake felt he "had to" marry Bakely because she had given birth to his baby. They signed a joint custody arrangement and Bakely took up residence in a cottage behind the star's home.

Prosecutors allege a miserable Blake tried several times to hire hit men to do in his bride. Bodyguards, friends, his *Baretta* stunt double—they all apparently turned him down, but not one of them turned him in. Six months into their sham of a marriage, the couple ate dinner at one of Blake's favorite spots,

Vitello's restaurant in Los Angeles. Blake says he walked Bonny to their parked car, located on a dimly lit street, and helped her into the passenger seat. He told her to wait while he went back to retrieve a gun he had forgotten in the restaurant, the same gun he claimed he carried because of Bakely's concerns for her safety. When he returned to the car moments later, he found his wife shot twice in the head, gurgling out her final breaths. A frantic Blake ran to a nearby home. The owner called police, but it was too late to prevent the actor from becoming a widower.

LA prosecutors eyed Blake as a suspect from the start, certain that his story about an unseen thug shooting Bonny and then vanishing during his brief trip back to the restaurant was as likely as Calista Flockhart joining Overeaters Anonymous. After spending nearly a year building a case, police arrested the Emmy award winner and charged him with murder, solicitation of murder, conspiracy, and the special circumstance of lying in wait—a charge that can carry the death penalty. However, the court has decided only Blake's freedom —not his life—is on the line. Blake's bodyguard, Earle Caldwell, also faces a conspiracy charge. Both men have pleaded not guilty.

Several issues had to be settled before trial, including whether Blake would be allowed to pay Caldwell's court costs—a situation that vaguely resembles coercion. Although Blake's attorney pleaded for bail, prosecutors described the actor as a flight risk. His attorney, Harland Braun, described his client as "very calm" about his predicament. Braun repeatedly pointed to Bakely's checkered past as the most likely source of such hatred against her.

Is Robert Blake a cold-blooded murderer? Was he so blinded by rage and his wife's deceit that he would risk missing out on parenting his beloved little Rose in order to rub out her mother? Captain Jim Tatreau of the LA police force thinks so. "He felt that he was trapped in a marriage that he wanted no part of," Tatreau claims. Failing to persuade any of his pals to do

> **HE TOLD HER TO WAIT WHILE HE WENT BACK TO RETRIEVE A GUN HE HAD FORGOTTEN IN THE RESTAURANT**

the deed, Tatreau says an exasperated Blake pulled the trigger himself. An audience raised on *LA Law* and *The Practice* will be glued to the details, anxious to learn if the accusation against an ex–TV cop can be proved beyond a reasonable doubt. ✪

DANNY **BONADUCE**

How refreshing! Here's a former child star who doesn't blame show business, his parents, or any other outside force for his many screwups, even though he has likely earned the right. This former *Partridge Family* kid has taken all of the responsibility for his life squarely onto his own shoulders.

Danny Bonaduce knows how lucky he was to have even appeared on a television show, let alone a hit network series that made him an icon along with costars David Cassidy, Shirley Jones, and Susan Dey. As ABC's Danny Partridge for four seasons, the freckled-faced, smart-aleck middle child was part of a Friday night TV staple in the early 1970s. (The show later moved to Saturday nights.) Regularly beaten by his real-life father, who was a writer for shows such as *Bonanza* and *All in the Family*, the boy's bruises became too numerous for his adult castmates to ignore. Danny was soon given temporary safe haven with Jones and eventually moved in with Dave Madden (Reuben Kincaid), while his own dad was banned from the set.

> **HE WAS DISCOVERED AT A DAYTONA BEACH CRACK HOUSE**

In the years following his sitcom's cancellation (which he learned about one day from a security guard while his mom was driving him to the set), Bonaduce filed back into life as a normal adolescent. School, girls, and spending his TV money took up most of his time. He once recalled that boredom led him to drugs. "I started recreationally," he said, "and the next thing I knew, it was the focus of my life." In 1985, Los Angeles police arrested then twenty-six-year-old Danny after finding fifty grams of cocaine in his sports car. Five years later he was discovered at a Daytona Beach crack house with a pocket full of twenty-dollar bills.

In 1991, he faced the law in Phoenix, Arizona, for assaulting a transvestite prostitute he picked up while high. Thinking he was engaging the services of a woman, the troubled star was surprised to discover under the harsh dome light of his car that the she was in fact a he. No longer interested, Danny called off the transaction. The hooker, however, refused to exit the vehicle without compensation for his time, prompting the actor to drag him out and pop him a time or two for good measure. Later that night, police arrived at Bonaduce's home to find him bleeding and shaking in his bedroom closet. The incident first sparked outcry as a possible gay-bashing, a theory Bonaduce quickly put to rest. That chapter ended with a plea-bargained charge of endangerment and assault.

Bonaduce admits to having served several stints in rehab, one as recently as the summer of 2001, although he refuses to use 12-step clichés like "addictive personality," "personal demons," and others as excuses for his behavior.

The bratty kid we remember from television is now a bratty adult on the radio in Los Angeles, a cohost on the TV chatfest *The Other Half*, and an occasional celebrity boxer who has kicked the famous butts of Donny Osmond and *Brady Bunch* star Barry Williams. He credits his wife and family for giving him a reason to keep trying to be a better man. ✪

MARLON BRANDO

A film legend who has uttered some of cinema's most memorable lines in classics like *On the Waterfront, The Godfather*, and *A Streetcar Named Desire*, Brando has endured more than his share of heartache. His son Christian served half of a ten-year prison term for shooting and killing his sister Cheyenne's fiancé, Dag Drollet; Cheyenne later hanged herself.

Marlon Brando is a three-time loser in marriage. The formerly great thespian is now fending off a $100 million claim from an alleged ex-lover. Maria Christina Ruiz says she lived with the girthy one from 1988 until December 2001, serving as maid, mistress, and mom of his three youngest children. Her lawyer describes the breakup as tantamount to a divorce and maintains his client is entitled to her fair share of the eccentric actor's millions.

BETTMANN/CORBIS

Sacheen Littlefeather (a.k.a. Maria Cruz) declines Marlon Brando's 1972 Academy Award

Reclusive and rather odd, Brando continues to make movies, coming out of seclusion only to take small parts for outrageously extravagant paychecks. But his latter-day performances convey the impression of a distracted, obese man captured in between bites of a hero sandwich rather than a player at the top of his game.

Marlon's most memorable hissy fit came during the 1972 Academy Awards broadcast, when he won Best Actor for his signature role as the Mafia kingpin Don Corleone in *The Godfather*. He didn't attend, deciding instead to boycott the show in protest of his country's treatment of American Indians in movies and television. In his place he sent a woman decked out in traditional First Nations attire. She identified herself as an Apache named Sacheen Littlefeather and took to the podium to decline Brando's Oscar in a perhaps laudable, if grossly out-of-place, demonstration, which later rang hollow when it was revealed that she was not Apache at all, but an actress—Maria Cruz—playing a role. Brando's carefully planned political statement was diminished to a barely audible whisper. As the great philosopher Alanis Morissette once crooned, "Isn't it ironic?" ✪

TODD BRIDGES

A former child star, Bridges forms one corner of the Hollywood triangle known as "the *Diff'rent Strokes* curse." (*See* Gary Coleman and Dana Plato.) Famous for being on the receiving end of the show's catchphrase, "What'chu talkin' 'bout Willis?" the California-born Bridges was the first of the trio to attract postshow attention—for all the wrong reasons.

In 1990, at age twenty-five, he was accused and eventually acquitted of assault with a deadly weapon and attempted murder in the near-fatal shooting of a Los Angeles drug dealer. His testimony during that court case revealed the depths to which he had sunk following the sitcom's 1986 cancellation by NBC. Disillusioned and depressed, Bridges turned to drugs, which led to his fateful acquaintance with the afore-mentioned gunshot victim.

> **HIS TESTIMONY DURING THAT COURT CASE REVEALED THE DEPTHS TO WHICH HE HAD SUNK**

After vehemently vowing at trial's end to stay clean of brushes with the law, Bridges found himself back behind bars in 1997 on an assault charge for ramming a friend's car (and several others parked nearby) in a dispute over a video game.

Bridges' spotty post–*Diff'rent Strokes* acting career mirrored that of his troubled former costars, but he dismisses the "curse" as coincidence. Now a husband, father, budding director, sometime celebrity boxer, and head of his own Todd Bridges Youth Foundation, he told TV's *Inside Edition*, "We were three kids in difficult situations." Ah, fame. It can be hard to endure, but it's even harder still when it's all you've known and it comes to a sudden halt. ✪

BOBBY **BROWN**

R&B singer Bobby Brown's rap sheet contains more hits than he has put on the charts. A former member of the group *New Edition* and a chart-topping solo artist (*My Prerogative*), Brown has defended himself in criminal court, but suspicions continue to plague him in the court of public opinion. He's been suspected of and investigated for, but never formally charged with, assaulting his wife, singer Whitney Houston, who continues to stand by her man. Rumors of hard drug use have swirled around the couple since they wed in 1992. In his case, it's fact: "I have a problem," he told a judge. "I'm an addict and an alcoholic." His wife, however, continues to simply baffle us with her seesawing weight and erratic behavior (*see* Whitney Houston).

> **IT'S FACT:**
> **"I HAVE A PROBLEM,"**
> **HE TOLD A JUDGE.**
> **"I'M AN ADDICT**
> **AND AN ALCOHOLIC"**

The long arm of the law grabbed Brown on several occasions, dating back to a lewd conduct citation stemming from getting too jiggy with it at a 1993 concert in conservative Georgia. Two years later he was charged with battery and subsequently sued by a man whom police say had to undergo an ear reattachment operation following a brawl with Brown, his publicist, and his bodyguard in a Florida nightclub. The singer's lawyer claimed Brown's bodyguard delivered the beating and ear removal while his client and the publicist were merely innocent bystanders. The melee was reportedly sparked when the victim made an unwanted pass at an unidentified woman in Brown's party. According to the Orange Country Sheriff's office, the new jack swing king proved himself to be anything but a model prisoner. Arresting officers claim he swore at police, urinated in the back of a patrol car, and carved a four-letter word into the seat cover. The trio faced three years each behind bars, but the case was eventually settled out of court for an undisclosed multimillion dollar sum that was reportedly far less than the $6.6 million originally sought in the suit.

Just a few months later, Brown found himself in front of a judge yet again for allegedly kicking and punching a security guard who was attempting to break up a rowdy party at his Georgia home.

Brown found more trouble after slamming his wife's Porsche into a street sign in 1996. Subsequent tests revealed his blood alcohol level was almost three times the legal limit. He hobbled away from the crash with a broken ankle, bruised ribs, and a court date. (The incident was in sharp contrast with his previous citation for driving the Porsche too slowly—30 mph in a 45 mph zone.) Despite shedding crocodile tears during the jury trial, his eventual DUI conviction two years later resulted in a rehab stint, five days in jail, community service, and a $500 fine. When his probation officer presented urine test results showing Brown was on cocaine, the humorless judge ordered Bobby front-and-center to face consequences for violating parole. The singer remained AWOL for nearly a year, but was finally nabbed at the New Jersey airport upon his return from a Bahamian vacation. Brown cooled his heels in jail, serving twenty-six days of a seventy-five-day sentence. Vowing to work on his life, he then left via limo, accompanied by wife Whitney and a good friend, comic Chris Rock. ✪

JAMES **BROWN**

Lawsuits, alleged drug addictions, gun offences, and a police chase: the Godfather of Soul has a strong kinship with the justice system.

Born into poverty in the American South, James Brown first ran afoul of the law in the 1940s with a conviction for armed robbery. Four decades later, with his star fading and his musical footnote all but written, the Hardest Working Man in Show Business found himself once again facing prison time. In 1988, his third wife Adrienne accused

> **"I GOT TO HAVE PROTECTION. I HAVE GUNS AND I'M GOING TO KEEP ON HAVING GUNS"**

him of assault and battery. Just a year later, allegedly whacked out on drugs, he terrorized a group of people by waving a handgun and then led police on a bizarre, interstate car chase. That episode resulted in a six-year prison sentence. He served half that term.

A decade later, Brown was forcibly taken to a mental hospital at his daughter's request over what he described as "a misunderstanding." His publicist released a statement acknowledging his client was addicted to painkillers prescribed for back pain (at the time, the sixty-four-year-old soul singer was still trying to perform his trademark splits). Authorities discovered a rifle and a semiautomatic handgun while carrying out the mental transport. Brown denied the pain pill addiction but admitted to the *Chronicle*, a Georgia newspaper, that he dabbled in "a little bit" of marijuana because he had "bad eyes."

And the guns? "I got to have protection. I have guns and I'm going to keep on having guns. Thank God we live in a free country," was the reply. The chapter wrapped with a ninety-day rehab stay and a fine for the firearms after Brown pleaded no contest to drug and weapons charges.

The frenetic performer behind the hits "(I Got You) I Feel Good" and "Sex Machine" also endured lawsuits for alleged improprieties. One former female friend accused the Godfather of using Mob-like power over her. She claimed he held her hostage for three days and subjected her to repeated sexual assaults. An ex-backup singer sued for sexual harassment, claiming Brown couldn't keep his jumpsuit zipped in her presence. The singer was cleared of wrongdoing in another case of alleged sexual harassment brought forward by the former West Coast president of James Brown Enterprises. A utility worker's lawsuit was later dropped due to insufficient evidence after he claimed the singer swung a steak knife at him and prevented him from leaving the South Carolina home to which he had been summoned to take care of a power problem. Brown claims he's a target for frivolous lawsuits because of his celebrity status, but mama always said, "Where there's smoke, there's fire." ✪

LENNY BRUCE

The original shock comic, Lenny Bruce was a stereotypical brash New Yorker: he made audiences blush and censors nervous, and forever changed the face of comedy.

No subject was taboo for Bruce as he unleashed his trademark tirades on sex, race, and religion in profanity-laced performances. Arrested several times on obscenity charges and banned from performing in Australia and the UK, he was convicted only twice and died of a heroin overdose at age forty—before he could see those convictions overturned on appeal. Bruce reveled in the notoriety he gained from pushing the envelope of decency. His colorful euphemisms for parts of the human body and their many uses that turned the establishment on its ear in the 1960s are now routinely used in comedy shows. Today, he is regarded by many as a cult figure in the battle for free speech. Perhaps the title of his 1965 autobiography, published the year before he died of a drug overdose, says it best: *How to Talk Dirty and Influence People.* ✪

HE UNLEASHED HIS TRADEMARK TIRADES ON SEX, RACE, AND RELIGION IN PROFANITY-LACED PERFORMANCES

NAOMI CAMPBELL

This sinewy supermodel gives new meaning to the Bell Telephone slogan, "Reach out and touch someone." It appears no one told Campbell not to take it literally.

The pressures of starring in her first movie on location in Toronto, Canada, proved too nerve-racking for the catwalk kitten in 1998. Frustrated with a long delay at Canadian customs upon her return to the *Prisoner of Love* set in December, the British-born model blamed her assistant for not hurrying things along. Georgina Galanis was just nine days into her job, still anxious to make a good impression on her beautiful, tempestuous boss. The dispute flared once the duo finally reached their hotel. The pretty poser had just ordered room service when her anger suddenly boiled over. She lunged at Galanis, grabbing at her throat and slamming her back to the wall. Then— not once, but twice—she bonked her thirty-

Naomi Campbell with a boyfriend in a Munich discotheque in May of 1997

nine-year-old assistant on the head with the telephone handset. In her subsequent $8 million lawsuit, Galanis claimed she ran from the room bleeding, crying, and screaming for help.

Three months later Campbell faced the criminal charge of assault causing bodily harm, a serious offence with a maximum sentence of six months in jail and a fine. Her publicist initially issued a terse statement claiming Galanis was a gold-digging opportunist who invented the assault. He added, "Naomi will vigorously fight these charges." My, my how a tune can change.

After several hearing delays, the supermodel finally pled guilty to beating Galanis in February 2000 in exchange for no permanent criminal record. The civil lawsuit brought by Galanis had been settled the previous year and the supermodel submitted to anger management classes. It was also reported that she took up boxing to channel her substantial aggression. The entire debacle inspired Campbell to assess her priorities, and just days before the assault case was settled she announced her retirement from the "very stressful" catwalks of London and New York.

One year later, the model's frustration at not being recognized resulted in her banishment from an exclusive London boutique. A tabloid report alleged Campbell turned up at the Voyage shop in Fulham, West London, and was kept waiting when staff didn't recognize her. Repeated rings of the doorbell got her nowhere, so the steamed diva chilled out in her car. When another customer arrived and was immediately allowed inside, Campbell reportedly stormed in, shouted at staff, and made a huge fuss over the perceived slight. Owner Rocky Mazzilli stood by his employees, exiled the model from the store, and revoked her membership.

Naomi had long dismissed claims that some of her troubles stemmed from drug abuse, but that suspicion turned into fact when the *Mirror* published a photo of her leaving a London Narcotics Anonymous meeting. A furious Campbell fired up her solicitor and sued the tabloid, claiming invasion of privacy. *Mirror* editor Piers Morgan insisted Campbell's refusal to admit an addiction made her ripe for a media exposé to disprove her claim. The model testified she felt "shocked, angry, betrayed and violated" by the account, which the *Mirror* countered was handled with sympathy to her plight. The court disagreed, awarding Campbell US $5,000 in damages

> **SHE LUNGED AT GALANIS, GRABBING AT HER THROAT AND SLAMMING HER BACK TO THE WALL**

and ordering the tabloid to pay court costs for removing the word "anonymous" from Campbell's personal life. Her lawyer said the token dollar figure would be donated to charity. (In the meantime, Campbell won the right to keep another potentially embarrassing case out of the courts. She alleges another former personal assistant sold details about her private life to the *News of the World* tabloid; the ex-PA claims Campbell physically assaulted her. The attack accusation will eventually be heard at a full trial.)

The judge also characterized Campbell as "manipulative and selective," however, pointing out that she has been less than truthful about several aspects of her life, including a 1997 hospitalization in the Canary Islands, which she claimed was to treat an allergic reaction (she was actually seeking help for a drug addiction). A spokesman for Britain's Society of Editors said the verdict did not set any precedent for future reporting: "Powerful people have to expect more attention from the media than ordinary people." Especially when they continue to do things that attract the spotlight. ✪

DREW CAREY

By all accounts, the star of *The Drew Carey Show* was superb in the role of celebrity King Bacchus at New Orleans's 1998 Mardi Gras celebration. Every winter, costumed tourists and locals crowd the streets for the annual festival, taking in live music, parades, and dining in the city's many fine restaurants. Scads of tales of misbehavior follow the rowdy party each year, but only Carey's drew the attention of a tabloid TV show.

A time-honored Mardi Gras custom carried out in the French Quarter well away from the parade route involves cheap beads and women's breasts. The locals say it began more than a decade ago with a boisterous group of college students who were drinking heavily and gleefully lifting their shirts to bare their assets. Now men can purchase plastic beads along with their beverages and taunt willing lovelies into trading a "flash" for the faux jewels. The later

> **CAREY YELLED REPEATEDLY TO A WOMAN, "SHOW US YOUR T— —S!"**

it gets and the more drunk they become, the more beads the women accumulate. In any other context it's a disgusting ritual, but in New Orleans during Mardi Gras, hard-core partygoers claim it's all part of the fun.

Caught up in the excitement during a balcony bash, Carey yelled repeatedly to a woman, "Show us your t— —s!" The spectacled TV star offered her $100 and a promise that no one would ever discover her identity. The young woman complied with the hoots and hollers of an adoring crowd—and was caught by a whirring video camera, which, unknown to Carey, recorded the whole episode. The footage made compelling tabloid fodder when it aired soon afterward on TV's *Hard Copy*. Carey offered no apologies in his book *Dirty Jokes and Beer*. His attitude was, When in Rome ...

Early in 2002, the cherubic comic nearly lost his livelihood when ABC threatened to shut down taping of a *Drew Carey Show* episode that took jabs at airport security guards. Carey whined to the *Los Angeles Times* that his character's bumbling buddies, Lewis and Oswald, were due to moonlight as security guards, but the network's censors took exception to the script. As Carey tells it, ABC's honchos intimidated the writers by threatening to scrap the entire episode if they didn't rework the lines so at least one of the guards would appear competent. Network officials routinely intervene and demand script changes, but such a warning was unprecedented. As one of the show's executive producers, Carey obliged, but his complaints to the *Times* about the network's stance rang hollow. Isn't it obvious? Jittery executives were worried about placating nervous travelers—and likely airline ad reps packing millions in revenue to keep Drew's show on the air—in the realities of a post-9/11 world. ✪

MARIAH CAREY

Hospitalization for "extreme exhaustion" is a privilege enjoyed only by the rich and pampered. It's difficult to muster up pity for a wealthy, supremely beautiful, sought-after artist when she claims the demands of her grueling work schedule, for which most folks would gladly offer up a limb, have sent her into a tailspin.

Mariah's meltdown in the summer of 2001 followed her first two film roles (in the widely panned *Glitter* and the more kindly reviewed *Wisegirls*) and the release of the *Glitter* soundtrack, recorded under a historical multimillion dollar deal with Virgin Music. Those who watched her prebreakdown appearance on MTV's *Total Request Live* knew something was up. A half-naked Carey pushed an ice-cream cart onto the set and deluged host Carson Daly with rapid-fire babble that included reading a supposed love letter from her mother to the host. In the days prior to her hospital stay, the songbird posted strange voice messages on her website, telling fans she needed time off and a good night's sleep. (Those messages were quickly deleted once word of them leaked to the media.) Some tabloids reported that Carey attempted suicide following a bust-up with her boyfriend, Latin singer Luis Miguel. Her publicist vehemently denied the claim. More than a year later, in an exclusive and supposedly revealing interview, Carey told MTV she simply burned out on too many career obligations and too little sleep.

Regardless of the details, Carey's incarceration left Virgin Music floundering with no star to promote its new album, as she cancelled all publicity while her psychiatric sessions continued on an outpatient basis. The *Glitter* CD sank like its celluloid counterpart, prompting Virgin to eventually buy out the diva's contract in a humiliating fashion despite a generous severance (reportedly $49 million).

> **A HALF-NAKED CAREY PUSHED AN ICE-CREAM CART ONTO THE SET AND DELUGED HOST CARSON DALY WITH RAPID-FIRE BABBLE THAT INCLUDED READING A SUPPOSED LOVE LETTER FROM HER MOTHER TO THE HOST**

People magazine claims Billy Blake, a producer on Carey's film *Wisegirls*, confided to them that the exhausted singer got into a catfight on the set with costar Mira Sorvino. It apparently began with a tossed salt shaker and ended with the two stars wrestling on the floor. Sorvino soon released her own account of events, admitting "words were exchanged" between the two when Carey arrived late one day for filming. Sorvino insists, however, that the encounter did not escalate to physical contact. Blake later denied making the statement, but *People* stands by its story. In the meantime, the public has been seeing less of Mariah Carey—her trademark handkerchief-sized dresses not-withstanding—as she creates her own record label to serve as a new musical home for her five-octave range. Hopefully the project will inspire some renewed self-respect and newfound support from fans and critics alike. ✪

Lon CHANEY JR.

Chaney Jr. spent his life chasing the successful career of his father, Lon Chaney Sr., a legendary silent movie star nicknamed The Man of a Thousand Faces. The younger Chaney was consistently described by costars and fans as the nicest guy in the world and a big man whose stories grew larger and more exciting with every telling. It was best to catch him in the morning, however. After his liquid lunch hour, it was difficult to engage the actor in any work, let alone civil conversation.

His film career began after his father's death in 1930. Reluctant to cash in on being the son of a celebrity, Chaney, who was born Creighton, refused to call himself Lon Jr. until he was "starved into doing it" to get better roles. He drew great notice as Lenny in the 1939 version of Steinbeck's *Of Mice and Men*, and his career took off.

> CHANEY AND FELLOW ACTOR BRODERICK CRAWFORD TRADITIONALLY SPENT THOSE EVENINGS IN THE DRESSING ROOM GETTING SMASHED, FOLLOWED BY PUSHING BACK THE FURNITURE AND BEATING THE CRAP OUT OF EACH OTHER

Nineteen forty-one's *The Wolfman* is a horror film classic and the lead was a plum role for Chaney. However, the three-week shoot was less than harmonious, with no love lost between the actor and his lovely costar, Evelyn Ankers. Their relationship was strained from the first day of filming, after Chaney discovered Ankers had been given his usual large dressing room as a star perk. He blamed her for ruining his Friday night fun. Chaney and fellow actor Broderick Crawford traditionally spent those evenings in the dressing room getting smashed, followed by pushing back the furniture and beating the crap out of each other. On- and off-camera, Chaney delighted in spooking his leading lady while in full makeup as the beast. Ankers was not amused.

The grueling process of transforming from man into wolfman sent the tired and frustrated actor deeper into the bottle. In what seems an archaic technique by today's standards, Chaney was forced to lie rigid for as many as twelve hours straight while bits of yak hair were glued to his skin. He would then be photographed, wait while more yak hair was applied, and so on. But by the time Chaney told his version of the story to interviewers years later, the length of the sessions had ballooned to twenty hours or more.

Chaney's heavy drinking caused his most embarrassing performance, which was carried on live television. It came during a 1952 episode of *Tales of Tomorrow*, which featured Chaney as the Frankenstein monster. Mistaking the live show for a dress rehearsal, the drunken actor mockingly strolled through his scene, failing to break props he was supposed to and appearing very un-scary. Told later of his mammoth error, Chaney was mortified and didn't recover from the shame for several gin-soaked weeks. Still, the beloved performer continued to work as a horror star and character actor in mainstream movies like *High Noon* virtually nonstop until his death in 1973 from liver failure. ✪

CHARLIE CHAPLIN

He was known as the Little Tramp and a genius filmmaker with a bowler hat, a funny walk, and a well-known preference for the company of young girls.

Charlie Chaplin was a true movie pioneer. Raised on the streets and in orphanages in England after the death of his father and his mother's nervous breakdown, he performed his way into the US and launched a film career in 1913. Many of his movies, which he wrote, directed, and starred in, are classics, including 1915's *The Tramp* and *The Kid*, circa 1921.

In 1915, twenty-six-year-old Chaplin made the acquaintance of Lillita McMurray, then six years old. After casting the wide-eyed child in several walk-on and bit parts, the engrossed director literally watched her develop through the camera lens. Fast-forward six years: Chaplin cast the young actress, who was going by the stage name Lita Grey, in *The Kid*. By age fifteen, she was carrying his child and became his second wife when he decided—as he told his friends—that a sham marriage was better than a statutory rape charge. When Lita and Charlie skipped the border to Mexico for a quickie wedding, dozens of reporters followed on their heels.

The couple had two children in quick succession and just two years later, McMurray filed for divorce. Her threats to name a half dozen other underage girls he had consorted with resulted in a $625,000 divorce settlement, the biggest to that date. The nasty split is considered the first real tabloid story, as it was eaten up by the press and the public. Lita took her rightful place in Hollywood history as the original Lolita. Some film historians say the actress's wily waitress mother actually facilitated her little girl's scandalous relationship with Chaplin and for her trouble, banked half of the divorce payment.

Although he lived in the US for decades, Chaplin never sought citizenship. In 1943, while briefly between wives, he lost a nasty paternity suit brought against him by actress Joan Berry. By the early 1950s, sickened by what he perceived to be persecution over his political views, back taxes, and moral character, Chaplin settled in Switzerland with his fourth wife and one-time teen costar, Oona O'Neill. Anti-Chaplin sentiment in America was so strong that his 1957 movie *A King in New York* couldn't find a home in US theaters until sixteen years later. His last major appearance stateside came after twenty years of self-imposed exile, when he received an honorary Academy Award. Charlie and Oona eventually had eight children and remained together until the Little Tramp's death in 1977. ✪

> **HE WAS KNOWN AS THE LITTLE TRAMP AND A GENIUS FILMMAKER WITH A BOWLER HAT, A FUNNY WALK, AND A WELL-KNOWN PREFERENCE FOR THE COMPANY OF YOUNG GIRLS**

BILL CLINTON

Who could forget the scandalous events of 1998 that rocked the Clinton White House? The revelation that the world's most powerful leader had carried on an affair with intern Monica Lewinsky three years earlier shook the administration to its core. The details had the allure of a Jackie Collins novel: a thong peek-a-boo; rushed encounters in the Oval Office carried out under the threat of discovery; DNA evidence inexplicably preserved on a dress; and bald-faced lies earnestly told to a supportive spouse and a stunned nation. And add to all of that the betrayal of Lewinsky by her former "best friend" Linda Tripp, whose secret tapings of conversations with the intern brought the whole sordid mess to light.

The investigation headed by Ken Starr very nearly cost the US president his job. Mrs. Clinton steadfastly supported her husband—in public, anyway—and no one will likely ever know if her defiant stance was in fact a means to an end for her own political aspirations. In 2000, Hillary Rodham Clinton became the first former First Lady to be elected to the US Senate.

There were other allegations leveled against Clinton, some acknowledged, some vehemently denied. The juiciest items on the list included an assertion of a long-term love affair with singer and beauty queen Gennifer Flowers; a complaint of alleged fondling by former White House volunteer

> **LEWINSKY ADMITTED SHE HAD THOUGHT SHE WAS IN LOVE WITH THE COMMANDER IN CHIEF**

Kathleen Willey; and a sexual harassment lawsuit filed by Paula Jones, which provided an occasion for Lewinsky's first actual testimony about her relationship with the president. The harassment grievance, while important, was quickly overshadowed by the Lewinsky-Clinton affair. Videotape of the young intern, a beret perched atop her raven-black hair as she embraces the president at a photo op, is forever burned into the brains of North Americans.

As the probe concluded and Clinton stayed on at the helm of government, the public was left with more questions than answers. Did he tell Lewinsky to lie about their sexual relationship as was alleged by many and denied by the former intern? Did he really believe, as he first told US citizens, that anything short of actual intercourse did not qualify as "sex"? Why did Lewinsky keep the stained blue dress in her closet? Was she strangely sentimental? And was the entire matter simply a case of two consenting adults—albeit one of them married—becoming involved in what sometimes comes naturally, or did the then forty-nine-year-old Clinton exert his influence and power over the naïve twenty-one-year-old Lewinsky?

Once her gag order was lifted, Lewinsky admitted she had thought she was in love with the commander in chief and, for a fleeting moment, believed he might leave his wife for her. She'll be dining out on that story for the rest of her life. ✪

KURT COBAIN

Most artists enjoy some sort of recovery after their tantrums. In the case of Nirvana's songwriter and lead singer Kurt Cobain, there was no coming back. Success, money, and the worship of a multitude of fans could not exorcize the demons of the distressed man who originated rock's Seattle, Washington, grunge movement of the early 1990s.

Poring over the history of Cobain's short life, it appears he never really had a chance. Born into a troubled family with a history of suicide and alcohol abuse, Kurt was a hyperactive, creative kid who was pumped with Ritalin as a toddler. A high school dropout, he sought solace in music and broke out in 1991 with bandmates Krist Novaselic, Dave Grohl, and Pat Smear to a success beyond their wildest dreams. The album *Nevermind*, propelled by the single "Smells Like Teen Spirit," sold in excess of ten million copies. It turned the spotlight on the Seattle music scene, sending industry executives scrambling to discover sound-alike bands with loud, crunchy guitars and angry, ranting frontmen. Fame and fortune didn't placate Cobain, however, who felt unworthy of his new role as music hero to millions of teens.

> **PORING OVER THE HISTORY OF COBAIN'S SHORT LIFE, IT APPEARS HE NEVER REALLY HAD A CHANCE**

Cobain's enduring heroin addiction appeared to take a firmer hold with the release of each subsequent Nirvana album. Nineteen ninety-three's *Insecticide* was a collection of early material while *In Utero*, released later that same year, marked an evolution in the band's sound from hard-edged grunge to mainstream rock. Nirvana proved their expert musicianship with an appearance on MTV's *Unplugged,* also in 1993.

Cobain's personal life seemed to be settling down, even if it was still steeped in rock and roll clichés. In 1992 he married Hole's Courtney Love, a rock star in her own right (*see* Courtney Love) and became father to daughter Francis Bean later that year. In their intense and volatile relationship, Love did not prove a calming influence on her man; rather, she joined him in his decadent, self-destructive ways and on at least one occasion accused him of spousal abuse. (She summoned police to their home but later refused to press charges.)

In March 1994, Cobain went AWOL from a drug treatment center, prompting his mother to file a missing person's report. His body was discovered on April 8, 1994, in a room above his garage by an electrician working a contract on-site. The self-inflicted gunshot wound to Cobain's head was so destructive that fingerprints were required to make a positive identification. Like fellow rock stars Jimi Hendrix, Janis Joplin, and Jim Morrison, Cobain checked out at just twenty-seven years old. Love went public with excerpts from her husband's suicide note, which essentially explained his loss of passion for life and music and his erratic moods. It echoed the famous phrase "It's better to burn out than to fade away." But Cobain's career flourished despite his absence. In 2002, the release of Nirvana's *Greatest Hits* CD pushed the band's total album sales up past fifty million. Cobain's achingly intimate, witty, and self-loathing *Journals* simultaneously topped the *New York Times* best-seller list.

> **LIKE FELLOW ROCK STARS JIMI HENDRIX, JANIS JOPLIN, AND JIM MORRISON, COBAIN CHECKED OUT AT JUST TWENTY-SEVEN YEARS OLD**

Conspiracy theorists continue to perpetuate a feeding frenzy on the circumstances surrounding Cobain's suicide. Among their evidence: no fingerprints were apparently found on the shotgun and the suicide note's final sentences appear to be written by someone else's hand. One popular scenario is driven by the outrageous accusation that Kurt's wife orchestrated his murder to dodge a pending divorce and the loss of millions of dollars. The official case is closed but for many of Cobain's fans, a question mark will always follow the conclusion of suicide. ✪

GARY COLEMAN

Talk about typecasting. Diminutive Gary Coleman couldn't unlock the shackles of stardom that bound him forever in our minds to his character on *Diff'rent Strokes*, the wisecracking adoptee Arnold Jackson. Unlike his sitcom siblings, the clean-living Coleman's frustrations didn't lead him to drugs, but to blackening the eye of a fan in LA.

As if admissions of personal bankruptcy and life-long virginity weren't embarrassing enough, Coleman had the misfortune of losing his cool when insulted by a so-called fan. Bus driver Tracy Fields approached the small star in July 1998 while he was shopping for a bulletproof vest. The actor–turned–mall security guard kindly consented to giving his signature, but when Fields asked him to personalize the scribble, Coleman tore up the paper and threw it in the trash. His "fan" responded with a comment that may have landed too close to the bone: "That badass attitude is the reason why you can't get a job as an actor."

Coleman later testified in a $1 million civil case brought against him by Fields before TV's Judge Mills Lane. The 85-pound actor claimed the 205-pound woman made him fear for his safety, so he decided to get in the first punch and make his getaway. The judge ruled that Coleman was out of line and ordered him to pay less than $2,000 in medical costs, but denied damages to the victim for pain and suffering. The little star had earlier pleaded no contest to criminal assault charges, was sentenced to a year's probation, and completed an anger management course. He was nabbed by police a few months following the plea bargain for neglecting to pay his $400 fine. As unseemly as the whole incident was, Coleman still reigns supreme as the least troubled of the three *Diff'rent Strokes* kids. ✪

PHIL COLLINS

It's a cold way to end a marriage, especially one that involves a child.

Having fallen in love with his twenty-one-year-old interpreter, Swiss heiress Orianne Cevey, the former Genesis drummer and lead singer reportedly asked his second wife, Jill, for a divorce—by fax. She complied and forty-eight-year-old Phil Collins was free to marry the sultry Cevey in the summer of 1999. The couple now live in Switzerland and have since had a son. Collins also has three children from his previous marriages. There is no truth to the rumor that Orianne has had her fax machine disconnected. ✪

SEAN "P. DIDDY" COMBS

Call him what you wish—Puffy, P. Diddy, or J-Lo's ex—but by any name, this multimillionaire rap music star and record label honcho was a magnet for trouble in 1999.

Smart, handsome, and charismatic, Puffy (as he was known then) was used to getting his own way. As CEO of Bad Boy Entertainment, he steered the careers of up-and-coming rappers—not to mention his own—and won accolades for his brilliance behind the board as a producer. He had the ear of the music industry elite and millions of fans. So when he had second thoughts about his cameo appearance in the Nas video "Hate Me Now" in April 1999, he expected to be spliced out. (In the video, Puffy was shown nailed to a cross saying, "I think I like this." The bit did eventually end up on the cutting room floor.) When Universal Records executive Steve Stoute resisted acting on Combs's concerns, Puffy grew huffy and allegedly clubbed the man with a champagne bottle, a chair, and a telephone, leaving the stunned Stoute with a broken arm and jaw.

The melee resulted in assault charges for Combs, who eventually pleaded down to second-degree harassment, thus avoiding a possible maximum seven-year jail term. His sentence? One day of anger management training. The civil case hit his wallet harder, but it was still a comparatively easy ride: $500,000, a fraction of the reported $12 million Stoute was seeking.

Just as memories of the boardroom brawl were beginning to fade, the Puffster found himself in another legal battle, one that would consume nearly two years of his life. December 1999 gunplay at New York's trendy Club NY left three clubbers seriously wounded. Combs and then girlfriend Jennifer Lopez were at the nightspot with some of Puffy's posse. His protégé, rapper Jamal "Shyne" Barrow, was arrested outside the club while Puffy, Lopez, and bodyguard Anthony "Wolf" Jones fled in a Lincoln Navigator. When police pulled the trio over, they claimed to have found a loaded pistol on the SUV's floor and allege another gun was tossed out the window during the wild ride. Only J-Lo escaped indictment. Barrow faced two counts of assault, two weapons offences, attempted murder, and one count of reckless endangerment for firing his pistol during the fracas. Combs and Jones were both cited for alleged criminal gun possession, and Puffy faced a further charge for reportedly bribing his driver to claim ownership of the firearm found in the Navigator. If convicted, he faced up to fifteen years in the slammer.

COMBS AND JONES WERE BOTH CITED FOR ALLEGED CRIMINAL GUN POSSESSION, AND PUFFY FACED A FURTHER CHARGE FOR REPORTEDLY BRIBING HIS DRIVER TO CLAIM OWNERSHIP OF THE FIREARM FOUND IN THE NAVIGATOR

Puffy hired the services of high-priced legal eagle Johnny Cochrane, the loudest mouthpiece on O. J. Simpson's Dream Team defense squad, and chose to testify on his own behalf. The verdict apparently hinged on the seesawing testimony of the driver, Wardell Fenderson, who attested the gun was his but later recanted. In March 2001, Puffy was finally cleared, as was Jones, but the jury found Barrow guilty on all charges except attempted murder. The young rapper's career was grounded before it ever took off. He is currently serving a ten-year stint in prison. It was the best of times and the worst of times for

Puff. Though his claims of innocence were vindicated, the publicity surrounding the case proved too much for his longtime relationship with Lopez. The couple announced they had officially split midtrial.

Claiming he needed a "fresh start," Sean Combs dropped the name Puff Daddy and adopted P. Diddy, the nickname given to him by the late rapper Notorious BIG. He has since launched a sideline acting career (he appeared in *Made*) and his own clothing line. He also formally shot down rampant rumors of a reunion with ex-lover Lopez after her brief rebound marriage to a choreographer fell apart. P. Diddy continues to venture out into New York nightlife, almost always accompanied by enough security to form his own street basketball league. ✪

SEAN CONNERY

As the first—and many say the only—James Bond, Sean turned the heads of millions of women in 1987 with his comment about physical abuse of the fairer sex. The remark came in December, just prior to winning the Academy Award for Best Supporting Actor in *The Untouchables*. During an interview with American broadcast legend Barbara Walters, Connery told Babs that he felt it was okay to hit a woman if she deserved it or needed to be kept in line. Tongues wagged, scribes scribbled, and fans fretted. Did the aging sex symbol believe in beating women? Was his wife, French actress Micheline Roquebrune, the recipient of actual blows to her body? Inquiring minds needed to know. Still, the puzzling questions didn't prevent *People* magazine from naming the aging thespian the Sexiest Man Alive for 1989.

> **CONNERY TOLD BABS THAT HE FELT IT WAS OKAY TO HIT A WOMAN IF SHE DESERVED IT OR NEEDED TO BE KEPT IN LINE**

Connery elaborated on the controversial comment in a 1993 interview for *Vanity Fair* magazine by saying, "To slap a woman is not the cruelest thing you can do to her. It's much more cruel to damage somebody psychologically, to put them in such distress they really come to hate themselves." Perhaps, but being tossed about by the one you love isn't exactly food for the soul.

Whether or not Sir Sean, who was finally knighted by the Queen in his native Scotland in 2000, actually practices the theory he preaches is up for debate. His admissions have not, however, put a dent in his popularity. He continues to make box office smashes and fans continue to flock to them. Early in 2002, a British poll showed he beat out much younger men, including Ewan McGregor and Jude Law, as the sexiest actor of the moment, a result that leaves most of us shaken, not stirred. ✪

COOLIO

An artist doesn't *have* to live the kind of life they sing about, but Coolio is apparently striving for authenticity. A run of trouble in the late 1990s helped this gangsta rapper live up to his title.

The Grammy award winner and his posse, called the 40 Thievz, made like bandits on a late 1997 trip to Germany and their leader was forced to face the music. Coolio, born Artis Leon Ivey Junior, and his hangers-on descended on a trendy shop in the German suburb of Boeblingen and helped themselves to the merchandise. The group was accused of trying on thousands of dollars' worth of clothes and then trying to leave—price tags still hanging from their hips. The multimillion-selling singer of "Gangsta's Paradise" allegedly slugged the shop owner when she tried to stop the group. Give Coolio his due, though. When it came time for court, he was the only one who showed up to face a possible sentence of four years in prison. His quartet of homies left their leader to take the heat alone.

Coolio coughed up $3,000 for the clothing in pretrial damages and later testified he was in the shop to sign autographs and had been promised free threads. The story didn't wash and the guilty verdict for being an accessory to robbery and causing bodily injury was accompanied by six months' probation and a $17,000 fine.

> **THE DOTING DAD WAS PULLED OVER IN HIS HUMMER FOR DRIVING ON THE WRONG SIDE OF A CALIFORNIA STREET WITH THREE OF HIS SEVEN CHILDREN ON BOARD**

Nearly a year later, the doting dad was pulled over in his Hummer for driving on the wrong side of a California street with three of his seven children on board. Police discovered more than one minor offence: an expired license and a small bag of marijuana, which he claimed belonged "to a friend." He readily told the cops he was transporting an unloaded semi-automatic pistol with several rounds of ammunition because he was en route to a shooting range. He entered a guilty plea on the weapons charge and served ten days in jail, two years' probation, and forty hours of community service. He later told fans during an on-line chat that the arresting officer was "overzealous."

The clean-living Coolio, who beat a cocaine habit before hitting the music charts, promotes up-and-coming artists through his own record label Crowbar, and has branched out into acting. You can see his trademark Pippi-Longstocking -meets-Bo-Derek-in-*10* hairdo in movies like *Get Over It* and *Exposed.* ✪

JOAN CRAWFORD

We may never have learned about many of legendary Hollywood actress Joan Crawford's transgressions on the home front if it weren't for her adopted daughter Christina's tell-all autobiography and subsequent movie, both titled *Mommie Dearest*. The 1978 best-seller inspired pop culture enthusiasts to shriek the now infamous phrase "No more wire hangers!" as a synonym for bad parenting.

Crawford, a Best Actress Academy Award winner in 1946 for *Mildred Pierce*, was a bit of a pioneer. She adopted her first child, Christina, in 1939, a time when adoption wasn't yet popular. She was also a single parent, although she would marry several times and, according to her daughter's famous book, would parade a long succession of "uncles" through her children's lives. The family would grow to include a son, Chris, and two more girls, Cathy and Cindy.

Under the old Hollywood studio system, actors and actresses were contractually bound to a single production company and obligated to appear exclusively in that studio's projects. By the time she reached her late thirties, fearing her fading looks and younger starlets, Joan found herself moving between studios for less pay and the promise of more on-screen opportunities. When there was a lull in her work schedule, her frustrations were taken out on Christina and Chris, often with little warning and startling viciousness.

> **THE CHILDREN WERE FORCED TO HELP THEIR MOMMIE CHOP DOWN AND CUT UP ROSEBUSHES, WITHOUT THE AID OF GLOVES**

The children lived in fear of the sudden bursts of anger and what they came to call "night raids." Joan, in a bout of insomnia, would turn her obsessive need to clean on her children in the wee hours. The "No wire hangers!" cry came during a late-night raid of Christina's closet, when Joan discovered her daughter had ill-advisedly hung her clothes with wire hangers—a no-no in Joan's books—and hit the scared child with one. During another episode, the children were forced to help their mommie chop down and cut up rosebushes, without the aid of gloves. Bruised, bleeding, and silent with fright, they worked through the night destroying a beautiful garden on their mother's command.

Intimidation ruled the Crawford home. If the family appeared serene when the press or an "uncle" came to call, it was only because the children had been sternly warned to be on their best, if fake, behavior. Mother and eldest daughter often dressed in matching outfits for on-camera publicity, but the ensembles were trotted out only for such occasions.

Life behind the Crawford mansion's closed doors was characterized by further startling contradictions. It was not unusual for a lavish birthday party to be followed by a terrifying beating. While they were handed the best of everything by day, on many nights Christina and Chris would be tied down to their beds. Even Christmas was a study in contrasts. The kids would receive dozens of the most expensive and trendiest toys only to be forced to pack them into a closet for regifting to others later in the year. They were allowed to enjoy only cheap playthings, despite Crawford's ability to easily afford anything her children wanted.

CRAWFORD RETALIATED BY SHREDDING CHRISTINA'S FAVORITE YELLOW DRESS WITH SCISSORS AND FORCING THE GIRL TO WEAR IT FOR A WEEK

Crawford's methods of discipline ranged from corporal punishment—severe spankings that would sting for a week—to cruel and unusual reprimands. Christina wrote about being locked in a linen closet and the time she was punished for absent-mindedly tearing off a piece of her bedroom wallpaper. Crawford retaliated by shredding Christina's favorite yellow dress with scissors and forcing the girl to wear it for a week. Seven days in kid time is an eternity. It was an unforgivable and extremely harsh act of revenge for a minor, childish transgression.

But Crawford's children weren't the only ones on the receiving end of her wrath. One of Hollywood's legendary long-running feuds was carried out on film sets and at parties by Crawford and Bette Davis (*see* Bette Davis). The competing and sometimes costarring actresses truly despised each other. Davis loathed Crawford's attempts to manipulate the press and the public into believing she was truly *the* movie star, complete with a glamorous, flawless life. She also despised Joan's neediness and her crippling insecurity, which drove her to constantly fish for praise.

Like the abuse of her children, Crawford's heavy drinking was done behind closed doors. Keeping up appearances was more important to Joan than her own kin. Christina once discovered that her mother had remarried when she heard it on the news; her mother had never mentioned her new husband's name, let alone her plans to wed. Crawford died in 1977 of heart failure and there was no mention of her children at the star-studded memorial service. Crawford's final word to her family left a legacy of confusion and hurt. Her will stipulated that token amounts of money would go to Cindy and Cathy but not a dime to Chris and Christina, "for reasons which are well known to them." ✪

RUSSELL CROWE

He's a paradox. When he finally realized his ambition of making it from Australia to Hollywood and was embraced by the acting elite (he won the profession's top prize, the Best Actor Academy Award, for *Gladiator*), he still bristled at the system that brought him his bounty. Charismatic but cagey, Russell Crowe is a gifted actor, the embodiment of cinematic cool and an artist who seems to take his work and himself very seriously.

There are a few accounts of Crowe's impatience with reporters from his earlier years working down under as a child actor and later as wannabe rocker Russ Le Roq and stage player in productions of *Grease* and *The Rocky Horror Picture Show*. The stories that have surfaced generally involve on-set quarrels over artistic differences, details that pegged him as particular and difficult—

LOVE CLAIMS CROWE SELFISHLY PRESSED HER TO MAKE PUBLIC THE FACT HE WAS NOT THE FATHER WHILE SHE WAS RECOVERING FROM THE LOSS OF HER CHILD

not unusual traits to find in those working in the high-stakes world of performing. Back then, he wasn't nearly bad-tempered enough and his star didn't shine brightly enough to warrant the media circus he now faces every day. It wasn't until he had starred in a Hollywood blockbuster that he was threatened with kidnapping in December 2000—surely a sign of megastar status. The mysterious warning was taken so seriously by the FBI that agents met with the actor's security staff. They even accompanied him down the red carpet for the Golden Globe Awards the following January. The case was never solved but more importantly, the threat was never carried out.

Crowe's first major US film was the Sharon Stone western *The Quick and the Dead*, but he didn't begin to carve out a reputation as a challenging and curmudgeonly interview until later that same year when he costarred in *Virtuosity*, one of Denzel Washington's rare box office flops. A bad boy in reel life becomes a bad boy in real life if the actor doesn't present a winning smile and genial attitude to the public. And so began the reputation that sticks with Crowe to this day.

His disdain for the promotional end of filmmaking is well known. He'll blow smoke into one reporter's face, lace another interview with so many blue words that it'll be rendered unusable, and do it all with an Eddie Haskell grimace. He's often short-tempered and he cannot tolerate the necessary evil of shilling for a movie, which requires an actor to answer the same questions over and over, ad nauseam, with a voice and manner that belies the fact that the "spontaneous" responses are being repeated for the two hundredth time.

It might be said that Crowe doesn't suffer fools, but unfortunately, he's quick to judge and often doesn't determine if he's dealing with an *actual* fool before he makes them suffer. Case in

Russell Crowe appears in video stills from a security camera outside The Saloon Bar nightclub at Coffs Harbour

point: during an interview with BBC reporter David Wills, the actor was asked if his reputation for rudeness might turn off Academy voters at Oscar time. In classic Crowe style the Aussie retorted, "You think I'm going to answer a question like that from a man in a yellow suit?" The star of *A Beautiful Mind* also stunned a Los Angeles reporter who asked, "What makes a mind beautiful?" "Is that what they taught you in journalism school—how to rephrase movie titles?" Crowe fired back. When the reporter replied that he didn't go to journalism school, the smug actor responded, "It shows."

One longtime observer of Crowe's career suggests that the temperamental star has no fear of damaging his reputation because he grew up on TV and film sets: because he's always been in the biz, he doesn't treat it with the same respect as other actors. Perhaps. But how does one then explain the charming personality of Crowe's director in *A Beautiful Mind*, the lovable, sweet, and gentle Ron Howard? Ron also had an early start in show business, but he remains one of Hollywood's most personable figures.

Accounts of Russell Crowe's most famous (so far) flare-up differ, but one thing is certain: he lost it, and soon found himself eating crow. The event was the 2002 BAFTAs, the British Academy of Film and Television Arts Awards, where he won Best Actor for his starring role as the schizophrenic mathematician John Nash in *A Beautiful Mind*. An excited Crowe ended his speech with a four-line poem, "Sanctity," by late Irish poet Patrick Kavanagh. Later, upon discovering the poem was edited out for the broadcast, Crowe became livid. He sought out show director Malcolm Gerrie, cornered him, and pushed him up against a wall while cursing the entire time. Witnesses said the surly actor had to be pulled off Gerrie by his own security personnel and was dragged away, kicking at chairs and shouting obscenities. This is not the way men in tuxes normally behave at an occasion as prestigious as the BAFTAs. Gerrie's press statement expressed his disgust over the incident and explained that he was forced to keep the show to time by cutting the poem. He claimed the immature thespian took the situation too personally. Word quickly spread and the intense scrutiny on Crowe cranked up a notch; everyone wanted to know if he was sorry.

> **"IS THAT WHAT THEY TAUGHT YOU IN JOURNALISM SCHOOL — HOW TO REPHRASE MOVIE TITLES?" CROWE FIRED BACK. WHEN THE REPORTER REPLIED THAT HE DIDN'T GO TO JOURNALISM SCHOOL, THE SMUG ACTOR RESPONDED, "IT SHOWS"**

"I've got nothing to apologize for," Crowe responded. "It was between him and me." Even days later, his hot fury not yet cooled, Crowe refused to acknowledge that he may have gone a bit over the top. It took several weeks before the actor finally swallowed his pride, picked up the telephone, and apologized to Gerrie. "I was unrepentant for a while there," he told reporters after his win as Best Actor for *A Beautiful Mind* at the 2002 Screen Actors Guild Awards. His mind was changed, he said, after learning Gerrie's twelve-year-old son was being given a hard time at school over his dad being manhandled. He even offered to buy Gerrie a drink the next time he's in the UK.

Although Crowe retreats to his farm near Coffs Harbour, Australia, whenever time permits, he doesn't impress the residents who witnessed his 1999 scuffle with a local DJ. After Crowe told the music spinner that his show was "crap," the man replied, "So are most of your movies." Crowe warned the DJ's wife that he was about to level her husband and then proceeded to do so, involving several other bar patrons and his older brother Terry in the altercation.

One witness told *People* magazine that Crowe was "kicking, punching and biting like a wild man." No charges were ever filed. A blurry video that purportedly shows Crowe biting the neck of a bouncer before fleeing the pub was at the core of a famous Australian lawsuit. The tape's owners allegedly attempted to blackmail the silver screen gladiator into paying up to have the slice of reality television destroyed. However, prosecutors ultimately had to back off when a judge acquitted the amateur cameramen of extortion charges.

The Aussie star's ire isn't reserved only for unknowns. Some of his fellow celebrities have felt his wrath and disdain, and in the case of singer and actress Courtney Love, his thoughtlessness. Love, lead singer of Hole and star of *The People versus Larry Flynt* and *Man on the Moon* (*see* Courtney Love), suffered a miscarriage in the spring of 2001, around the same time she was photographed on the town with Crowe. Love claims Crowe selfishly pressed her to make public the fact he was not the father while she was recovering from the loss of her child. For the record, Crowe was not the impregnator; the duo did not have that kind of relationship. Love says she was shocked that a so-called "friend" would worry about his image at such a sensitive time.

Australian actor Samuel Johnson apparently ran into Crowe in the men's room during the annual Film and TV Awards down under. The excited Johnson thrust out his hand for a shake only to be insulted by a stream of four-letter words from Crowe that centered on hygiene and washing one's hands following a pee. Johnson later said that if the opportunity presents itself again, he will keep his hand to himself.

Crowe's love life made headlines around the world during the filming of 2000's romantic thriller *Proof of Life*. The on-screen chemistry between the Russell and Meg Ryan, his very married costar, inspired an intense, short-lived affair that reportedly contributed to the end of Ryan's nine-year union with actor Dennis Quaid.

Russell Crowe's tremendous movie success now allows him to dabble in dreams of rock stardom. He fronts the band 30 Odd Foot of Grunts and the group continues to record and tour, largely buoyed by their leader's notoriety. Crowe admits, however, that he's merely passable as a guitar player. In November 2002, with another reported brawl putting his name back in the tabloid headlines, Crowe announced the surprise cancellation of a Grunts tour so he could take some much needed time off to spend with his family and girlfriend Danielle Spencer. His reputation as a perennial troublemaker has inspired at least one British tabloid writer to make a tongue-in-cheek diagnosis that Crowe suffers from a newfound condition called irritable male syndrome (IMS), which was first detected in Scottish sheep. IMS manifests itself in male animals as grumpiness and irrationality after a sudden drop in testosterone levels, and is most commonly brought on by illness or stress. IMS is not a proven phenomenon in humans, but whatever the cause of his surly demeanor, Russell Crowe is sure to confound, entertain, and probably shock us for years to come. ✪

MATT **DAMON**

If Matt Damon had a dime for every time "staying friends" was used to describe a celebrity breakup ... wait a minute, Damon likely has that many dimes! As one half of the Academy Award–winning screenwriting duo behind the 1997 sleeper hit *Good Will Hunting*, Damon has loads of change to spare, as well as a juicy breakup story of his own.

On the big screen he has been a soldier reluctant to leave battle (*Saving Private Ryan*), an angel (*Dogma*), and a lovelorn cowboy (*All the Pretty Horses*),

> **DAMON WAS APPARENTLY A CAD IN REAL LIFE WHEN HE DUMPED MINNIE DRIVER, HIS *HUNTING* COSTAR AND GIRLFRIEND OF SEVEN MONTHS, ON LIVE NETWORK TELEVISION**

but Damon was apparently a cad in real life when he dumped Minnie Driver, his *Hunting* costar and girlfriend of seven months, on live network television. It happened during Damon's appearance on a January 1998 episode of *The Oprah Winfrey Show*. When Her Oprahness asked the Oscar winner if he had a girlfriend, Good Will became Bad Matt when he replied, "No." Reports say Minnie Driver was the one most surprised by the admission. At the time she still believed she was very much his girlfriend and wasn't impressed to find out publicly— along with the entire continent—that she wasn't.

Damon insists Driver knew their relationship was over before he admitted as much to Oprah, but the actress is sticking to her story. Her hard feelings for her ex showed all over her face a couple of months later when a camera caught her in a close-up as Damon and friend Ben Affleck bounded up the steps to accept their Oscar for *Hunting*. Either that or she had been recently sucking on lemons. The night was a major disappointment all around for Minnie, save for her stunning red gown. She also lost in the Best Supporting

Actress category to Juliette Binoche in *The English Patient*. Still, her spokesperson released a statement claiming Damon and Driver would remain "good friends," a Hollywood cliché that brings to mind all of those dimes. ✪

TED **DANSON**

No man is immune to an occasional momentary lapse in judgment. However, when the man is as famous as former *Cheers* star Ted Danson, such a lapse becomes news that will follow him as long as he lives.

The occasion was a 1993 Friars Club Roast of Danson's then girlfriend, comic Whoopi Goldberg. The unlikely pair met the year before on the set of *Made in America* and quickly fell in love. Danson, who earned his place in TV lore as the womanizing ex-baseball player Sam Malone on *Cheers*, felt sure enough in his new relationship to end his fifteen-year marriage and move out of the home he shared with wife Casey and their two children.

The actor and the comedienne say they endured public scorn and racial discrimination against their intense love affair and, in response, they developed what Danson called "gallows humor" as a defense shield. Despite their previous individual fame, neither performer had yet experienced the kind of media scrutiny they endured as a couple. That special brand of humor, said Danson, prompted him to appear at Whoopi's roast in blackface and deliver a monologue laced with racial slurs and bawdy jokes. Danson claimed the performance was staged in the spirit of Al Jolson, but it was horribly out of context. Goldberg, in on the gag and a shocking comedy force in her own right, was delighted and laughed loudly. Some audience members weren't as amused and stomped out in disgust, proclaiming the routine racist. As Ricky used to tell Lucy, there was a lot of "splaining" to do.

Danson called his performance "brave" and Whoopi defended her man, now accused of being a bigot, by turning the critics' questions back on them. It didn't make sense, explained Whoopi: If Danson were truly a bigoted white man, how could he possibly date a black woman? That's what everyone else was wondering, too.

> THAT SPECIAL BRAND OF HUMOR, SAID DANSON, PROMPTED HIM TO APPEAR AT WHOOPI'S ROAST IN BLACKFACE AND DELIVER A MONOLOGUE LACED WITH RACIAL SLURS AND BAWDY JOKES

The relationship quickly fizzled out, but in press statements both performers insisted the blackface brouhaha didn't cause their split. Whoopi quickly took up with a dentist while Ted reportedly fled briefly back to his wife before later settling into a more comfortable, less combustible life with actress Mary Steenburgen. ✪

BETTE DAVIS

Bette Davis was a big screen idol to many actresses who were inspired by her box office reign in the 1930s and 1940s, including Whoopi Goldberg. The comic is a fan who delights in telling the story of her classic Davis experience.

Goldberg was very excited to be on the exclusive guest list for a party given by Elizabeth Taylor because Davis, her ultimate role model in movies, was also due to attend. As she mingled among the guests, Goldberg heard a tiny voice angrily denouncing the "stars" of today: "And that Whoopi Goldberg! She's been in the business five minutes and she's a star? I've never heard of her." Whoopi, becoming more agitated by the second, edged closer to the voice's source only to discover in horror that it was her idol, Miss Davis, the grumpy, self-righteous diva of the silver screen.

> DAVIS WAS A CRUSTY BROAD AND A BRILLIANT PERFORMER WHO'S REMEMBERED EQUALLY FOR HER ON-SCREEN PROWESS AND HER OFF-SCREEN ANTICS

Davis starred in dozens of films, won two Academy Awards, and at one time was the highest paid actress in Hollywood. At five-foot-two, Davis was a tiny package packed with dynamite that she lit for anyone who dared to tell her what to do, including some who had the right to do so, such as directors, producers, and heads of studios. Davis was a crusty broad and a brilliant performer who's remembered equally for her on-screen prowess and her off-screen antics.

Bette's well-earned reputation as an "actress who walks" began in 1934 when she refused to show up for wardrobe fitting and other production duties for the film *Housewife*, claiming the role assigned to her was too trivial. Her job action was in clear violation of her contract with Warner Bros. A letter from the studio's lawyers ended the protest more than ten days later. She soon attempted the same stunt for a movie titled *The Case of the Howling Dog.* That time Warner Bros. released Davis from the project and in her mind, a precedent was set: if she wanted out, all she had to do was hold out long enough to get her way.

Her tug of war with management escalated in 1936 when, fresh from a Best Actress Academy Award win for *Dangerous*, Davis decided that she was underpaid and her talent was being wasted. She wanted the freedom to choose projects from other studios, a privilege that was taboo at the time. When Warner Bros. balked, Davis pulled another no-show and pleaded illness and nervous exhaustion from making too many films back-to-back. She retracted the illness claim when the studio offered to send its physician to conduct an examination and fled to England while her agent held firm for a new contract.

Her words to the press, uttered with contempt during her holdout, echoed through the halls of all Hollywood studios: "I don't take the movies seriously and anyone who does is in for a headache. I really don't like the work but it's amusing, even if it is hard." Her loose-lipped publicity stunt backfired; her dedication was called into question, which encouraged Warner Bros. to dig in its heels. Davis was suspended and the case went before a judge, who sided with the studio. A defeated Bette grudgingly went back to work.

It wasn't long before her old antics resurfaced, and Davis once again refused to report for filming and other obligations, resulting in further suspensions. In 1937, she claimed her absence was due to a mysterious case of sunstroke; later, it was the flu; then, the recurrence of a puzzling nervous condition. When she revived complaints about being stifled by her contract in 1939, Warner Bros. enticed her back to work by threatening to replace her with Vivien Leigh, who was fresh from a triumphant performance as Scarlett O'Hara in *Gone with the Wind*. Despite the animosity between the studio and the actress, Warner Bros. managed to continue squeezing tremendous performances out of Bette. She won her second Oscar in 1939 for *Jezebel*.

> UNDER THE CONSTANT STRESS OF DAVIS'S FLARING ANGER ON THE SET OF 1943'S MR. SKEFFINGTON, SHERMAN'S HAIR BEGAN TO FALL OUT AND HE DEVELOPED INSOMNIA. "I WANTED TO KILL HER," HE SAID. INSTEAD, HE APPARENTLY STARTED SLEEPING WITH HER AGAIN

In 1941 she was at it again, stomping off the set of *The Little Foxes* following arguments with director William Wyler, her former lover. It took yet another threat of replacement—this time with Tallulah Bankhead, who originated Davis's *Foxes* role on stage—to coerce the rebellious star into returning.

Observers called Bette Davis strong willed. Those who chose to take her on called her a control freak. At least one married director, Vincent Sherman, reportedly discovered the only way to tame the savage beast was to sleep with her. His reprieve from Davis's wrath was short-lived, however; when Sherman called off the affair, his star's temper was whipped into a tornado. Under the constant stress of Davis's flaring anger on the set of 1943's *Mr. Skeffington*, Sherman's hair began to fall out and he developed insomnia. "I wanted to kill her," he said. Instead, he apparently started sleeping with her again.

The actress's claims of boredom, restlessness, and treatment unbefitting a star of her stature continued in varying degrees throughout her career. Likewise, her personal life remained just as unsettled and was peppered with extramarital affairs, abortions, and four marriages.

Some film historians attribute the tremendous success of the 1962 classic *Whatever Happened to Baby Jane?* as much to the real-life feud between its unpredictable stars, Bette Davis and Joan Crawford (*see* Joan Crawford), as to their performances. "That bitch hated working with me on *Jane* and vice versa," Davis said of Crawford. The ill will began soon after they were both cast with a tug-of-war over the lead roles. Davis said there was "no way" she would play the wheelchair-bound former film queen, lobbying instead for the darker role of the sister who torments her. Once production began, the stars went to great lengths to torture each other. Crawford strapped on weights before shooting a scene in which Davis had to drag her across a room, hoping the extra load would strain her rival's back. An on-screen kick from Davis that sends Crawford down the stairs is reported to have been real. They even fought over the size of their dressing rooms and the temperature in the studio. Yet somehow they managed to pose together with fixed grins for publicity photos. The dueling divas reunited for 1964's *Hush ... Hush, Sweet Charlotte*, but Davis's volatility reportedly drove Crawford to withdraw from the picture. She was replaced by Olivia de Havilland.

In her later years, Davis grew increasingly compulsive about her routine and cleanliness, and she smoked and drank heavily. Like the offspring of her old nemesis Crawford, Bette's daughter wrote two tell-all books about her mother. However, B. D. Hyman unleashed the embarrassing tomes while Bette

> **CRAWFORD STRAPPED ON WEIGHTS BEFORE SHOOTING A SCENE IN WHICH DAVIS HAD TO DRAG HER ACROSS A ROOM, HOPING THE EXTRA LOAD WOULD STRAIN HER RIVAL'S BACK**

was still alive and battling breast cancer, causing a permanent rift between them. Davis succumbed to cancer in 1989, four years after B.D.'s first hardback, *My Mother's Keeper*, was published.

In a fitting end to her career, Davis walked off the set of her last job, a film called *Wicked Stepmother*, in 1988. At age eighty and very frail, Davis admitted as she viewed the daily rushes that she was no longer up to the task. Her dentures clicked, she forgot her lines, and she appeared addled. But true to form, the ailing actress later complained—aloud and often—that the project was bungled and therefore she, the true professional, could not be expected to continue amid such incompetence. ✪

KIM **DELANEY**

The star of the legal drama *Philly* and the former cop on *NYPD Blue* obviously picked up a thing or two about the justice system from her day jobs. Kim Delaney's brush with the law wrapped up neatly in less than one short month.

It began in February 2002 with a 911 call from a California motorist who recognized the beautiful Emmy-winning actress and claimed she was behind the wheel of a weaving Mercedes-Benz on Malibu's Pacific Coast Highway. Just to be sure, this Good Samaritan (or Star-Struck Samaritan?) followed Delaney home and confirmed to cops that it was indeed former Detective Diane Russell from *NYPD Blue* in control of the car.

Delaney inadvertently summoned more police by setting off her home's burglar alarm. Now a gaggle of cops was on the way! The actress declined to submit to a blood alcohol

THE ACTRESS DECLINED TO SUBMIT TO A BLOOD ALCOHOL TEST AND WAS ARRESTED ON SUSPICION OF DRUNK DRIVING

test and was arrested on suspicion of drunk driving. The charge was later reduced to reckless driving, a misdemeanor, due to a lack of evidence to support the claim of intoxication. And the alarm? She tripped it because someone changed the code without telling her, claimed her lawyer. She pleaded no contest to the charge, resulting in two years' probation, a $300 fine, and enrollment in a driver's safety class.

The actress released a statement after the case wrapped, thanking the District Attorney's office for clearing her of the drinking and driving allegation, which she maintained from the start was bogus. What would Detective Andy Sipowicz have to say about that? ✪

SHANNEN DOHERTY

Is this star a spoiled brat or an innocent magnet for trouble? Ever since Shannen Doherty rose to fame in 1990 as an advantaged teen on the hit drama *Beverly Hills 90210*, she has drawn more attention for her bad girl reputation than for her acting skills.

At age ten, Doherty was a regular on *Little House: A New Beginning*. By eighteen, she was a seasoned show business veteran nestled under the wing of *über*producer Aaron Spelling. The TV impresario with the golden touch was responsible for several successful programs, including *The Love Boat*, *Dynasty*, *Sunset Beach*, and the preteen megahit *Beverly Hills 90210*. He's also to blame for unleashing his daughter Tori's one-dimensional acting style on an unsuspecting public, but we digress.

Reports concerning Doherty's foot-stomping, diva-like outbursts abounded from the *90210* set. In a nutshell, she apparently always had a bad attitude packed in her makeup kit; she refused to follow direction and regularly showed up late to the set to play Brenda Walsh. What *is* it with young stars who lose sight of the fact that they've beaten the odds in a lottery-like entrance to an incredibly privileged life? Her whiny, clingy character inspired some of the show's fans to create "I Hate Brenda" clubs. Doherty would later explain that people confused her with her on-screen persona, but her renown as a self-absorbed leading lady persisted. *90210* and Doherty parted company in 1994 due to "creative differences," a phrase synonymous according to some with, "She can't get along with anybody else." The actress also claimed she wanted to spend more time with her new husband, actor Ashley Hamilton, son of Alana Stewart and George Hamilton. The young couple split a few months later, citing "irreconcilable differences" (read: "We married before we got to know each other").

> **HER WHINY, CLINGY CHARACTER INSPIRED SOME OF THE SHOW'S FANS TO CREATE "I HATE BRENDA" CLUBS**

In the following years, Doherty became well acquainted with the court system through a wide array of charges. She was accused of bouncing checks, participating in a brawl at a Los Angeles nightclub, trashing a rented house, bailing out on back rent, and allowing her dogs to bite a woman who came to the door of her parents' home. She also completed a court-ordered anger management class and was placed on probation after smashing a car with a bottle.

Still, she worked. Some directors, like Kevin Smith of *Mallrats*, hired her *because* of her reputation rather than in spite of it. She now says her brat status was overblown and largely invented by the media.

Spelling took another risk with his troubled protégé in 1998 by casting her in a series called *Charmed*, which centered on three sisters with supernatural powers. The magic of *Charmed* didn't last for Doherty, who reportedly clashed with costar Alyssa Milano. With a wave of his wand, Spelling caused Shannen to disappear after three seasons and replaced her with Rose McGowan, whose film credits include *Scream* and *Monkeybone*. Doherty's departure came shortly after pleading no contest to drunk driving charges, a switch from her original plea of not guilty. The actress was pulled over in the wee hours after her Ford pickup drifted over several lanes of a California freeway. She refused a Breathalyzer, but a test revealed her blood alcohol level was .05 over the legal limit. Her sentence included research into the effects of alcohol, a fine, and five days of community service—all standard rulings in that state for a first DUI conviction.

The raven-haired siren spun another quickie romance into a wedding in February 2002. Reports say her new husband, film producer Rick Solomon (*Traffic*, *I Am Sam*), once wrecked a nightclub and was tossed out. It sounds like a marriage made in Hollywood. ✪

ROBERT **DOWNEY JR.**

One of the lowest points in Robert Downey Jr.'s battle against the demon of drug addiction manifested itself in a version of *Goldilocks and the Three Bears* —except Downey's experience was no fairy tale and we're still waiting for a happy ending for this gifted actor.

Robert Downey Sr. admits to instilling his son with a sense of permissiveness concerning drugs by offering the boy a joint when he was nine years old. Whatever Downey Jr. did between that time and 1996 he did within the bounds of the law (or, he just wasn't caught), but it all blew wide open in June of that year when a traffic stop revealed hard stuff inside his car: cocaine, heroin, and a loaded gun. Fast-forward one month and Downey's neighbor experienced the fright of her life when she discovered the inebriated actor unconscious in her child's bed. Ordered to rehab, Downey went AWOL three days later and found himself back before a stern-faced judge, who sentenced him to three years' probation.

His attraction to drugs proved more compelling than an obligation to the State. Downey violated probation terms several times and wound up behind bars for six months—a drug-addicted Academy Award nominee warehoused alongside common criminals. Recovery programs didn't stick. He attempted several times to kick the monkey off his back, all the while uttering an explanation for his behavior that he wore like a badge: "I've got a shotgun in my mouth and my finger on the trigger and I like the taste of gunmetal." Downey's career stayed on remarkably sure footing through it all with a steady roster of film and TV projects, including a Golden Globe–winning guest stint on *Ally McBeal*. However, long separations from his son Indio were taxing on the devoted dad. His wife Deborah formally ended the separation that began in 1996 and filed for divorce in 2001.

Meantime, the devil on Downey's shoulder kept encouraging him to give in to his impulses. In November 2000 an anonymous 911 caller tipped off police that Downey was in party mode and high on drugs at the swanky Merv Griffin Resort in Palm Springs. Police confirmed the tip when they discovered the actor in a luxury suite with cocaine and, inexplicably, a Wonder Woman costume in the closet. Facing another possible stint in the slammer, Downey became inconsolable and sought medical treatment for depression. When the gavel was lowered the following summer, Downey was spared a jail term thanks to a plea bargain. Instead, he was sent instead to rehab for one year with an extension on his probation.

> **POLICE CONFIRMED THE TIP WHEN THEY DISCOVERED THE ACTOR IN A LUXURY SUITE WITH COCAINE AND, INEXPLICABLY, A WONDER WOMAN COSTUME IN THE CLOSET**

The judge received periodic updates on the actor's progress and was pleased to find a more mature, settled Downey affirming his commitment to good health and a clean life. Downey stayed faithful to the live-in recovery routine and seems ready to finally stare down his demons. Downey was ecstatic when his 1996 drug charges were eventually dismissed by an impressed and optimistic judge. His fans are hoping the star has lost his taste for gunmetal. ✪

ELVIS

The King sang like nobody's business and adored his mama, but try as he might, he couldn't keep a grip on his small town values. What's a poor boy from the American South to do when his "aw shucks" background clashes with the glitz of superstardom?

From 1956 on (except for the two years he served as the world's most famous soldier), Elvis Presley's life was one marked by excess. One stroll through Graceland, his Memphis home, tells visitors all they need to know about Elvis's taste, best described as over-the-top. Gobs of campy decor plus multiples of the era's latest electronics reveal a man with far more money than style. Graceland is now the shrine where the faithful come to worship The King. Seemingly endless hallways snake through the back of the mansion. On the walls, hundreds of gold and platinum records, well-preserved stage wear, and other Presley memorabilia are encased in glass.

> **GRACELAND'S VIEWING ROOM WAS OUTFITTED WITH THREE TVS; THE LATTER-DAY STONED ELVIS WOULD WATCH THEM, ZOMBIE-LIKE, INTO THE WEE HOURS WITH A LOADED PISTOL BY HIS SIDE. IF A PROGRAM WASN'T TO HIS LIKING, HE SHOT THE TV**

Elvis's taste for all things tacky even extended to his choice in snacks. His love for late-night kitchen raids is well documented, and who isn't familiar with the rumor about his favorite comfort food? It's true: nothing but fried banana sandwiches, eaten by the plateful.

As the man his friends called E grew increasingly dependent on drugs, his weight ballooned out of control and his reclusive world revolved around watching television and getting the next fix. Surrounded by his protective and indulgent gang of cousins and friends known as the Memphis Mafia, The King developed another bad habit. Graceland's viewing room was outfitted with three TVs; the latter-day stoned Elvis would watch them, zombie-like, into the wee hours with a loaded pistol by his side. If a program wasn't to his liking, he shot the TV. It was The King's expensive and frightening alternative to the remote control.

In 1997, on the twentieth anniversary of his death in Graceland's powder room, we learned of Elvis's desire to become a federal agent. He met with FBI officials in December 1970 and offered to rat on fellow celebrities and anyone else he felt was "un-American." He candidly told agents that the Smothers Brothers, Jane Fonda, and the Beatles were responsible for the sorry state of the nation's young people. The Bureau's notes characterize The King as "serious and sincere," but also mention his "bizarre personal appearance." Federal agents don't usually meet with men who are wearing rhinestone jumpsuits.

The world still copes with conspiracy theories surrounding Elvis's overdose. The possibility that Elvis is still alive was renewed in 2002 as he topped the British pop charts with a disco version of "A Little Less Conversation" shortly before the twenty-fifth anniversary of his death in August. Depending on your particular view, E is either buried outside his Memphis mansion or he's alive and well and working the drive-thru of a burger joint in Poughkeepsie or Cleveland or Tulsa or Orlando ... you get the idea. ✪

EMINEM

Eminem's sophomore CD, *The Marshall Mathers LP*, was released in May 2000 and became the fastest selling rap album in history. It followed a stunning debut, *The Slim Shady LP*, which drew fire from all corners for its angry rants about homosexuals, boy bands, and wives—the standard food groups rap stars tend to feast on. Soon Marshall Mathers III was changing his tune from the angst of a poor white boy to the trappings of the emotionally unprepared rich and famous. His life began to read like the headlines on a tabloid cover.

> EMINEM CLAIMS HIS MUSIC MERELY HOLDS A MIRROR UP TO SOCIETY AND TELLS IT LIKE IT IS— NOT NECESSARILY LIKE IT OUGHT TO BE

In June 2000, the then twenty-eight-year-old rapper allegedly pistol-whipped a man he claimed to have discovered "intimately kissing" his wife Kim in a Michigan café. He stood accused of more gunplay on that same weekend for his involvement in a modern-day Wild West standoff with a member of rival Motor City rap act Insane Clown Posse. The stress on the overnight star and his family was palpable. Kim, his high school sweetheart and troubled wife of less than two years, attempted suicide in July and a fed up Eminem soon filed for divorce. In soap opera style he withdrew the petition, then stepped aside when Kim decided to refile. The settlement became sticky over money (what else?), with both parties claiming they wanted to do right by their daughter, Hailie Jade.

Eminem pleaded not guilty in the Posse fracas and worked out a deal with prosecutors over the alleged pistol-whipping. His total punishment was three years' probation.

The foul-mouthed star, who draws from real life for his music, quickly became a legal target for some of the people he immortalized on CD. Kim sued for $10 million, claiming her ex-husband's songs about fantasies of killing her caused emotional distress. He deftly deflected lawsuits from a former school bully and even his own mother, who sued her little boy Marshall twice. One claim was for unfair depiction in her son's music; the second was to toss out the first $25,000 settlement after her new lawyer advised her to try for something more lucrative. A judge saw through mommy's money-grubbing ruse and denied the claim. The accused wife-kisser also hired a legal eagle and eventually forced Slim Shady to kiss off $100,000. All the while *The Marshall Mathers LP* was perched atop the music charts.

The performer and his angry, in-your-face songs have been pulled off the air, banned, censored, scorned, edited, and vilified. A French composer claimed some of the sampled riffs from the Eminem anthem "Kill You" were plucked from his own jazz-fusion music. Columnists banged out pre-ceremony protests against Eminem's scheduled performance with Elton John at the 2001 Grammy Awards. Gay and lesbian groups joined in the chorus. But the powerful duet "Stan," Slim Shady's hip-hop rant about an obsessed fan, was exciting and flawless. It featured John on piano and singing parts of Dido's hit "Thank You," which had been sampled on the recorded version. The only questionable part of the performance was the finale, punctuated by the rapper offering his upright middle finger. Eminem claimed to be previously unaware of John's sexual orientation and later said he was gratified that a gay man would offer his support in the face of relentless criticism from pro-gay organizations like GLAAD. Eminem claims his music merely holds a mirror up to society and tells it like it is—not necessarily like it ought to be. ✪

LINDA EVANGELISTA

At the height of 1980s excess, the Canadian-born supermodel remarked to an interviewer that she didn't "wake up for less than $10,000 a day." That haughty statement has lived on as a symbol of arrogance, making Evangelista a little less beautiful in the eyes of a global population, many of whom are forced to wake up very early and work long days in real jobs—ones that don't involve a sycophantic photographer cooing, "Work with me, baby"—if they hope to earn ten grand. ✪

FARRAH FAWCETT

The ex-*Charlie's Angels* actress made several surprising career moves to dash her ditzy image, but none so regressive as her 1997 appearance on the *Late Show with David Letterman*.

In the 1970s Fawcett spun a pink bathing suit, feathered hair, and a million-dollar smile into a best-selling poster that became a mandatory wall covering in the bedrooms of red-blooded teenage boys everywhere. In years to come she would prove her talent with a spate of serious acting roles and her enduring beauty with two *Playboy* video specials that went behind the scenes of her magazine photo shoots. But her spaced-out appearance with Letterman confused us all.

In a mesmerizing and weird seventeen-minute interview, the actress tripped on her way to the chair, fidgeted, giggled, and lost

> IN A MESMERIZING AND WEIRD SEVENTEEN-MINUTE INTERVIEW, THE ACTRESS TRIPPED ON HER WAY TO THE CHAIR, FIDGETED, GIGGLED, AND LOST HER TRAIN OF THOUGHT

her train of thought. She rambled about the joys of body painting (rolling on a canvas, using her body as a brush) and became transfixed by Dave's faux Manhattan skyline backdrop. Speculation ran rampant that she was drunk or high on drugs. Not so, said Fawcett and her people, although no consistent reason for her oddness emerged. Her manager said it was his fault, as he advised her to act like Marilyn Monroe in *Gentlemen Prefer Blondes* during the interview. The *Late Show* producer chimed in and said it was a simple case of nerves. And Fawcett herself told the Television Critics Association her mom was to blame for telling her obedient daughter to loosen up with Dave and have a good time.

When she submitted to Letterman's scrutiny again two years later, Fawcett claimed she would "never have been in an altered state" on television and explained that during the earlier appearance, she had been "nervous and visceral."

Perhaps the whole strange episode can be attributed to severe stress. Just a few months before her wacky appearance, Fawcett and her lover of fifteen years, actor Ryan O'Neal, had called it quits. She was also accused (and acquitted) of stealing $73,000 worth of clothes and beaten up by her new boyfriend, director James Orr, after she turned down his marriage proposal. Fawcett declined to press charges, but police pursued the matter; Orr was convicted in the criminal case for slamming the former Angel's head onto a concrete driveway.

The beautiful fifty-something actress might have a more difficult time erasing smirks off the faces of those who read Joe Eszterhas's 2000 best-selling *American Rhapsody*. In the *Basic Instinct* screenwriter's scathing commentary on Hollywood indulgence (though the book's scope expanded to include an attack on Bill and Hillary Clinton), Eszterhas takes aim at a crowded Tinseltown party during which the lineup for the loo became too much for delicate Farrah to bear. Eszterhas contends — and Fawcett strongly denies — that the lady in question hitched up her cocktail dress and relieved herself on the lawn as half a dozen people watched dumbstruck through the window. If the actress were a dog, Eszterhas alleges her owner would have been required to stoop and scoop.

A steamed Farrah furiously disputed the claim by providing anecdotes from the too-much-information file, namely that she's unable to relieve herself in airplane bathrooms, let alone outdoors on someone's sod in full view of strangers. But if it's true, Eszterhas's tale remains the most notorious incident ever of celebrity lawn fertilization. ✪

FLESH-N-BONE

The music stopped for one-fifth of the Grammy-winning rap quintet Bone Thugs-N-Harmony with a September 2000 gun conviction. Flesh-N-Bone, born Stanley Howse, is serving an eleven-year sentence in a California state prison, an epilogue to a truly sad tale of a promising life gone horribly wrong.

Flesh-N-Bone and fellow Bones Layzie, Bizzy, Krayzie, and Wish won a 1997 Grammy for Best Rap Performance thanks to their spirituality-infused hip-hop single, "The Crossroads." Poised for superstardom, their CDs were selling platinum and their future was looking golden until Stanley's love for guns got in the way. A friend named Tarrance Vickers accused the singer of pulling an AK-47 from a baby crib and taking aim at him during a dispute in December 1999. A year earlier, Flesh was up on probation violation charges for another quick-draw firearm incident during an argument with a neighbor. On still another occasion, police reportedly caught him with a loaded sawed-off shotgun at a relative's home and claimed he refused to leave when asked.

FLESH PROPHETICALLY POSED BEHIND BARS FOR THE COVER OF HIS SOLO CD, 5TH BONE LET LOOSE, RECORDED PRIOR TO HIS IMPRISONMENT AND RELEASED IN THE FALL OF 2000

The presiding Van Nuys Superior Court Judge deemed Howse's life story one of the worst cases of child abuse she had ever read, full of beatings and other physical and mental traumas. Still, the rapper took responsibility for his actions by apologizing and describing himself as a nonviolent person who simply enjoys guns. He got ten years for the AK-47 incident, plus another for violating probation. The prerequisite anger management course that accompanies the majority of celebrity prison sentences was also tossed in for good measure.

Flesh prophetically posed behind bars for the cover of his solo CD, *5th Bone Let Loose*, recorded prior to his imprisonment and released in the fall of 2000. He may be down, but his lawyer says we shouldn't count him out. Despite incarceration, "Stanley will continue to write music and interact with people in the music industry," the lawyer claims. Meantime, Bone Thugs-N-Harmony continues to record and tour without him. ✪

ERROL FLYNN

The clichéd phrase "In like Flynn" was born of a scandalous episode in the swashbuckling actor's life. He never did live the incident down; rather, he embraced it.

A hot leading man in the late 1930s and into the 1940s, Flynn was described by many as too good looking. The Tasmanian devil's chiseled features and wash board abs made ladies swoon and men pack movie theaters for exciting, action-filled movies like *The Adventures of Robin Hood* and *They Died with Their Boots On*. Flynn was a natural in these films, having led an adventurous young life working his way from Tasmania through Australia, New Zealand, and England as a schooner-master, reporter, and diamond smuggler before landing in Hollywood. A hard drinker and a renowned ladies' man, he once remarked, "I like my whiskey old and my women young." The echo of that statement soon lost its glibness.

> **"I LIKE MY WHISKEY OLD AND MY WOMEN YOUNG." THE ECHO OF THAT STATEMENT SOON LOST ITS GLIBNESS**

Flynn's life on the high seas nearly sank in 1942 when two underage girls accused him of seduction. Charged with statutory rape, the actor faced a maximum twenty-five-year sentence and the near ruination of his reputation in the press. Strangely, the seriousness of the supposed crimes evolved into something of a joke. The phrase "In like Flynn" crept into the vernacular as a sexual reference, mockingly referring to the alleged rapes. One press report at the time praised the actor as "a wild man of the mattress." Flynn was eventually acquitted, but the slang and the stigma hung over him like a cloud. Humiliation finally gave way to acceptance, and with an if-you-can't-beat-'em-join-'em philosophy, Flynn eventually adopted "In like ..." as his personal motto.

Errol Flynn's career wilted in the 1950s with less buckling of his swash and several second-rate television jobs, taken with the sole purpose of keeping his yacht afloat. The actor seemed oblivious to the joke he had become. He died in Vancouver, Canada, of a heart attack in the fall of 1959. Married and divorced three times, Flynn's companion during his final years was a teenage girl. ✪

JANE FONDA

In the early 1970s, the actress-turned-activist lived to regret becoming the poster girl for the antiwar movement and propagandizing on behalf of the Viet Cong during America's controversial involvement in the Vietnam War.

The Oscar-winning star of *Coming Home* and *Barbarella* still draws hate mail (and now hate Internet postings) for sticking her movie star's nose into the conflict in Vietnam. There were scads of protests on the home front, but Fonda kicked it up a notch by traveling to the war zone in the summer of 1972 and shoving her so-called liberal views in the faces of her countrymen, the soldiers who were far from home and fighting for their lives. During her two-week visit to Vietnam the message was peace, but the messenger was stigmatized a traitor.

> IN THE EARLY 1970S, THE ACTRESS-TURNED-ACTIVIST LIVED TO REGRET BECOMING THE POSTER GIRL FOR THE ANTIWAR MOVEMENT AND PROPAGANDIZING ON BEHALF OF THE VIET CONG DURING AMERICA'S CONTROVERSIAL INVOLVEMENT IN THE VIETNAM WAR

In August of 1972, Fonda delivered a broadcast to US troops that was filled with emotional impressions from her fortnight with the Vietnamese people and details of their suffering during the war. Branding President Richard Nixon a criminal and a killer, she pronounced the campaign essentially unwinnable by American forces. Her words were like ammunition, wounding the soldiers' spirits like the enemy's bullets were wounding their bodies. In a decision she has since characterized as "thoughtless," she also posed with North Vietnamese soldiers for a now famous photo on an antiaircraft carrier. Americans were angry, confused, and outraged by her obvious lack of loyalty. She was an actress, a person who pretends for a living—what right did she have to opine on the realities of 'Nam, they wanted to know. The mocking moniker "Hanoi Jane" follows Fonda to this day. For some, the deep cut of her perceived betrayal has never healed.

The ex–Mrs. Ted Turner also turned her tongue on her own state, angering the governor. At a 1998 United Nations meeting, Fonda compared the living conditions in some parts of rural Georgia to those in Third World countries. Governor Zell Miller was not amused and sarcastically suggested via letter that she come down from her Atlanta penthouse on occasion to get a closer look at the rest of the state. Fonda retracted her comments and apologized, calling her actions "ill advised." However, the furor surrounding the incident was a mere blip on the screen compared with her days in the limelight as Hanoi Jane.

The scab of the Hanoi Jane experience was picked off after September 11, 2001, amid a renewed focus on terrorism and war. Fonda once again opened up about her opposition to conflict, revealing herself to be soft on terrorism at a time when vengeance was on the nation's mind. In the sensitive first few days following the September 11 terrorist attacks, she apparently told an Atlanta radio station that the US should not rush into war. Instead, said Jane, the underlying roots of terrorism need to be understood and then the acts themselves must be dealt with as criminal activity. Full military action, in her view, was not warranted to avenge the deaths of thousands of innocent civilians. There are countless grieving families who apparently feel differently. ✪

FRANK **GIFFORD**

Some say the measure of a man isn't in what he'll do while you're watching, but what he'll do when he thinks there are no witnesses. If that's the case, Frank Gifford doesn't measure up.

Shame on the *Globe* tabloid and TWA flight attendant Suzen Johnson, but most of all, shame on Frank Gifford, a man old enough to know better. In 1997, the *Globe* allegedly set Frank up, hiring a sexy, married, forty-six-year-old flight attendant for a reported fee of $75,000 to lure the very married, sixty-six-year-old football commentator and former professional player into a New York hotel room. The suite was wired for sight and sound, and the duo's steamy liaison was videotaped and recorded. The *Globe* then gleefully released still photos of the couple's neck-nibbling hugfest and doled out lurid pillow talk from their conversation.

> IN 1997, THE *GLOBE* ALLEGEDLY SET FRANK UP, HIRING A SEXY, MARRIED, FORTY-SIX-YEAR-OLD FLIGHT ATTENDANT FOR A REPORTED FEE OF $75,000 TO LURE THE VERY MARRIED, SIXTY-SIX-YEAR-OLD FOOTBALL COMMENTATOR AND FORMER PROFESSIONAL PLAYER INTO A NEW YORK HOTEL ROOM

While thousands of readers were snapping up the scandalous edition of the *Globe*, some major department store chains refused to stock it, claiming its contents—a married man liaising with a married woman who was not his wife—violated their sense of ethics. The stores' stand didn't hurt sales. It seemed everyone wanted to see the husband of sickly sweet Kathie Lee misbehaving in the extreme. Meanwhile, even Johnson was outraged, claiming she didn't consent to cameras. She later sued the tabloid for invasion of privacy.

For Gif, the fallout was a nightmare. He and Kathie Lee, married for eleven years at the time, were forced to wear perma-grins and repeatedly wax on to the media about the "solid" state of their marriage. If the situation was particularly painful for Kathie Lee, she kept her dirty laundry in the hamper. Then a top-rated TV chatstress alongside cohost Regis Philbin on *Live*, she had anchored her career on sharing intimate details from her happy home life with Frank and their children, Cody and Cassidy. Still, she stood by her man throughout the humiliating episode, which was prolonged by Suzen Johnson's fifteen minutes of fame spinning off into a *Playboy* pictorial later in the year. Johnson was photographed in—you guessed it—a hotel bedroom.

The FBI is reported to have briefly investigated whether or not Johnson violated prostitution laws by essentially having been paid to have sex. No charges were filed.

More than a year after his imprudent tryst, Gifford admitted that fooling around on his supportive spouse was the dumbest thing he had ever done. Kathie Lee has forgiven her wayward mate and hopes others will do the same. She reasons, "I would hate for him to be defined by one mistake." ✪

GARY **GLITTER**

Never was a piece of music so quickly pulled from sports arenas around the world as "Rock and Roll Part II" when news spread of Gary Glitter's arrest on child pornography charges. The crunchy, mostly instrumental 1972 anthem with rhythmic "Hey!"s in place of actual lyrics was a staple at sporting events where crowd excitement was paramount to the thrill of the contest. Perhaps only golf and chess were exempt from its thumping, clap-along beat.

During a routine shop repair in late 1997, a PC belonging to Glitter, born Paul Francis Gadd, was found to contain disturbing pictures of children. A raid on the singer's home turned up more photos of boys and girls under the age of sixteen, described by police as "indecent." Glitter was released on bail, but repercussions came quickly. His name was instantly removed from the lineup of a planned benefit concert for underprivileged children. Once his arrest and the dozens of counts against him made headlines, a woman came forward claiming the star had sexually abused her nearly two decades earlier. However, the accuser's credibility immediately developed more holes than a colander when it was revealed that she accepted cash from British tabloids for her story and stood to earn more if Glitter was convicted.

> **HE SERVED TWO MONTHS AND EMERGED FROM JAIL SHAKEN, PALE, AND LOOKING VERY OLD WITHOUT HIS TRADEMARK HIGH-TOP WIG. CHOKING BACK TEARS, GLITTER ADMITTED TO HIS SINS AND PROMISED THAT HE HAD LEARNED HIS LESSON**

The abuse and porn cases were tried separately, a long year and a half later. Acquitted first of all counts of sexual abuse, Glitter then faced charges for trading porn, where he didn't fare as well. After pleading guilty to fifty-four counts, the glitter was gone for Gary as he accepted a sentence of four months in a Bristol prison. He served two months and emerged from jail shaken, pale, and looking very old without his trademark high-top wig. Choking back tears, Glitter admitted to his sins and promised that he had learned his lesson. He eventually dropped a planned appeal and accepted his fate along with his place on England's list of registered sex offenders.

Glitter moved to Cambodia, a country with an unfortunate reputation for being a haven for those involved in the sex trade. He was deported in December 2002 for what officials will describe only as a "violation of Cambodian law." ✪

BOBCAT
GOLDTHWAIT

It's considered a compliment to tell a stand-up comic that they've "set the house on fire." The night he appeared on *The Tonight Show* with Jay Leno, hyperactive comedian Bobcat Goldthwait *actually* set fire to the house, scaring the heck out of his host and getting himself into a rat's nest of trouble.

Few TV hosts can handle an unpredictable guest as well as Jay Leno. Funny men and women who are notorious for really letting loose and stick-handling outside their prearranged material—Jim Carrey, Robin Williams, Whoopi Goldberg, and the like—have given *The Tonight Show* some of its most memorable moments and Leno is always up for the challenge. But when Bobcat Goldthwait gave his own brand of ad-libbing a try, it went horribly wrong.

Screeching, angst-riddled Goldthwait is still best known for appearing in several *Police Academy* movies. Five days prior to his appearance with Leno, the *Shakes the Clown* star had, as part of his impulsive act, destroyed thousands of dollars' worth of sound equipment on *The Arsenio Hall Show*. Goldthwait insists Leno's staff was aware that he would do something outrageous on *The Tonight Show* and he admits his plan was premeditated—he arrived at the NBC studios carrying a can of lighter fluid.

While on stage, Goldthwait startled Leno and the audience by setting a chair on fire as the cameras rolled and onlookers gasped in amazement. What may have seemed funny to the comic in theory didn't get him many laughs in practice. Leno was livid and in fear for everyone's safety if the fire spread. Fortunately, the blaze was contained to a single unfortunate piece of upholstered furniture.

THE NIGHT HE APPEARED ON *THE TONIGHT SHOW* WITH JAY LENO, HYPERACTIVE COMEDIAN BOBCAT GOLDTHWAIT ACTUALLY SET FIRE TO THE HOUSE, SCARING THE HECK OUT OF HIS HOST AND GETTING HIMSELF INTO A RAT'S NEST OF TROUBLE

The fire department and other authorities didn't look kindly upon Goldthwait's little display of spontaneous combustion either. The comedian was fined $4,000, placed on probation, and forced to appear in televised public service announcements about fire safety. Further humiliation befell the recreational pyromaniac when the Burbank fire marshal refused to approve the first set of spots, saying Goldthwait's performance was insincere. A less sarcastic Bobcat was forced to reshoot all the commercials from scratch.

Now that he's over forty, Goldthwait is settling down professionally and personally. The man who once shot a fire extinguisher up Kathie Lee Gifford's skirt and stripped naked on *Dennis Miller Live* has toned down his act. He ventured into sitcom territory, costarring in the short-lived *Nikki* for the WB network and emerging with a fiancée—none other than the show's star, Nikki Cox. "If they come out to see a freak show now," says the once frenetic comic, "they'll be disappointed." ✪

HUGH GRANT

"What the hell were you thinking?"

Jay Leno asked the question for all of us when a bashful Hugh Grant submitted to his first interview, on *The Tonight Show*, just days after he stunned the free world by engaging the services of a Los Angeles street walker—and getting busted for it.

In his June 1995 mug shot, Hugh Grant looked like any other sorry John—sorry that he got caught. Sporting a striped T-shirt and the sagging shoulder stance of a little boy who's been very naughty, it was likely the only time the cocky star of *Bridget Jones's Diary* has looked so uncomfortable in front of a camera.

While in La-La land to promote the movie *Nine Months*, Grant exercised inexplicable bad judgment and taste by soliciting the services of hooker Divine Brown in his rented, white BMW convertible. The twosome turned into a three-some when their activity attracted the attention of the Los Angeles Police Department. Brown's company came cheap at $50, but the lesson Hugh learned was exceedingly expensive.

SPLASH NEWS/KEYSTONE PRESS

The mug shot of Hugh Grant taken after his solicitation arrest

Headlines around the world screamed out the lurid details. Everyone wondered why a dashing gent with a bright future and a longtime super-model-actress girlfriend (Elizabeth Hurley) would roll the dice on his charmed life for a moment's purchased pleasure with a stranger.

An apologetic and deeply embarrassed Grant flew home to England after being formally charged in LA with solicitation. The tabloids chomped on his anticipated banishment by Hurley, who told interviewers she felt as if she'd been shot when she heard the news. Those same tabs recoiled in shock before summer's end when Hurley professed forgiveness and acceptance of her partner's dalliance.

To his credit, Grant didn't duck the tough questions. Following his sentencing—a fine of $1,180 and two years' probation—he made the talk show rounds while his adorable mug appeared on virtually every major magazine cover. The actor claims he was even offered a role in family-friendly Disney's *101 Dalmatians* the day after his arrest.

Divine Brown squeezed every second out of her fifteen minutes of fame after serving her 180-day jail sentence and paying a fine for lewd conduct charges. She became the darling of morning radio talk shows, starred in a porn film, and vowed to give up prostitution to become a serious actress. That change in vocation didn't last; a year later she was once again busted for soliciting, and apparently went broke after confusing fame with wealth and acquiring a taste for caviar and expensive hotel rooms she couldn't afford.

Grant and Hurley continued their relationships, both personal and professional, and produced and starred in the film *Extreme Measures* together. British tabloids speculated Hurley's mercy on Grant was spawned by guilt—she allegedly had had an affair four years earlier. However, their thirteen-year love story ended in the spring of 2000. Friends of the couple claimed they never really recovered from the hooker hoopla. The official reason for the breakup was cited as a disagreement over starting a family. Hurley has since given birth to a baby boy while Grant, the author of his own unusual destiny, recently whined that his fame has taken the thrill out of dating. ✪

TOM GREEN

As a man who makes his living by being outrageous, shock comic Tom Green has to go pretty far to surprise anyone. After all, this is the goateed MTV star who routinely humiliates his own parents on his show by phoning them at 3 A.M. just to freak them out, not to mention holding his panicked father's face still so he can give him a saliva-soaked French kiss. Followed by cameras, he shows up in unexpected places to impersonate ordinary people doing ordinary jobs (e.g., bingo caller, sandwich maker, sports coach) until he's forcibly removed from the establishment. When his road crew happened upon a dead moose on a rural roadside, Green naturally allowed them to capture him on film humping the blood-soaked carcass. He proved nothing is off limits by designing a comedy special around his own, real-life battle with testicular cancer. His movie *Freddy Got Fingered* anchored many Worst Movies of 2001 lists, centering as it did on a boy's false accusations of child molestation against his father. But Green crossed a line when one of his unexpected stunts actually ground a TV talk show to a halt.

The occasion was an appearance on *Open Mike* with Mike Bullard, on Green's home turf in Canada. The host was braced for outlandish behavior, having entertained Green before. On a previous show, Bullard watched helplessly as the comic sprayed the studio with milk. Bullard learned to anticipate virtually anything, including losing control of his own program. But on his November 1998 visit, Green presented his host with an unexpectedly disgusting gift: the corpses of a squirrel and a raccoon. The aromatic presents were of the vintage variety, reeking of rotting flesh and teeming with maggots and other life forms. Green unceremoniously slapped the dead animals on Bullard's desk and all hell broke loose. The host fled the studio to get sick in a nearby alley. Guests ran, the production crew sprayed air freshener, and taping was halted. Bullard told the *Toronto Sun*, "I threw up for 10 minutes."

WHEN HIS ROAD CREW HAPPENED UPON A DEAD MOOSE ON A RURAL ROADSIDE, GREEN NATURALLY ALLOWED THEM TO CAPTURE HIM ON FILM HUMPING THE BLOOD-SOAKED CARCASS

Amazingly, Green was allowed to stay and finish the taping. He has been welcomed back to the Bullard show since the road kill debacle, although producers now ask more questions about his plans. Since the incident, Green has graduated from comedian cult hero to magazine and tabloid cover boy, thanks to his brief marriage to actress Drew Barrymore. We can hardly wait for the comedy special about his divorce. ✪

Tonya **HARDING**

This figure skater's life, once brimming with potential, has become a sad and sorry mess. Hardened by disappointment and harsh consequences, Harding has no one to blame but herself for her dashed dreams.

Two descriptors will forever be spoken in the same breath as the name Tonya Harding: disgraced skater and knee-clubber. The two-time US champion was banned for life from figure skating after she claimed her then husband Jeff Gillooly hatched a plan to oust her number one domestic rival, Nancy Kerrigan. Gillooly and some friends conspired to attack Kerrigan at the US championships in Detroit, Michigan, hoping a good whack to the knees would end her bid for the Olympics, if not her entire career. The plan backfired in spectacular fashion and Harding ended up with much more than she had bargained for: a conviction on a charge of hindering prosecution, a $110,000 fine, and 500 hours of community service. Kerrigan went on to finish second in the Lillihammer Olympics while Harding struggled into eighth place. In the years to come, things would only get worse.

Broke, divorced, and barred from the sport that had been her means of support, Harding's life took a southward slide, a decline often aided by too much booze. In 2000, she spent a few nights behind bars for bopping her boyfriend with a hubcap during a drunken brawl. She was turfed from her Washington home a year later for failing to pay back rent. In the spring of 2002, Harding was cited for alleged drunken driving after she plunged her pickup truck into a Battle Ground, Oregon, ditch. The ex-skater failed field

Tonya Harding and Paula Jones pose before their match on Celebrity Boxing

sobriety and breath tests, logging in at twice the state's legal alcohol limit. She and her passenger, a twenty-three-year-old man, were unhurt in the accident. Harding made a plea bargain with prosecutors that kept her out of jail in return for her admission of guilt and a promise to complete a two-year alcohol counseling program. This time, thankfully, everyone's knees were spared.

Harding recently joined other notorious personalities on the TV special called *Celebrity Boxing*, a mock sporting spectacle that is really just a dustbin for has-beens. The perennial tough girl dominated and pummeled her opponent Paula Jones (*see* Bill Clinton) in front of millions of transfixed viewers. It was arguably a more constructive outlet for the violent side of Harding's peculiar personality. ✪

RENNY HARLIN

Finnish director Renny Harlin wrote dark chapters, both personal and professional, in the life story of Oscar-winning actress Geena Davis. As a member of the high IQ society Mensa International, perhaps Davis ought to have caught a whiff of her rogue mate's pending betrayal. But as a woman blinded by love, she didn't have a hope of avoiding the speeding train wreck poised to crumble her career and her emotions.

> **FINNISH DIRECTOR RENNY HARLIN WROTE DARK CHAPTERS, BOTH PERSONAL AND PROFESSIONAL, IN THE LIFE STORY OF OSCAR-WINNING ACTRESS GEENA DAVIS**

Harlin and Davis wed in a lavish September 1993 ceremony; the marriage was her third and his first. They vowed to work together as much as they could, citing all of those superstar couples who fail to go the distance because of too much time spent apart. They appeared poised to become a tour de force in filmmaking, with Harlin behind the lens and his statuesque, ex-model wife out front. But something went wrong on the road from concept to completion. The collaboration between *The Accidental Tourist* star and the *Cliffhanger* director resulted in some of the most poorly received films, both critically and financially, of the early 1990s. From the disappointing action-thriller *The Long Kiss Goodnight* to the sorry swashbuckling *Cutthroat Island*, the couple couldn't seem to make a go of it as a coproducing team. Despite an outward appearance of solidarity, their marriage was stumbling along a similar path.

After separating in April 1997, they formally announced plans to divorce in August. In a typically classy move, Davis didn't lay blame and instead pledged a desire to continue a working relationship with her former prince charming. In October, Harlin proved to be more rat than royalty when it was revealed that an assistant from his production company had given birth to his child. No one needed a calculator to work out that equation. Geena's spokesperson issued a terse statement, saying only, "The facts speak for themselves."

Since the divorce, Harlin has gone on to orchestrate such duds as *Deep Blue Sea* and *Driven*. Davis, meanwhile, has enjoyed a career revival in gems like *Stuart Little*. She married for a fourth time in 2001 to a surgeon fifteen years her junior, and gave birth to a daughter the following year. It seems the cosmos occasionally believes in a karmic conclusion, even in Hollywood. ✪

WOODY HARRELSON

Woody Harrelson is definitely not the same man as Woody Boyd, the lovable, dim-witted bartender he played so convincingly for eight seasons on *Cheers*. His off-camera time is most often spent far away from celebrity parties, movie premiers, and other exclusive see-and-be-seen events, as he'd rather support causes he feels are worthy. Among them is promoting the benefits of eco-friendly hemp to a population purportedly duped into thinking hemp and marijuana plants are one and the same. But attempting to change the world has cost Woody his time, money, and reputation.

> **HARRELSON BECAME A FARMER IN 1996 BY PLANTING FOUR—COUNT 'EM, FOUR—HEMP SEEDS IN BEATTYVILLE, KENTUCKY, IN HOPES OF CHALLENGING THE LOCAL LAWS, WHICH FORBID HEMP PRODUCTION**

Harrelson became a farmer in 1996 by planting four—count 'em, four—hemp seeds in Beattyville, Kentucky, in hopes of challenging the local laws, which forbid hemp production. The case went through several courts and was even delayed so the good folks of Beattyville wouldn't miss their annual Wooly Worm Festival on account of jury duty. The *White Men Can't Jump* star milked his arrest for all its worth, saying he was willing to go to jail on behalf of cash crop farmers whose kin had made a living from growing hemp before it was unjustly outlawed 150 years ago. The case proceeded only after a naïve state judge ruled there was no difference between hemp and marijuana. That decision was a major setback for Harrelson, who owns a hemp goods company and has a vested interest in educating a nation about harvesting hemp as an alternative to destroying old-growth forests. (His support of marijuana is also well known, but his activism on that issue is smaller-scale.) Once the hemp seeds were classed the same as marijuana, a possession conviction ran Woody the risk of a possible jail term.

The actor rejected a prosecutorial deal that would have quashed the case in exchange for a thirty-day jail sentence and a small fine. Although the agreement would have served Woody the individual, it wouldn't have served his higher purpose. Four years and several trips to Beattyville later, a jury deliberated for less than half an hour before finding Harrelson not guilty. Perhaps they were swayed by their former governor and hemp activist Louie Nunn, who testified on Woody's behalf.

Harrelson proved that white men can climb in the winter of 1996, when he joined eight other eco-minded crusaders and scaled San Francisco's Golden Gate Bridge in demonstration against the destruction of a redwood forest. The resulting misdemeanor charge was settled with a $1,000 fine and a day's worth of community service. He also came to the aid of a stranger arrested for housing a marijuana grow operation in his Los Angeles home. The actor put up half a million dollars to spring the man from jail.

Meantime, he continued a stubborn attempt to order a new trial for his own father, who was convicted in 1979 of murdering a San Antonio federal judge. Spending his own money, Woody hired private investigators and lawyers to work on substantiating his father's alibi of being in another city at the time of the killing. Woody actually persuaded a judge on the case to recuse himself due to conflict of interest during a one-on-one basketball game. The actual decision came in court, with lawyers and other officials present, but the camaraderie established on the b-ball court certainly didn't hurt the decision-making process.

Not too long ago, the star of *The People versus Larry Flynt* found himself on the receiving end of a lawsuit following a scuffle with tabloid shutterbugs at the Martha's Vineyard airport. After repeatedly requesting that his daughter, then a toddler, not be photographed, the actor snatched away a camera and film when his pleas were ignored. A Boston judge ruled in favor of the photographers, calling the camera confiscation "assault" and fining Woody $4,800. It was considered a judicial loss but a moral victory due to the paltry penalty.

WOODY ACTUALLY PERSUADED A JUDGE ON THE CASE TO RECUSE HIMSELF DUE TO CONFLICT OF INTEREST DURING A ONE-ON-ONE BASKETBALL GAME

In spring 2001, Harrelson and pals took their passion to the pavement and launched the Simple Organic Living (SOL) Tour. Designed to prove the merits of an ecology-minded lifestyle that doesn't compromise modern conveniences, the bicycle tour from Seattle to Los Angeles was accompanied by Woody's own bus, which was fueled with a mixture of hemp and vegetable oils. SOL stopped at college campuses to demonstrate the bus's solar-powered kitchen and other features. Woody's wife Laura was struck by a car midtour, but was not seriously hurt. Woody himself was stopped by a cop after cycling through a stop sign; no charge was laid, however.

Woody made headlines in 2002 in London, England, for allegedly trashing a taxi and running off, leaving hundreds of dollars' worth of damage. The cab's owner, who told the tabloids that the actor went "berserk" during the incident, decided not to press charges after Woody compensated him for repairs. At the time, Harrelson was anticipating the release of his next film, *Anger Management.* ✪

JOHN **HEARD**

Celebrities often level charges of stalking against deranged or obsessed fans, but it's unusual for one star to make the claim against another. Being cast as a stalker was certainly a role reversal for versatile actor John Heard, best known as Macaulay Culkin's dad in the 1992 family blockbuster *Home Alone*. His accuser: his equally famous ex, Melissa Leo; the alleged prey: Leo and their son.

Heard, a sought-after character actor whose face is still more recognizable than his name, found himself playing the part of defendant in 1997. Ex-love Leo, former star of *Homicide: Life on the Street* and mother of the former couple's son John, claimed the actor was persistently pestering her and their young boy. She further alleged telephone harassment and trespassing at the child's school, and her live-in boyfriend claimed to have been clubbed by Heard. During their bitter breakup three years earlier, Heard was denied custody of the boy and evidence emerged that he physically abused Leo during their relationship. Citing his volatile temper and lack of parenting skills, a judge allowed the actor access to his son only three days a month. Apparently Heard felt that was not enough.

> BEING CAST AS A STALKER WAS CERTAINLY A ROLE REVERSAL FOR VERSATILE ACTOR JOHN HEARD, BEST KNOWN AS MACAULAY CULKIN'S DAD IN THE 1992 FAMILY BLOCKBUSTER HOME ALONE

Leo testified that she felt victimized by Heard's constant, unexpected visits and his alleged spying on John while the child was at school. Unable to properly concentrate on her work as Detective Kay Howard on the *Homicide* set, Leo claimed she felt as if she were living at the core of a "war zone." A frustrated Heard challenged the charges, maintaining his rights as a father were being denied. He claimed the legal system had failed him—had failed all dads, in fact—and left him with no other option but to steal furtive moments with his son.

Heard's head hung low in a Baltimore court when all in attendance listened to more than two dozen of his taped phone messages to Leo, which ranged in tone from solicitous to angry, proving Leo justified in having earlier secured a restraining order against the unpredictable star.

The most serious charges—stalking, assault, harassment—were all dropped, but an anguished Heard was found guilty of trespassing and improper use of a telephone. Spared a maximum six-year prison sentence, he was put on probation and ordered into psychological treatment for habitual abusers. Terms also included keeping clear of Leo and her boyfriend except during the routine business of picking up and dropping off his son for specified court-ordered visits. Throughout the ordeal, Heard proclaimed the case one of "father's rights," rights that in his narrowly focused mind were being wrongly denied. ✪

ANNE HECHE

Love at first sight apparently exists, but how about lesbianism at first sight? In the wacky world of Anne Heche, it does indeed—alongside aliens and spaceships.

When the astral-planed actress first laid eyes on comic Ellen Degeneres across a crowded room at an Oscar party and proclaimed herself instantly in love, she inspired a million parental "I told you so" lectures. Moms and dads who didn't believe their offspring's same-sex orientation was genetic were suddenly vindicated by this ditzy performer who, as a supposed adult, clearly chose to suddenly become gay. Then, like a light switch, three and a half years later she flicked back to straight mode.

She has strained our sympathy so many times that it's difficult to drum up any more for Anne Heche. The Six Days, Seven Nights star, now happily married to a cameraman and the mother of her own youngster, rode the crest of the Anne-Ellen couplehood to starring roles opposite the likes of Harrison Ford and Robert DeNiro. Who could blame us for our suspicions that likable, funny Ellen was being duped by a fake dyke? As a couple, they orchestrated Ellen's infamous coming out and together mourned the subsequent cancellation of her suddenly

> **LOVE AT FIRST SIGHT APPARENTLY EXISTS, BUT HOW ABOUT LESBIANISM AT FIRST SIGHT? IN THE WACKY WORLD OF ANNE HECHE, IT DOES INDEED —ALONGSIDE ALIENS AND SPACESHIPS**

unfunny sitcom *Ellen*. Their relationship, long-lasting by Hollywood standards, offered us Tinseltown's first camera-friendly lesbian lovers and presented a united force against intolerance of homosexuals. When that bigotry didn't evaporate, they even vowed to leave Hollywood for good (a promise they didn't keep). The duo bought a house together and waxed on mushily about wanting to get married and adopt a baby—regular couple stuff.

But then whiffs of a rift surfaced and the official announcement of their breakup came in August 2000. "We have decided to end our relationship," read the official statement. "It's an amicable parting and we greatly value the three and a half years we have spent together." What we thought was Heche's strangest hour came just hours following the press release. (Little did we know, then.) A resident of a rural home near Fresno, California, was startled to discover the babbling *Psycho* star, dazed and confused, wandering in just her bra and shorts after having abandoned her car beside a highway a mile away. A sheriff's deputy who was called to the scene reported that Heche was cooperative, introduced herself as God, and claimed to be gathering recruits for a spaceship trip.

A SHERIFF'S DEPUTY WHO WAS CALLED TO THE SCENE REPORTED THAT HECHE WAS COOPERATIVE, INTRODUCED HERSELF AS GOD, AND CLAIMED TO BE GATHERING RECRUITS FOR A SPACESHIP TRIP

The lawman said she appeared to be under the influence of a controlled substance, which was later determined to be the drug Ecstasy. The kindly homeowner was sympathetic to her alien guest, who was later diagnosed with dehydration on account of her long stroll in the summer heat. While the incident made headlines and provided fodder for countless jokes, Heche was spared a criminal investigation. Two days later, she was on a plane bound for Canada, ready to costar in the medical drama *John Q*.

More than a year after her visit to Fresno, Heche would explain to Barbara Walters that the bizarre episode began prior to popping E, with voices that compelled her to take the drug (she was not a drug abuser), travel to the mid-California town, and wait for a spaceship. She was eventually taken away, true, but it was in an ambulance, not the Enterprise.

What to do when you are, for the moment, the most misunderstood person in show business? Simple. Write a book about it. In her autobiography *Call Me Crazy*, Heche attributed her many years of "insanity" to long-term sexual abuse at the hands of her choir director father, who died of AIDS in 1983. She acknowledged splitting off into a second personality, an alien named Celestia, whenever her real life became too much to bear. Heche's furious mother and sisters vehemently denied the sex abuse claims; her mom was particularly incensed by Anne's assertion that she ignored her husband's continued misuse of her daughter. Now, having found joy in newly formed family ties and finding no more need for distracting alien adventures, the star has pronounced herself mentally fit.

Is Anne Heche a survivor and thriver despite unimaginable atrocities put upon her by the man who should have been protecting her? Or is she an insufferable attention seeker, willing to humiliate and hurt anyone for the sake of fame? Only Celestia knows for sure. ✪

JIMI **HENDRIX**

Drugs have been the downfall of many a fine rock and roll artist. They were the root cause of James Marshall Hendrix's premature checkout at the tender age of twenty-seven.

While Jimi Hendrix's biography contained scads of typical tales about rock star excesses (most involved women, wine, and weed), a wily promoter's attempt to spin Jimi into a wholesome, family-friendly performer charted the strangest paragraph in his brief life story. Jimi's unique techniques with a guitar—playing with his teeth and occasionally setting an instrument on fire for pure shock value—caught the attention of Mickey Dolenz, himself a serious musician trapped in the role of teen idol as a star on TV's The Monkees.

Seattle-born Hendrix had launched his assault on rock and roll in the UK and was ready to return stateside. In the strangest concert pairing until crooner Anne Murray shared a bill with Bruce Springsteen, Hendrix and his band were signed on to blare powerful, feedback-laced licks as the opening act for adoring Monkee-focused crowds. It was the debut US concert tour for both groups, and a very short-lived stint for Jimi. Even as his signature classic "Purple Haze" was poised to climb the pop charts, the guitarist was booed by the teenybopper

> JIMI HENDRIX'S BIOGRAPHY CONTAINED SCADS OF TYPICAL TALES ABOUT ROCK STAR EXCESSES (MOST INVOLVED WOMEN, WINE, AND WEED), A WILY PROMOTER'S ATTEMPT TO SPIN JIMI INTO A WHOLESOME, FAMILY-FRIENDLY PERFORMER CHARTED THE STRANGEST PARAGRAPH IN HIS BRIEF LIFE STORY

audience on his first night out. As Dolenz remembers it, an exasperated Jimi gave up and stomped off the stage midset. He reluctantly muddled through only a few more dates with the Monkees before asking to be released from his contract. The Monkees relented and soon Jimi was headlining a tour of his own.

At the time of his stupid and wasteful demise in 1970 (official cause: choking on his own vomit while under the influence of barbiturates), he had recently reunited his band, The Experience, which had broken up a year earlier. In an all-too-brief five-year career, Jimi Hendrix created more magic and myth than most musicians can hope to accomplish in a lifetime. ✪

DENNIS HOPPER

If not for the monkey on his back, Dennis Hopper could have been one of the biggest stars of his generation. Instead, he'll have to settle for being one of its better, albeit troubled, actors. Hopper's drug-fried memory cost him dearly where it hurts the most.

Hopper eased into an acting career in the 1950s, but his strong start hit a snag. His taste for pharmaceuticals and a falling out with director Henry Hathaway on the set of 1958's *From Hell to Texas* led to what Hopper claims was an eight-year blackball from Hollywood productions. He finally came back

HOPPER'S DRUG-FRIED MEMORY COST HIM DEARLY WHERE IT HURTS THE MOST

with a vengeance, peaking early as a director with *Easy Rider*, 1969's ode to freedom and the open road, which he cowrote with Peter Fonda. The film defines the era, earning the rare, concurrent status of cult classic and true classic. It also brought us Jack Nicholson in a memorable, if brief, Academy Award–nominated movie debut. Hopper was feted at Cannes, winning the Best First Film prize. He triumphantly returned to Hollywood only to submerge himself in drugs and booze.

His reputation fell from celebrated cinematic prodigy in films like *Rebel Without a Cause* and *Apocalypse Now* to semireliable character actor due to uneven performances that varied in quality depending on the amount of chemicals swimming in his bloodstream. His love life was equally unpredictable and included a weeklong marriage to *Mamas and Papas* singer Michelle Phillips.

Hopper eventually happened upon a trump card in his deck of talents: a rare ability to translate sinister intensity onto the screen as the lead character or supporting character in memorable roles. He made being the spooky bad guy his niche. Cleaning up his act in the early 1980s proved a renaissance for his career, allowing him to act in *Blue Velvet, Speed*, and countless other films. He returned to directing and climbed behind the camera in 1988's *Colors*, among others. Dennis Hopper was reinventing himself as a respectable force in film, but his past was about to come back to bite him in his chinos.

It happened on the *Late Show with David Letterman* in June 1994. Hopper told Dave a tale from the casting process behind *Easy Rider*, claiming actor Rip Torn was up for the Nicholson part, but lost the role for pulling a knife on Hopper during dinner. Apparently the drugs had altered Hopper's memory of the event. Torn was livid, remembering the incident in reverse—it was Hopper who pulled the knife, said the former Artie from *The Larry Sanders Show*. Torn argued that the talk show allegation hurt his career and he filed a defamation lawsuit. In a decision that sent drug-addled stars scrambling to begin diaries, Torn won nearly a million dollars from Hopper's coffers: $475,000 for loss of income and emotional distress, later doubled for punitive damages.

Recently Hopper has won respect and admiration for his talents in photography and painting, though that hasn't stopped him from sparking up the occasional fattie. The sixty-something actor was charged with marijuana possession after Canadian police discovered less than an ounce of pot on his person as he entered the country en route to a movie set in 1999. When drug-sniffing dogs pawed his luggage out of the lineup, Hopper readily admitted to carrying the contraband. Citing his age and cooperation with authorities, a judge granted Hopper an absolute discharge. "Don't confuse the man with the movie," said Hopper's lawyer, referring to the drug-taking biker in *Easy Rider*. Perhaps we should heed the lawyer's advice—it seems like Hopper has. ✪

WHITNEY **HOUSTON**

She looks like a goddess and sings like a bird but despite a career that's gone big-time and an image that oozes glamour, when you get right down to it, Whitney Houston hasn't evolved much beyond her New Jersey roots. She may appear high-gloss, but when she dishes with friends, her speech punctuated with four-letter words, it's clear Whitney is still very much a homegirl. Her looks are straight out of *Vogue*, but her vocabulary is right off the street.

She's a vocalist with few peers; she spun her debut 1985 self-titled album into a record-breaking hit, and has followed it up time after time with award-winning and multimillion-selling successors. Her soundtrack to *The Bodyguard*, a film she costarred in with Kevin Costner, was the biggest selling album of the 1990s. However, her choice of a husband has illuminated the true woman within. In 1991, Houston married R&B singer and perennial bad boy Bobby Brown, sending tongues wagging about the attraction of opposites when, as we have come to learn, they're more like birds of a feather.

Whispers and rumors have dogged Houston for nearly two decades: Does she do drugs? Is she a closet lesbian? Does her troubled hubby have the market cornered on misbehavior? In January 2000, some of those questions inched closer to an answer when Houston was reportedly stopped by customs officers at the Keahole-Kona airport in Hawaii. Nearly half an ounce of pot was discovered in her carry-on bag, but the diva dashed to her San Francisco–bound flight before police could arrive. Authorities in the Aloha state cited the singer on the misdemeanor charge, to which her lawyers entered a plea of no contest, brushing off the threat of a thirty-day jail sentence. Instead, Houston was ordered to pay charitable contributions to several Hawaiian causes, in amounts totaling the loose change at the bottom of her Gucci bag, about $4,000. The case was dismissed early the following year after she completed her court-ordered duties.

> SOME REPORTS CLAIMED THE SINGER'S FRIENDS HAD ATTEMPTED, AND FAILED, AT AN INTERVENTION, HOPING TO SHAME THE SINGER INTO VOLUNTARILY ENTERING REHAB. STILL, SHE CONTINUED TO DENY HAVING ANY PROBLEMS WITH DRUGS

Still, lingering concerns about the state of Houston's health were exacerbated by her no-show at the Academy Awards two months following the airport pot incident. Diva-in-waiting Faith Hill was a last minute fill-in for Whitney, who allegedly flubbed her rehearsal of "Over the Rainbow" so badly that she was asked to steer clear of the ceremony. An Oscar spokesperson blamed her missed cues on a sore throat, but whatever the reason, Houston was out and Hill was in.

Some reports claimed the singer's friends had attempted, and failed, at an intervention, hoping to shame the singer into voluntarily entering rehab. Still, she continued to deny having any problems with drugs.

Worries about Whitney grew to new heights after her show-stopping performance at Michael Jackson's thirtieth anniversary concert at Madison Square

Garden. She appeared gaunt, bony, and malnourished, and when she didn't show up for the second show, a "Whitney is dead" rumor began to circulate. Her publicist claimed Houston was fine and bewildered about all of the fuss over her health. "She has been under stress and when she's stressed, she doesn't eat," came the official word in a tone that intimated merely a few skipped meals despite clear evidence that the singer was emaciated.

Meanwhile, her home life seemed to seesaw between bliss and near break-down. More than once we held our collective breath following leaks to the media that a Brown-Houston separation was imminent. The couple revel in their roles as parents to daughter Bobbi, but they've mourned more than once over tragic miscarriages. And Whitney's devotion has been tested more than once while forced to endure her husband's painfully long incarcerations (see Bobby Brown).

> **SHE APPEARED GAUNT, BONY, AND MALNOURISHED, AND WHEN SHE DIDN'T SHOW UP FOR THE SECOND SHOW, A "WHITNEY IS DEAD" RUMOR BEGAN TO CIRCULATE**

Whitney claimed to "set the record straight" during an exclusive television interview with ABC's Diane Sawyer, in which she evaded questions about her health and deftly denied any problems at home. She admitted to a history of doing drugs but she (and Bobby) claimed there has never been violence in the marriage. The diva was in obvious damage control mode, hoping to salvage some positive vibes in advance of the release of her widely panned *Just Whitney* CD, her first release in four years.

Whitney Houston's enigmatic persona continues to confound her many fans. Touted as a main attraction at the star-studded Liza Minelli-David Gest circus/wedding in the spring of 2002, she once again gave last minute regrets, blaming a recording commitment in Florida. Natalie Cole crooned to the happy couple in her stead. Houston has become that unreliable friend with whom you optimistically make big plans, only to have her bail on you at the eleventh hour, leaving you dateless and alone on a Saturday night. Perhaps Whitney's grown weary of the scrutiny, but she's going to have to eventually face the music. ✪

ROBERT ILER

It was an awful lot like an episode of his hit mobster show *The Sopranos*, only not quite as sinister—*The Sopranos Lite* or *The Sopranos Take Manhattan*, maybe. Call it what you will, Iler, who plays gang leader Tony Soprano's rebellious son on TV, was facing a very threatening reality: a possible fifteen-year prison sentence and a certain end to his budding career.

In the summer of 2001, seventeen-year-old Iler and three New York buddies were accused of shaking down two teenage Brazilian tourists, family style, for a grand total of $40. He and his "Mob" were arrested a few blocks away when the sightseers fingered them to police as their robbers. The arresting officer testified to discovering a still-warm marijuana pipe and bag of pot on Iler and a boxcutter in one of his friends' pockets.

> IN THE SUMMER OF 2001, SEVENTEEN-YEAR-OLD ILER AND THREE NEW YORK BUDDIES WERE ACCUSED OF SHAKING DOWN TWO TEENAGE BRAZILIAN TOURISTS, FAMILY STYLE, FOR A GRAND TOTAL OF $40

From the moment of Iler's arrest, his lawyer pleaded for calm, claiming the facts of the case would "come out" eventually. Iler himself denied any involvement in the crime. That claim led *Sopranos* fans to believe it was all a mistake, that TV's A.J. Soprano was innocent, possibly even being framed. His "mom," actress Edie Falco, stood by her "son" and expressed complete disbelief that he'd run afoul of the law. His "dad," actor James Gandolfini, was even compelled to write a heartfelt letter to the presiding judge, pleading that the magistrate have mercy on the wayward boy. Star power didn't sway the court, however, and the case proceeded.

But Iler switched gears in April 2002 when he had his day in court and delivered an outright confession to his role in the incident. The young actor testified that he and his friends decided to "hassle" the young out-of-towners. He wasn't the stickup man, he said, but he did aid and abet by blocking the tourists' escape route. By agreeing to plead guilty to petty larceny, Iler avoided much more serious charges of second-degree robbery and marijuana possession. His real-life mother still contends her son is a good fella, and told the *New York Post* he copped to the crime only to avoid further media scrutiny. But that's what mothers do; even the hardest criminals are backed by deluded moms who, despite stacks of concrete evidence, don't believe their precious little boys are capable of doing anything illegal. The boy's father wasn't so easily fooled. Iler later told *Fox News*, "My Dad was very tough with me. Now I have to watch my step and be careful who I associate with."

If Robert successfully finishes three years of probation, he'll get his record wiped clean. It was the plea bargain prosecutors had proposed from the start, but it took months for Iler to realize it was an offer he couldn't refuse. ✪

JERMAINE JACKSON

Granted, it must have been tough on a familial level to be a member of The Jackson 5 if you were anyone other than Michael. Try as they might, the group couldn't get off the ground until their little brother with the angelic face and perfect pitch joined them as the frontman in 1964. Michael was showered with attention and praise and from that point on, Jermaine, Tito, Jackie, and Marlon were destined to be edited down to mere footnotes in *The Michael Jackson Story*. Eventually petty jealousies were put aside and, by and large, the Jackson men got over being relegated to bit players. Only Jermaine continues to struggle publicly with letting go of the past.

> IN 1991 HE RELEASED A MEDIOCRE SINGLE TITLED "WORD TO THE BADD," NOTABLE ONLY FOR ITS BITING LYRICS AIMED DIRECTLY AT HIS RIDICULOUSLY SUCCESSFUL BROTHER MICHAEL'S MANY ECCENTRICITIES: "DON'T KNOW WHO YOU ARE/ONCE YOU WERE MADE/YOU CHANGED YOUR SHADE/WAS YOUR COLOR WRONG?"

Michael's big brother Jermaine once proclaimed, "I could have been Michael. It's all a matter of timing and luck." That attitude continues to gnaw away at his psyche. In 1991 he released a mediocre single titled "Word to the Badd," notable only for its biting lyrics aimed directly at his ridiculously successful brother Michael's many eccentricities: "Don't know who you are / Once you were made / You changed your shade / Was your color wrong?" Jermaine's ex-wife claims the tune was his jealous response to producers who abandoned his recording project to work with Michael instead.

One of the highlights of Michael's heavily hyped thirtieth anniversary concerts in New York City was to be the J-5's first reunion since the 1984 Victory Tour. Everything was on track until Jermaine tossed a spanner in the works by staging a lone wolf holdout, ostensibly over the high cost of tickets. For a moment, the world turned its attention to Jermaine as he publicly threatened to boycott the shows because "the exorbitant ticket prices being charged by promoters will prevent some of our most loyal fans from attending." The tickets were admittedly steep, topping out at $2,500 each. However, Jermaine soon gave up his lame protest, admission charges stayed as they were, and fans and Jacksons alike were left scratching their heads. All Jermaine succeeded in doing was temporarily drawing press attention away from Michael, which seems likely to have been his goal all along.

After he returned to the fold, Jermaine issued a statement claiming all was well, and there were no lingering rifts between any Jackson family members. In fact, it looked just like old times: Jermaine and his brothers found themselves on stage as supporting players for their little brother, the superstar. ✪

LATOYA JACKSON

Every family has one: a difficult member who breaks away from the pack and does his or her own thing—damn the torpedoes. LaToya Jackson made an art form out of individuality and revenge. She has become a verb: to disgrace your family is to "LaToya."

Possessing virtually no discernable talents of her own, LaToya did contribute backup vocals for the latter-day Jackson 5. An attempt to go solo hit a sour note, and after hooking up with fast-talking manager Jack Gordon—her Svengali or copilot depending on the version of events you believe—they made a career out of pursuing celebrity together. When they realized the surest route to fame was to hitch a ride on the Jackson family bandwagon, they launched the second eldest Jackson daughter's desperate campaign to become a star.

> LATOYA JACKSON MADE AN ART FORM OUT OF INDIVIDUALITY AND REVENGE. SHE HAS BECOME A VERB: TO DISGRACE YOUR FAMILY IS TO "LATOYA"

After the plastic surgery and stomach crunches (and who knows what else) worked their magic, LaToya set out to shock us. That she did in 1989 with a nude spread in *Playboy*. The issue flew off the shelves, selling seven million copies in one month. Later that year, she and Gordon married. They were an odd couple: a beautiful, lithe, young black woman and a balding, paunchy, middle-aged white man. Her family hated Gordon, believing he had some sort of hold over LaToya and was manipulating her into doing things she wouldn't ordinarily consider. The *Playboy* layout was a family tragedy and it was only the beginning.

In June 1990, the girl her siblings called Toy-Toy let loose with her first tell-all about the secretive Jackson clan. The book, *Growing Up in the Jackson Family*, was a hit and spent nine weeks on the *New York Times* best-seller list. In it, she revealed a miserable childhood rife with physical abuse at the hands of her parents. She offered detailed accounts of the fear Joseph Jackson instilled in his nine children, a fear so strong that even as adults they remained uncomfortable in his presence. Whether readers ate up her allegations or dismissed them as hogwash, LaToya certainly had their attention. What she lacked was support for her claims from her kin.

When brother Michael's 1993 concert tour came to a sudden stop amid accusations of child molestation (*see* Michael Jackson), LaToya's initial statements expressed support for her younger brother. However, she quickly retracted that backing and replaced it with declarations of his "perversion." Is it any wonder brother and sister are no longer on speaking terms?

LaToya continued on her career path of skin and scandals, hosting a *Playboy* video, working clubs as a celebrity stripper/host, and launching her own $3.99 per minute psychic phone line. She and Gordon had a colossal fight in 1993 that involved a knife (her) and a chair (him) and resulted in assault charges that were eventually dropped. She would later set up a "Jackson family secrets" 900 phone number to hype the release of her second book, *Shocking and Controversial Expose of Life in the Jackson Family*.

During their intense 1996 divorce proceedings, LaToya Jackson and Jack Gordon were forbidden to talk *to* each other, but that didn't stop them from talking *about* each other. She accused him of forcing her to take gigs in seedy little clubs and insisting that she perform even when she was sick. He accused her of lying. She said he was lying about her lying, and so on. What was clear to the Jackson family was that Jack had hit the road and they had their LaToya back. Katherine, her relieved mother, forgave her daughter's transgressions and welcomed her home. An alleged link was later uncovered between Gordon and organized crime. He had apparently been under investigation by the FBI during his marriage to LaToya. The other Jacksons—even Michael—will have to pick up the pace if they hope to catch up with LaToya's string of disgraceful acts during the six years she was Mrs. Jack Gordon. ✪

MICHAEL JACKSON

From his ever-evolving looks to the unanswered questions about his sexuality and the baby-dangling incident that shocked the world, the self-proclaimed King of Pop continues to baffle us. The little boy who worked long and hard fronting his brothers' band eventually became the biggest star on the planet. And such a strange ride through life inevitably comes with a few nasty bumps along the way.

As a solo artist, Michael Jackson created the single most phenomenal piece of vinyl ever to grace the airwaves. Nineteen ninety-two's *Thriller* sold forty million copies, racked up several top ten hits, and won shelves full of awards. His follow-up albums were unfairly compared to *Thriller* in terms of sales and substance, and had no hope of ever coming close. Still, his magic left virtually no corner of the world untouched. A real-life Peter Pan who was robbed of his childhood by a taskmaster father, he lives a childlike existence at his home, Neverland. The sprawling California ranch is part sanctuary, part zoo. His former pal Bubbles the Chimp, the Elephant Man bones, and the face mask he wears in public are all indications of an eccentric and very rich personality at work. But lurking behind that oft-molded visage is a ruthless businessman.

> THE KING OF POP MARRIED THE KING'S DAUGHTER, LISA MARIE PRESLEY, IN A SECRET CEREMONY IN THE DOMINICAN REPUBLIC... WAS MICHAEL JACKSON TRYING TO DIVERT OUR ATTENTION FROM QUESTIONS ABOUT HIS SEXUALITY?

In 1985 the gloved one proved friendship was not among his top priorities by buying ATV Music Publishing out from under Paul McCartney's nose for $47.5 million. The publishing company controlled the catalog of hundreds of Lennon and McCartney tunes from their Beatles days. The betrayal was especially painful for Paul, as it came just a few years after he and Michael enjoyed tremendous success as a duo with the hit records "The Girl is Mine" and "Say, Say, Say." McCartney felt especially foolish for tipping off Jackson to the songbook's upcoming sale; he had complained to his old pal that Lennon's widow, Yoko Ono, was dragging her heels and fighting him on their planned bid together. Recent estimates put the catalog's value up around $500 million, a shrewd investment indeed. However, there have also been rumblings that Jackson has been experiencing money problems and is worried that Sony Music will use his vulnerable financial state to gain full control of the catalogue, something the company strongly denies. McCartney never forgave his old friend and even refused to include their duets on his career retrospective called *Wingspan*.

Meanwhile, Jackson took those alleged financial difficulties to the streets of New York City in July 2002. He arrived at a news conference on a double-decker bus and announced to a throng of fans and media that Sony's chief, Tommy Mottola, had intentionally scuttled his 2001 release *Invincible*, rendering it invisible. The accusations were very serious. Brandishing a sign depicting Mottola with a set of red horns and a forked tail, Jackson called the executive "racist, mean and very devilish." Though some say Jackson turned his back on his roots several plastic surgeries ago, the artist went on to announce, "When you fight for me, you fight for all black people, dead or alive."

Sony responded by calling the accusations "ludicrous, spiteful and hurtful," and further claimed Mottola was a consistent champion of Jackson's waning career. The King of Pop also alleged the company held back his charity single "What More Can I Give?" (Several reports claimed the "We Are the World"–type tune was a victim of bad management, led by a producer with a history in pornography.) The outburst was expertly timed. Jackson owed Sony one more CD, a greatest hits collection, and was reportedly looking to sweeten his already industry-leading deal on his cut of its sales. *E!* reported Jackson was cash poor and, even more scandalous, that his one-time best pal Bubbles the Chimp had been sent off to live out his days in a private zoo. Whatever the reason, Jacko's anger had lured him willingly and without his usual surgical mask into the public eye to state his case, however thin or ill-advised.

Michael Jackson's affinity for children has always been part of his persona. In a touching moment on the highly rated 1993 Oprah TV special, Jackson showed off the comfy barracks he erected on his property specifically to accommo-

> A REAL-LIFE PETER PAN WHO WAS ROBBED OF HIS CHILDHOOD BY A TASKMASTER FATHER, HE LIVES A CHILDLIKE EXISTENCE AT HIS HOME, NEVERLAND

date children with cancer for overnight stays. Dozens of little kids, bald and weakened by chemotherapy and radiation, were invited to watch movies, eat their favorite foods, meet the King of Pop, and forget their troubles for a while. His closest buddies were child stars, past and present: Macaulay Culkin, Elizabeth Taylor, and Emmanuel Lewis, to name a few. Photographers commonly captured him surrounded by gaggles of young fans while he extolled his "passion" for kids. It all seemed too good, too sweet, and a little bit creepy. But this was a man we couldn't begin to relate to, so what to say? Most gave him the benefit of the doubt.

Then, in 1993, while Jackson was on a world concert tour, a thirteen-year-old "friend" dropped a bombshell. The young boy claimed he was sexually abused by the star during a stay at Neverland. Suddenly all of those photos lost their rosy glow and took on a much darker hue. A criminal investigation was launched and although it was eventually dropped without any charges filed, the unconfirmed accusations came to a legal rest only after Jackson agreed to an out-of-court settlement with the boy's parents. He didn't admit to any wrongdoing, but wrote a check for an estimated $15 million nonetheless.

As the dust was settling, another boy came forward claiming he and Jackson had shared a bed. The Los Angeles District Attorney dropped that case due to lack of evidence, although some claim it fell apart only when the youngster refused to testify. Jackson released a statement thanking his fans the world over for their "overwhelming support," but his closest friends remained strangely silent. Several business deals fell apart on Jackson, including his lucrative endorsement contract with Pepsi. The focus once again shifted from his music to his personal life and he responded the following year with a surprise wedding. The King of Pop married The King's daughter, Lisa Marie Presley, in a secret ceremony in the Dominican Republic. They made a grand public show of their affection, but the timing was suspect. Was Michael Jackson trying to divert our attention from questions about his sexuality? The marriage lasted only twenty months, but he is said to still be pining for Lisa Marie.

> **THOUGH SOME SAY JACKSON TURNED HIS BACK ON HIS ROOTS SEVERAL PLASTIC SURGERIES AGO, THE ARTIST WENT ON TO ANNOUNCE, "WHEN YOU FIGHT FOR ME, YOU FIGHT FOR ALL BLACK PEOPLE, DEAD OR ALIVE"**

Jackson followed up the star-crossed marriage with a seemingly utilitarian union. Debbie Rowe was an ordinary dermatologist's assistant who had apparently treated the star's skin pigmentation problem for fifteen years. The bride was already pregnant with their son, Prince Michael Jr., when they married in a November 1996 shotgun wedding. Jackson's foray into fatherhood only inspired more interest in his ambiguous sexuality, causing many to wonder if the couple had actually done the deed or used artificial insemination. The bride's own father blabbed to tabloids that conception was carried out in a beaker, not a bed. Barely a month after Prince's birth, Rowe was pregnant again with daughter Paris. She didn't even try to hide the couple's living arrangements, openly explaining that she stayed in her own apartment while Michael cared for the children at Neverland. She raved about his devotion to kids and said she hoped they'd have a large brood, but the odd couple divorced after only three years. Rowe went back to living in obscurity; no one knows how often she sees her children, who live at Neverland and travel with their dad. In the summer of 2002, Jackson began turning up at events with a six-month-old baby in tow, introducing the tot as his third child, also named Prince. Jacko has declined to reveal the identity of the baby's mother, but it's suspected she is ex-wife Debbie Rowe. In the fall, global audiences were subjected to repeated viewings of the flailing baby's chubby white legs after a manic Jacko inexplicably dangled the tot in a loose, one-armed hold over a fourth-floor balcony railing in Berlin. Hundreds of fans below watched in disbelief. Authorities decided the frightening incident wasn't unlawful and Jackson responded to subsequent worldwide criticism with an apology for the "terrible mistake" and a declaration that "I'd never put my children's lives in danger." But as one father so aptly put it, "A loving Dad doesn't hold his baby that way."

Through it all, Jackson's throngs of fans the world over have remained loyal and thanks to the endurance of *Thriller*, he can still sell out the biggest arenas on a whim. And after several false starts, it seems Michael Jackson is finally poised to make movies. He recently announced a major production deal and plans to produce and direct several features. Whatever he chooses to do, he can be sure we'll continue to watch—and wonder. ✪

RICK JAMES

The Buffalo, New York–born father of funk rock and master of the 1981 hit "Superfreak" enjoyed the tremendous extravagances that come with living the rock star life. Leather-clad James flaunted his wealth and reveled in his image as a sexual superhero. Although he was quickly off the charts as a singer, he became a sought-after producer and sat behind the board for hits by artists like Teena Marie and the Mary Jane Girls. He even produced Eddie Murphy's "Party All the Time," which was a song title James took to heart. But the good-time dude went very bad after getting caught in the grasp of a cocaine addiction.

In 1993, James and his then girlfriend, model Tanya Hijazi, brought a woman to their hotel room for a business conference. In a cocaine haze, James tied the woman up and beat her intermittently for twelve hours while Hijazi flitted in and out of the proceedings. The singer, already out on bail for a previous assault conviction, crashed hard from his high.

The sheepish, fearful man who later appeared in a Los Angeles courtroom didn't resemble the confident, strutting singer of yesteryear. James faced a shopping list of charges and garnered convictions on assault, kidnapping, torture, and drug offences. He claims to have written hundreds of songs while serving half of his five-year prison sentence. Tanya was convicted of assault and received a two-year term. Their victim also won $2 million in damages from a civil lawsuit brought against the couple.

> **JAMES FACED A SHOPPING LIST OF CHARGES AND GARNERED CONVICTIONS ON ASSAULT, KIDNAPPING, TORTURE, AND DRUG OFFENCES**

Out of the slammer for two years, the repentant singer was all cleaned up and working hard for a second chance at success in 1998. During a show in Denver, a blood vessel popped in his neck and when he later experienced numbness upon returning home, he was rushed to Cedars Sinai Medical Center. Doctors discovered the fifty-something funkmaster had suffered a stroke. James's publicist explained the condition was caused by "rock and roll neck," a condition sometimes suffered by performers who repeatedly whip their heads back and forth. At first the stroke left him unable to walk, but he has since recovered and resumed recording and touring.

James married Hijazi in 1997, after she dealt with a brief jail stay for a shoplifting charge. The two have a young son, Tazman. The Grammy award winner has been shopping his life story to publishers; it's tentatively titled *Memoirs of a Superfreak.* ✪

ELTON JOHN

More than three decades' worth of hits makes Elton John truly one of popular music's greatest treasures. He's also one of its most notorious divas, a shopaholic, and a gossiping, tantrum-throwing prima donna. However, unlike most divas, John is the first to mock his own eccentricities, which makes it impossible not to love him, no matter what he does.

It's the same old song: drugs got in the way of good judgment for the rock legend, born Reginald Kenneth Dwight. He blamed substance abuse for several lousy decisions, including his blind trust in the "suits" who took care of his money while he took care of the music. His outrageous spending habits came to light during 2000's lawsuit against a former tour manager and accountants for alleged misappropriation of his many millions.

Reportedly flirting with bankruptcy, he cleaned out his closets and auctioned off millions' worth of old pinball wizard costumes and giant glasses through Sotheby's as his finances came under scrutiny. The eye-popping calculations included $200,000 annually for fresh flowers alone, not to mention costs incurred for several homes, lavish vacations, and generous donations. And despite a highly paid team employed to oversee his money, most of the expenditure it seemed, was by John himself. The former flamboyant dresser admitted to blowing $57 million in less than two years because, as he explained in a typical understatement, "I like spending my money." But that memorable spree and others he could recall occurred *after* he kicked his drug habit. Elton testified he was having memory problems regarding any big debits prior to that time. His accounting firm kept records, however, and the artist lost the lawsuit, costing him an estimated $5 million, or twenty-five years' worth of flowers. He has since revived part of the legal battle in a high court appeal.

> **THE EYE-POPPING CALCULATIONS INCLUDED $200,000 ANNUALLY FOR FRESH FLOWERS ALONE, NOT TO MENTION COSTS INCURRED FOR SEVERAL HOMES, LAVISH VACATIONS, AND GENEROUS DONATIONS**

Sir Elton (he was knighted in 1996) has threatened to quit music more often than some people change their socks. In calmer moments, he admits that when things don't go his way, he pouts and threatens to pack it in—just like a diva. It's where he chooses to do his foot-stomping that makes it unsettling. Sometimes it's on stage, midconcert, in front of a sold-out crowd.

Witness the packed house he stunned in late 2000 at New York's Madison Square Garden by announcing his retirement, "within a year." There was no discernable reaction from his band, who were likely used to their boss crying wolf and venting every time someone hit a flat note or stage lights got too hot. But it became the announcement heard around the world as he told subsequent audiences that he was fed up with the industry and was quitting. He loved the music but hated the music business, he said, and it was time to get out. International pundits pontificated on the end of an era in rock history. But like the retirements of Celine Dion, Barbra Streisand, The Who (several of them), and Garth Brooks before him, John's "retirement," if it ever existed, certainly didn't stick for more than a cosmic moment. He soon released another album, *Songs from the West Coast*, and hit the road with old pal and fellow temporary retiree Billy Joel.

John, named an "honorary diva" by the folks who assemble the *VH1 Divas Live* performances, single-handedly scuttled a highly touted tour with Tina Turner. During rehearsals, the songstress felt John needed a few pointers for his piano playing on "Proud Mary." Insulted, Elton flew into a rage and ended any hopes of launching the elaborate, coheadlining tour. He eventually apologized to his old friend Tina, but it was too late.

The rocket man was the first to shout out what others were whispering regarding the rushed and extravagant nuptials of Liza Minelli and David Gest in early 2002. John giggled as he claimed that the groom set off his "gaydar." It was an odd toss of a stone for a gay man living in a fragile glass house. Elton himself once walked the aisle with someone of the female persuasion. In February 1984, a closeted Elton married Renate Blauel; the relationship lasted barely a year.

There is, arguably, no more honored or appreciated popular music artist than Sir Elton John. We can only hope he'll be wailing, gossiping, and stomping his feet for another three decades at least. ✪

DON **JOHNSON**

Does the legend make the man or does the man make the legend? Actor and erstwhile ladies' man Don Johnson boasts of losing his virginity at age twelve —to his babysitter, no less. At sixteen, he moved in with a woman who was twenty-five. At twenty-two, he and fourteen-year-old Melanie Griffith set up house before embarking on their stormy and brief first marriage four years later. They divorced after only one year and another decade-plus passed before they reconciled for a second set of "I do's." That union was even rockier, if longer lasting, ending in another divorce after seven years. Since then he has dated teen costars (one who was cast as his daughter at the time) and romanced up the food chain to Barbra Streisand during a short-lived stint as a pop star. After a decade-long lull in his career, he was reborn as a sex symbol in pastel suits and no socks on the hip 1980s hit cop show *Miami Vice*. If Don Johnson were a cat, he'd have used up most of his nine lives while on the prowl. And yet he always landed on his feet.

In more recent times Johnson has enjoyed another rebirth (again as half of a police duo) on TV's *Nash Bridges*. He's also waded through some nasty court battles whose secret settlements have left a hint of suspicion lingering over his perfectly coiffed head.

But it's hard even for a star to find reliable help these days. In early 1997, Johnson filed a lawsuit against two former young female employees. The actor claimed the chauffeur and production assistant were conspiring against him to hatch a $1.5 million extortion plan by spreading damaging gossip that his long-buried drinking problem had reemerged. The twenty-something ex-staffers shot back with a lawsuit of their own for sexual harassment, claiming

> **ACTOR AND ERSTWHILE LADIES' MAN DON JOHNSON BOASTS OF LOSING HIS VIRGINITY AT AGE TWELVE—TO HIS BABYSITTER, NO LESS**

they were axed after spurning Johnson's sexual advances. After the actor, the women, and the press endured several months of legal tug-of-war, a secret deal finally settled the suits. Both parties withdrew their claims, agreed to keep the quiet about the details, and walked away—likely without shaking hands.

Another claim surfaced in the summer of 2001. A self-confessed *Miami Vice* fan claimed Johnson grabbed more than a spicy spring roll when the two met at a Los Angeles sushi bar. The plaintiff's lawsuit said a drunken Johnson fondled the woman and rudely propositioned her. His publicist called the suit a groundless attempt to extract money from the star. A criminal probe was conducted and closed with no charges filed. A gaggle of supporters rallied to the actor's side, including his wife, fellow patrons, and one of the restaurant's co-owners, who insisted Johnson hadn't been dining long enough to get blotto and belligerent. However, witnesses reported seeing the emotionally distraught woman and Johnson chatting near the restroom. The merits of the case—or lack thereof—are still to be argued in court. Or perhaps history will repeat itself and the sorry mess will quietly be put to rest with a conclusion known only to those directly involved. Pity. ✪

R. KELLY

Whether or not Chicago musical force R. Kelly is allowed the privilege of continuing his career as melodic hero to millions of kids is still to be decided. Some say he should start looking for a new line of work. Even in the permissive business of popular music, there are things that can't be overlooked. It appears the songwriter, producer, and soul singer may have placed some questionable activities under the heading of "fun."

Each year, the prestigious Grammy Awards show offers up one breakout performance that blows away the crowd. The ceremony that in past years gave us a moon-walking Michael Jackson, a shimmying Ricky Martin, and a newly resurrected Carlos Santana showcased Robert Kelly in 1998. The performance of his powerful anthem "I Believe I Can Fly" sent shivers down spines before it sent him home with an armful of golden gramophones. He has been the helmsman for dozens of hits by top artists such as Céline Dion, Janet Jackson, Whitney Houston, and Mary J. Blige. As an artist he's sold millions of albums worldwide, commanding an impressive slice of the record industry pie. But now there are whispers that his glorious train ride is going to derail.

SEVERAL MUSIC INDUSTRY INSIDERS WHO HAVE SCREENED THEM SAY IT'S DEFINITELY KELLY IN AT LEAST ONE AND IN AS MANY AS THREE SEX TAPES BEING INVESTIGATED BY CHICAGO POLICE

Several music industry insiders who have screened them say it's definitely Kelly in at least one and in as many as three sex tapes being investigated by Chicago police. Home sex videos made by the man who once described the inspiration behind a new song as "taking it back to the bedroom" wouldn't be of much legal interest if not for the suspected age of his partners, who are all reportedly teenage girls under the age of consent. And the private performances are as much about power as they are about sex. On the most curious of the tapes, a twenty-seven-minute romp, the man in question receives a laundry list of sexual favors from his partner before things take a turn for the perverse. (He urinates on the girl's face and body, an act obviously completed for his benefit alone.) A spokesperson for the Philadelphia group called Racial Unity, one of several associations organizing boycotts of Kelly's music, viewed the now infamous tape and concluded that the man in it had to be stopped. The look of shame and anguish on the participating girl's face convinced members that the scenario was very wrong.

Kelly's preference for the company of teenage girls has apparently been a longtime open secret in the record industry. Two previous civil lawsuits against him were settled out of court and paid as much as $250,000 to one of the young plaintiffs who claimed she suffered emotional pain following seduction and subsequent liaisons with Kelly. An intern at a record label, she says she was sixteen and a virgin when Kelly first used his position of authority to establish a sexual relationship with her. The other claimant was a teen choirgirl whose acquaintance he made at a high school music class. In 1994, twenty-seven-year-old Kelly married then fifteen-year-old singer Aaliyah in a secret ceremony at the same time he was producing her debut CD. The songbird, who died in a 2001 plane crash, later admitted to lying about her age to obtain the marriage license. In just a few weeks, the sham union was annulled.

Kelly maintains the most disgusting of the three tapes is a fake. He claims it's a ruse for the purpose of blackmail, created by jealous and vengeful music industry rivals. He has hired his own private investigator to clear his name. However, singer Sparkle, who collaborated with Kelly on a 1998 record, came forward to identify the girl in the film as her teenage niece. Sparkle admitted to introducing the then twelve-year-old budding rapper to her producer in 1998, and expressed guilt for not watching them more closely. Chicago police confirm they've been in touch with the girl's family, but won't yet admit that she is the reluctant and at times humiliated-looking teen on the tape.

SEVERAL MONTHS OF INVESTIGATIONS FINALLY CULMINATED IN CRIMINAL CHARGES OF CHILD PORNOGRAPHY

Several months of investigations finally culminated in criminal charges of child pornography. R. Kelly spent a night in jail before posting $750,000 bail. He maintains he's not the man in the tapes and is pleading for patience. He's even using his music as a platform for professing his innocence (the message in his single "Heaven, I Need a Hug" is fairly transparent). His lawyer says the girl on the most heinous of the tapes is not underage. Bootleg copies of the tapes continue to sell over the Internet and on street corners, despite warnings from police that anyone who views them could be subject to child porn charges. The twenty-one counts against Kelly carry a total maximum penalty of fifteen years in prison. The singer of "Bump 'N' Grind" and "Feelin' on Yo Booty" says he's looking forward to having his day in court, "so people will see that I'm no criminal." ✪

MARTIN LAWRENCE

Foul-mouthed stand-up comic-turned-movie star Martin Lawrence is creating a career centered on lowbrow comedies that critics routinely loathe. Fame has been a rough ride for the troubled *Bad Boys* star, who has logged more time in the courts than some of his movies have in the theaters.

Lawrence got his movie start in the 1990 comedy *House Party*, but he didn't enjoy widespread acclaim until the release of his stand-up video *Martin Lawrence: You So Crazy* four years later. His tasteless humor won him scads of fans despite its being so juvenile at times that it borders on banal. In February 1994, his horrifyingly sexist and repulsive monologue on *Saturday Night Live* actually inspired producers to implement a change in policy: no more free-form comedy will ever open the show.

Still, movie offers poured in and Lawrence seemed to turn nothing down.

HIS PHYSICIAN CLAIMED THAT EXHAUSTION AND DEHYDRATION CAUSED LAWRENCE TO WANDER INTO LOS ANGELES TRAFFIC IN 1996 WHILE WAVING A HANDGUN AND SHOUTING OBSCENITIES

His physician claimed that exhaustion and dehydration caused Lawrence to wander into Los Angeles traffic in 1996 while waving a handgun and shouting obscenities. When police arrived, he resisted arrest and put some wrestling moves on an unimpressed officer. Fortunately for Lawrence, the fracas was treated as a medical emergency rather than a criminal case. Nonetheless, the *Life* star's loaded 9 mm handgun made a reappearance only weeks later as he was trying to board a plane at the Burbank airport.

Lawrence busted a move—and a lip—on the dance floor of an LA area club in 1997. He pleaded no contest to slugging another clubgoer who bumped into him while they shook their respective booties. That infraction netted him a mere slap on the wrist—two years' probation and a bit of community service.

That same year, Lawrence lost two wives. Tisha Campbell, his small-screen mate on the Fox TV series *Martin*, walked off the set and charged her costar with sexual harassment. Lawrence countered that he was merely a pawn in Campbell's contract dispute with producers of the show, then in its fifth season. She stood her ground and sued Martin, claiming he made the *Martin* set unbearably tense with his subtle threats of violence. He countersued and once they came to an out-of-court settlement, Campbell returned to the show and resumed playing his loving wife. *Martin* was soon cancelled. Around the same time, Lawrence divorced his real-life wife after twenty months of marriage.

There have been a few blank lines on the rap sheet of the little man from *Big Momma's House* since his near-death experience in August 1999. Lawrence's girlfriend opened their front door to discover the star had collapsed and was gasping for breath after jogging in heavy clothes in 100-degree summer heat. Immediate hospitalization followed. His body temperature was 107 degrees and the situation was touch-and-go; Lawrence remained in a coma, on a ventilator, for several days. It was, he later explained, a stupid attempt to quickly lose weight for the movie, in which he played dual roles of a small cop and a big momma. Drastic as it was, it seems that frightening life lesson has at least temporarily tamed the former bad boy. ✪

TOMMY LEE

Tommy Lee is proof positive that one's troubles don't go away with the arrival of fame and money; sometimes, the headaches only multiply.

Drummer and babe magnet for the heavy rockers Mötley Crüe, Tommy Lee was the wild child that beautiful good girls tried desperately to domesticate. The scrawny, tattoo-covered hooligan wannabe dated—and even married—the sex symbols of the moment. He counts equally stunning actresses Heather Locklear and Pamela Anderson as his ex-wives. His split from Locklear was quick and quiet. Anderson was a different story.

> **LEE PROGRESSED FROM LEGENDARY PARTY ANIMAL TO TABLOID FODDER WHEN HE AND BIKINI-CLAD *BAYWATCH* STAR ANDERSON WED ON A MEXICAN BEACH IN 1995, FIVE DAYS INTO THEIR COURTSHIP**

Lee's explosive relationship with wife number two entered the intensity scale at ten; it had now-here to go but down. Lee progressed from legendary party animal to tabloid fodder when he and bikini-clad *Baywatch* star Anderson wed on a Mexican beach in 1995, five days into their courtship. Cementing their love with tattooed wedding bands, they preserved their erotic honeymoon on videotape. A construction worker allegedly stole the explicit thirty-nine-minute home video. The couple sued, but eventually abandoned their fight to prevent its release on the Internet. The Tommy and Pam sex tape became an instant cult classic.

Anderson, who hyphenated her last name with Lee's while they were wed, filed for divorce after less than a year of wedded bliss. But when Tommy sought counseling for alcohol abuse, Pam rushed back to his side. His notorious temper cost him his freedom on a number of occasions. Several photographers, a security guard, and his wife were all on the receiving end of blows. It seems multiple mandatory enrolments in anger management classes didn't take.

The most memorable and horrifying of the Lee-Anderson incidents led directly to the end of the brief marriage. Lee was convicted of spinning out of control during an argument and kicking his pregnant wife as she held their infant son in her arms. A six-month jail term and strict probation followed, accompanied by a court-ordered donation to a battered women's shelter. Terms of Lee's release included regular appearances before the judge to prove he was staying off drugs, out of the booze, and 100 yards away from his fearful ex-wife.

LEE SAYS SHE'S UNWILLING TO ACKNOWLEDGE HOW MUCH HE HAS CLEANED UP AND CALMED DOWN

The threat of losing access to his sons scared Tommy Lee straight, but his checkered past came back to haunt him as Pamela fought for sole custody. She claims Lee is an unfit, uncooperative coparent who doesn't properly supervise the children. Sadly, she was given fuel for her fire in the summer of 2001 when a little playmate of their oldest son drowned in Lee's pool in the midst of a backyard celebration. Several adults were present during Brandon Lee's fifth birthday party, and the death was ruled accidental with no blame laid on the host. However, the tragedy occurred under Lee's watch, and the victim's parents are suing him for wrongful death.

Tommy Lee no longer rocks with the Crüe, but he fronts his own badass band named *Methods of Mayhem*. He has complained that Pam's relentless pursuit of sole custody was tied to her relationship with his old rival, Kid Rock. Lee says she's unwilling to acknowledge how much he has cleaned up and calmed down. He claims he just wants to be a good dad to his sons. Anderson says she'll spend her last day and her last dollar to protect her boys and recently agreed to a joint custody arrangement. It remains to be seen if a judge will determine that the kids need protection from their fast-living father. ✪

JERRY LEE **LEWIS**

On his forty-first birthday, Jerry Lee Lewis plugged two shots into his bass player and later showed up at Graceland waving a pistol. He isn't called The Killer for nothing.

Even in the wild, budding days of rock music, Lewis's story stands out as one characterized by extremes. The Killer spun a dirt-poor childhood steeped in gospel into eventual musical gold in that unholiest of genres, rock and roll. Hot-tempered and arrogant with a penchant for partying, Lewis hit the road from his hometown in Ferriday, Louisiana, for Nashville, Tennessee, when he was still a teen, having heard that a record label there took a chance on Elvis Presley. Lewis figured the label might do the same for him. Within a year, he had outsold The

> **ON HIS FORTY-FIRST BIRTHDAY, JERRY LEE LEWIS PLUGGED TWO SHOTS INTO HIS BASS PLAYER AND LATER SHOWED UP AT GRACELAND WAVING A PISTOL**

King at Sun Records and earned a reputation for energetic and wild stage show antics. When "Whole Lotta Shakin' Goin' On" hit the nation's airwaves in 1957, it raised the ire of the conservative majority for its suggestive lyrics (and sold over a million copies nonetheless). In the meantime, Lewis himself was burning up the concert stage—literally. One particular Lewis legend recalls The Killer setting fire to his piano in a desperate bid to upstage Chuck Berry, who was headlining that particular concert.

Even more shocking was how Lewis managed to revive his sagging career in the wake of his scandalous marriage to his thirteen-year-old second cousin Myra Gale in December 1957. Although wedding a relative sounds very trashy by today's standards, taking vows with one's kinfolk was routine in the South at that time. It was twenty-two-year-old Jerry's third marriage and it nearly sank his career for good during his triumphant concert tour of England. A blissful Lewis naïvely shared his newfound happiness with London's ravenous tabloid reporters who delighted in putting the worst possible spin on the union. Songwriters stopped sending him their best material, concert ticket sales dwindled, and record sales declined. Miraculously, Lewis's fortunes eventually came out of freefall, although it took nearly a dozen years, a new record label, a new producer, and a foray into country music.

Drink and drugs dogged Lewis throughout his early career. Following his 1970 divorce from Myra, he briefly reunited with The Lord and cleaned up his life only to fall back into the bar scene after his mother's death a year later.

There's still a lot of speculation surrounding Lewis's nickname. He claims it has been with him since childhood, but some say it was his fondness for firearms coupled with his piano stool kicking and key-punishing playing style that inspired the lifelong handle. In 1976, the quick-tempered Lewis shot his bass player Norman "Butch" Owens twice in the chest, wounding him, but not fatally. The official story has Lewis as a terrible shot—he was really trying to pop a soda can with his .357 Magnum. The unofficial story seems more likely: in a fit of rage during band rehearsal, Lewis, who was frustrated with Butch's performance, lost his cool and pulled out his piece.

> **JUST A FEW WEEKS LATER, LEWIS DRUNKENLY PITCHED HIS ROLLS ROYCE INTO A DITCH AND LANDED IN JAIL**

Just a few weeks later, Lewis drunkenly pitched his Rolls Royce into a ditch and landed in jail. Only ten days after his release, despondent over the end of yet another marriage and the deaths of his parents, Lewis once again found himself on the wrong side of the law. He turned up hammered, howling, and waving a loaded Derringer at Elvis Presley's Graceland home, and demanded an audience with The King. He had long thought Elvis his chief rival, and music scribes often described him as The King's evil twin. Elvis's bodyguards, not knowing whether to believe the friendly words or the unfriendly looking gun, called the authorities and The Killer found himself behind bars yet again.

The lows of Jerry Lee's roller-coaster life have often been triggered by personal tragedies, including the deaths of two of his children. In 1962, his three-year-old son drowned in the family swimming pool. Eleven years later his only remaining son, Jerry Lee Jr., was killed in a car crash. Two of his five wives died under mysterious circumstances. Jerry Lee himself nearly died in the spring of 1981 following stomach surgery.

Today, his hard-living days are long past and Jerry Lee Lewis enjoys a quiet country life on his ranch in Nesbit, Mississippi. He shares the great outdoors and a guitar-shaped swimming pool with his sixth ex-wife, Kerri, their son, and countless barnyard critters. Following an amicable split in April 2002, Kerri also agreed to stay on as president of their company, J.K.L. Enterprises.

Lewis continues to perform "Great Balls of Fire," "Whole Lotta Shakin' Goin' On," and his many other hits at select events, including an annual convention in his name, attended by his very active and loyal fan base. But The Killer has definitely mellowed with age. When recently asked to confirm some of the more colorful events from his past, he barked in reply, "Hell, son, why can't y'all write something positive?" Well shucks, Jerry, the truth is so much more interesting! ✪

DEREK LONGMUIR

When apathy finally forced members of Scotland's teen dream band The Bay City Rollers to fold up their tartan trousers, founding drummer Derek Longmuir traded sticks for thermometers and became a nurse. The group had had a good run on the pop charts, most notably with the 1975 anthem "Saturday Night," known for its catchy, spelling bee–style chorus. Latter-day reunion tours carried on without nurse Derek, who wanted out of the Roller derby for good.

> **REGARDLESS, CHILD PORNOGRAPHY IS NOW PART OF LONGMUIR'S PERMANENT RECORD**

He stayed successfully out of the limelight until child porn charges thrust him into the role of suspected cyber perv.

Longmuir claims he pleaded guilty to possession of pornography involving minors in 2000 to avoid a media circus. Derek apparently believes that being branded a deviant is more desirable than publicity. Police allege Longmuir downloaded repulsive kiddy porn pictures and videos from the World Wide Web. The former heartthrob claims an American friend duped him into receiving the material. Regardless, child pornography is now part of Longmuir's permanent record. He was court-ordered to fulfill 300 hours of community service and the UK nursing license board considered prohibiting him from continuing on as a caregiver. However, they instead decided to issue a warning and allow him to keep his job—presumably not on a children's ward. ✪

LISA "LEFT EYE" LOPES

Diminutive and beautiful, Lisa Lopes of girl group TLC adopted the nickname Left Eye after a boyfriend noticed her left eye was slightly larger than her right. Capitalizing on the unique trait in early performances, she wore a condom instead of a lens in the left half of her glasses to promote safe sex. At the end of her brief but colorful life, obituaries confirmed that she wouldn't be remembered solely for her talent. The scrappy rapper is best recalled for one moment in 1994 when she was hell-bent for revenge after a fight with her boyfriend.

The singer who put the "L" in the chart-topping trio TLC and her longtime on-again, off-again pro football player boyfriend Andre Rison made a pact not to talk about "it." The "it" in question? The afterglow of a lovers' quarrel, when Lopes decided Rison's $1.3 million Georgia mansion was a "house of evil" and burned it to the ground. If it was attention she wanted, she got her wish. Her flaming outburst made headlines; news helicopters circled to capture the fiery destruction and a homeless Rison dropped her like a hot potato. The singer and sometime TV host went directly to jail and followed up her incarceration with a stint in alcohol rehab.

> **LOPES DECIDED RISON'S $1.3 MILLION GEORGIA MANSION WAS A "HOUSE OF EVIL" AND BURNED IT TO THE GROUND**

TLC also endured their share of group strife, having filed for bankruptcy protection from more than $3 million in debts. The year was 1995, and echoes of their number one single "Waterfalls" still hung in the air. Despite the appearance of tremendous success—being seen at all the right events in sexy outfits—they blamed bad management for their financial losses. Left Eye's million-dollar IOU to insurers Lloyds of London for the ruins of Rison's house had also pushed her partnership with bandmates Chilli and T-Boz too far into the red.

In spite of rumors that Lopes would marry an interim male-model boyfriend, her relationship with Rison eventually heated up again. At the 2000 Grammy Awards, the "No Scrubs" singer tried to explain: "You know, me and Andre, we just have a bond that no one will understand. Sometimes even I don't." While the flamboyant diva blazed a new trail as the first TLC member to go temporarily solo, the couple announced they'd marry in July 2001. The lavish nuptials were scrapped at the last minute as Left Eye begged off to work on her oft-delayed album. The couple's statement said they'd do the deed "eventually." That day never came. Lopes was killed instantly in an April 2002 car crash while driving a rented SUV on vacation in Honduras, a few weeks shy of her thirty-first birthday.

Shortly before her death, Left Eye's debut solo effort, *Supernova*, finally made it to market, but it failed to grab either radio airplay or substantial sales. Lopes had moved to a new music label, planned a second solo CD, and, following in the footsteps of Puff Daddy and The Artist, took on a name change. Lisa Lopes had decided to call herself NINA. The acronym stood for "New Identity Not Applicable." She had also reunited with Chilli and T-Boz to start work on another TLC album.

Most fans and friends lovingly recall her as the "crazy" in *CrazySexyCool*. But even as tributes to her vocal talent poured in from around the world at her memorial, it was obvious that many will remember her first and foremost as the furious woman who torched her boyfriend's house. ✪

COURTNEY LOVE

Black widow. Selfish shrew. The Yoko Ono of the 1990s. Raging bitch. Courtney Love has been called those names and much worse by some of the people who claim to know her best. She's been accused of latching on to Kurt Cobain's wild ride to fame, only to expedite his premature demise.

Talented actress. Expressive vocalist. Brilliant lyricist. Devoted single mom. Those are the monikers her fans use to describe her. As she raises Frances Bean (her daughter with Cobain) and struggles in what she believes to be a noble fight for artists' rights, she has found a clear voice distinct from the muddled croak of others within the music industry.

So is Courtney Love a sinner or a saint? She's probably a bit of both.

Outside of her careers as an actress and frontwoman for the rock band Hole, Love is involved in an ongoing and probably never-ending battle with her late husband's Nirvana bandmates, Seattle's original grunge rockers. When Kurt checked out of this astral plane via a self-inflicted gunshot wound in 1994 (*see* Kurt Cobain), Love was left with the lion's share of his holdings—namely, stakes in Nirvana's music. Her widowhood made her an unwilling business partner with

> **SO IS COURTNEY LOVE A SINNER OR A SAINT? SHE'S PROBABLY A BIT OF BOTH**

minor shareholders Dave Grohl and Krist Novoselic, with whom she formed a holding company, Nirvana LLC. Under that umbrella, the three dealt with Nirvana business. All decisions about licensing, trademarks, copyright, and so on, required unanimous consent. None of the trio was ever too pleased with the arrangement, but each appeared willing to tolerate the other until Grohl and Novoselic made a move to include a previously unreleased track, "You Know You're Right," on a Nirvana box set. Love voted against the proposal.

Grohl and Novoselic maintained the previously unheard song could sell millions of copies and renew interest in the group. What's good for one is good for all, right? Wrong, said Love, who claimed Kurt *was* Nirvana. She downplayed the other musician's roles in the legendary band as mere replacement parts, implying a new single wouldn't fly given Kurt's permanent absence. A they said, she said battle went on for several months and climaxed with Grohl and Novoselic's submission to a judge requesting that Love undergo a mental health evaluation. In short, they said she was crazy. Their evidence: the stripper-turned-singer's own admission that she was "impaired" when she signed their three-way partnership; her tendency to hire and fire managers based on whims; and a history of proving herself unreliable as a businesswoman. The request was denied. Meanwhile, "You Know You're Right" and Nirvana master recordings remained in legal limbo until the trio reached a surprise agreement in the fall of 2002. Several US radio stations suddenly began airing "You Know You're Right" after it surfaced on the Internet. Love admitted that the truce with her late husband's old bandmates was finally called with the help of "a lot of money."

> **RIVAL SINGER KATHLEEN HANNA WAS ON THE RECEIVING END OF A VIGILANTE LOVE PUNCH IN 1995; COURTNEY WAS ORDERED INTO ANGER MANAGEMENT COUNSELING FOLLOWING THE INCIDENT**

Never one to hold back, Love is seemingly quick to pounce on any suspected foe. Whether she takes justice into her own hands (literally) or sics a legal team on her perceived enemies, Courtney has proven that as a plaintiff or defendant, she's willing to pull out all the stops to get her way.

Rival singer Kathleen Hanna was on the receiving end of a vigilante Love punch in 1995; Courtney was ordered into anger management counseling following the incident. Hole's leader allegedly roughed up a celebrity photographer three years later as the shutterbug attempted to snap Love's picture at a fashion show. That incident ended in a suit/countersuit, with Love's contention that she is merely an obvious target for every money-hungry nutbar she encounters. Another lunge at a journalist's wife at the 1999 Sundance film festival was cut short when Love's boyfriend, Jim Barber, stepped between the two women.

Barber's ex-wife is among those who have felt Courtney's wrath in the courtroom. Love alleged she was the target of a bitter Lesley Barber's rage following the demise of the woman's marriage. Her lawsuit contended that while attempting to mow her down with a Volvo, Barber left tread marks on her foot. The tender tootsie cost Love a starring role in *Ghosts of Mars*. In hindsight, considering the movie's poor box office performance, perhaps a bouquet of flowers would have been more appropriate than a summons.

Love's legal problems escalated in 2001 when Hole's record label, Geffen/Universal, sued the band leader for breach of contract. The company claimed she failed to fulfill a deal that required her to provide the company with five more albums. The two sides entered an extended and likely endless process of mediation.

A self-appointed purveyor of the essence of rock, Love launched a bitter missile at the Rock and Roll Hall of Fame in 2000 for passing over acts she favored for induction. They included Patti Smith, Lynyrd Skynyrd, and AC/DC. Her correspondence also chastised the Hall for "stealing" memorabilia that belonged to her and her late husband, and demanded the articles be returned.

Three of Love's former employees—a butler, a nanny, and a jill of all trades —successfully sued the star for back pay. Their varying lengths of time in Love's employ were apparently anything but enjoyable. According to documents obtained by *The Smoking Gun* website, one of the trio wrote to Love's management team, "I believe that Courtney thrives on a chaotic household and micromanaging people with ... self-esteem that can take this type of abuse."

On a positive note, the former Mrs. Cobain has proven she can act, having easily and successfully assumed a variety of big screen personas. She even captured a Golden Globe nomination for a starring turn in *The People versus Larry Flynt* and good reviews for *Man on the Moon* and other films. Now she's looking to the future, having purchased the rights to *Bye Bye Baby*, the story of one of the 1970s' biggest musical phenomena, Scotland's The Bay City Rollers. Perhaps she's planning on taking a spot behind the camera as director or producer when the film is eventually made. Whatever she decides will come next, it's a sure bet that she won't let anything stand in her way. ✪

ROB LOWE

The West Wing star's directorial debut was a direct-to-video effort. Officially untitled, it was commonly called *The Rob Lowe Sex Tape*. Duped by two wanton women into frolicking with them on film, Lowe found himself ankle deep in quicksand once it was revealed that one of the lascivious ladies was still just a girl.

The year was 1989. Lowe was barely twenty-four, a fresh-faced Brat Packer reeling from the success of several movies including *St. Elmo's Fire* and *Youngblood*. He traveled to Atlanta to campaign on behalf of US presidential candidate Michael Dukakis and found himself with some free time one night. While sipping suds at a nightclub, Lowe met two pretty young females who suggested they could accompany the hunky star to his hotel room, where they would join him in a video-taped ménage à trois. Far from home and in need of a little companionship, Lowe decided to seize the moment. It was a decision he would live to regret.

> THE WEST WING STAR'S DIRECTORIAL DEBUT WAS A DIRECT-TO-VIDEO EFFORT. OFFICIALLY UNTITLED, IT WAS COMMONLY CALLED THE ROB LOWE SEX TAPE

In the morning, the girls—and the tape containing the trio's performance —were gone. When the crude home movie finally surfaced (as the fearful actor knew it would), it sold like crazy for $29.95 until it caught the attention of one girl's mother. Her daughter, carelessly cavorting all over the screen with the famous actor, was a minor. Mom sued and the case settled out of court with community service for Lowe as one provision of the settlement.

The star's career sputtered in the aftershocks. He didn't find his footing on the comeback trail until Mike Myers cast him in 1992's *Wayne's World*. Lowe looks back on the scandal as "a test" and proudly recalls that he earned a passing grade. He immediately sought help for his drug and alcohol problem, got married in 1991, and evolved into a loving husband and doting father. His amateur performance in Atlanta behind him, Lowe spun disgrace into a second shot at stardom as Deputy Communications Director Sam Seaborn on *The West Wing*, one of TV's most popular dramas. He exited the show in the fourth season after his requests for a salary hike were rebuffed. The "amicable parting" was the second blow to Lowe's career in 2002. Lowe was the lone *West Wing* star to be overlooked for an Emmy Award nomination; each of his nine costars was honored in their respective categories. ✪

MADONNA

She's a chameleon, revolutionary, trendsetter, and megastar. The misadventures of the Material Girl could easily fill up an entire book. And, in fact, they have—several times over. But since this book is a collection of highlights—or rather lowlights—let's look at the few that stand out.

It's not really surprising that Madonna's bad girl antics have always revolved around sex. After all, the sexual content in some of the best rock and roll (if Madonna's sound can even be called rock and roll) annoys parents, angers the church, and pushes the boundaries of decency. And that's what Madonna loves to do. If mixing sex and music is a crime, pronounce this Catholic-raised rebel guilty as charged.

Once the motherless, determined little girl from Detroit, Michigan, burst onto the music scene in the 1980s, she spread her tentacles into other media

Despite her protests, "Madonna Condoms" hit the US market in August of 2001

with varying degrees of success. Next to the 1986 movie flop *Shanghai Surprise*, an attempted comedy with then husband Sean Penn (for more on their brief, volatile relationship *see* Sean Penn), her biggest misstep was reinventing herself as some sort of sexual guru with the 1992 coffee-table book titled *Sex*. The target audience for her racy how-to manual was unclear. Music fans who snapped up millions of copies of the songs "Like a Virgin" and "Papa Don't Preach" were largely teens and preteens. But sales of the shrink-wrapped, graphic *Sex*, complete with live action nude photos involving guest sex object Vanilla Ice and others, were restricted only to adults. In a puzzling response to the obvious question *Why?*, Ms. Ciccione boasted, "I'm going to teach you how to f———." With her fans' idolatry gone straight to her head, she apparently felt qualified to fill in gaps left by the *Kama Sutra* and *The Joy of Sex*. That those earlier tomes left no erogenous zone unturned evidently eluded her. Yet give the girl credit; the project gave her another niche to wriggle into while capturing newspaper headlines at the same time. Now, the few remaining factory-sealed copies of *Sex* are considered collector items and sell to the faithful for hundreds of dollars each on the Internet.

There were hints of the book's genesis two years earlier during her Blond Ambition tour. On the company's stop in Toronto, Canada, the conservative local police force was called up to investigate the singer for suspected public indecency. It seems they caught wind that Madonna simulated sex on stage during the performance. Officers were prepared, if necessary, to stop the show. She later described the fake act, which involved an actual bed being rolled out onto the stage for the deed, as an extended middle finger to her father and conservatism. The scene was shrewdly designed for shock value and to inspire exactly the kind of outrage it sparked in Toronto. It afforded the envelope-pushing artist yet another opportunity to rail against her censors. Following a tense standoff, police finally decided not to file charges and the sold-out concert went on as planned. The whole sordid event is chronicled in Madonna's award-winning, behind-the-scenes rock-u-mentary *Truth or Dare*. (Watch also for her classless reaction to a gushing Kevin Costner.)

> **IF MIXING SEX AND MUSIC IS A CRIME, PRONOUNCE THIS CATHOLIC-RAISED REBEL GUILTY AS CHARGED**

Madonna claims racism and right-wing Christianity were to blame for the outrage generated by her 1989 video "Like a Prayer." In another bid to goad her detractors into a negative reaction, it featured the sultry singer writhing among burning crosses, sporting stigmata, and kissing a religious statue that morphed into a gorgeous black man. The controversy—which she also claims was never intended—cost her a lucrative endorsement deal with Pepsi, but propelled the song into the stratosphere of success. "Like a Prayer" ranked second overall to Michael Jackson's "Thriller" on music channel VH-1's 2001 ranking of all-time best videos.

Now a married mother of two (her husband is British film director Guy Ritchie), the Material Mama finds herself a forty-something superstar who worries more about her family's safety than her record sales. She cried foul upon learning that her face appears on a popular brand of condoms, an advertising scheme she might have cooked up herself in days past. The rare leak in her strict image control could not be plugged due to a release form signed in legal fashion for a photographer long before she hit it big. It's likely not the concept of her famous features appearing on condom packages that bothers her as much as a lack of power in the situation. It may be the only marketing ploy that wasn't her own idea. ✪

MARILYN **MANSON**

There are no halfway reactions to androgynous, outrageous Marilyn Manson. People either think he's creepy or cool, the devil incarnate or a rock icon worthy of worship. Here's another way to look at the divide: on one side of the fence are disenfranchised teenage boys who think the sultan of shock is, like, totally awesome; on the other side is everyone else. Pasty-faced societal outcast and Satan-loving Manson, who ditched his hopelessly normal birth name Brian Warner, may be the most vilified performer of his time. Consider the evidence.

Not once, but twice, the g-string-clad performer allegedly mock-humped the head of an unwitting security guard for an audience's amusement. One incident on a Michigan tour stop in 2001 inspired the humiliated sentry to sue, and resulted in criminal charges. The most serious charge of criminal sexual misconduct, which carried a probable jail sentence, was eventually dropped. Accusations of disorderly conduct and assault and battery, however, stuck. The judge explained he reduced the allegations after determining the "act" was designed for shock value only, and not for sexual gratification. That's likely of little comfort to the security guard. Manson eventually pleaded no contest and was handed a paltry fine and court costs totaling $4,000. The cadaverous performer still faces civil lawsuits from both the Michigan guard and another bouncer

AFP/CORBIS

Marilyn Manson at a preliminary hearing on charges of sexually assaulting a security guard

based in Minneapolis. Each claims Manson intentionally inflicted emotional distress for the amusement of others. With a watchful eye on his bank account, Manson isn't laughing.

On a tour swing through upstate New York, Satan's favorite son and his band apparently went medieval on the concert venue and in their hotel rooms. A T-shirt-burning ceremony in their dressing room set off smoke alarms, summoning the local fire department. Smokey the Bear's lecture obviously didn't take, because the rugs in their rented rooms later suffered the same fate. The group also redecorated their accommodations by leaving behind hair dye–stained bathroom fixtures and holes in walls. The New York Post reported that Manson paid up for the eve of destruction. The grand total: $25,000. Strangest of all was that Manson's parents were with him, staying only a few rooms away. Even mom and dad Warner couldn't keep their odd little boy in line.

Two weeks into a coheadlining 1999 tour, Courtney Love announced that she and her band Hole were bailing on Manson, calling his performances "evil." Love said she was caught unaware by the intensity of his antichurch, antireligion songs and stance.

The former editor of *Spin* magazine claimed he was manhandled by several of Manson's bodyguards in an overreaction to a change of heart. As legend has it, *Spin* had originally planned to place Marilyn on the cover of a year-end issue and then reneged. The dark prince allegedly hissed threats at the editor and his family, telling him, "That's what you get when you disrespect me." The Gothmeister's goons then reportedly tossed the editor against a wall. The *Spin* head filed a $24 million lawsuit, which Manson countered with his own $40 million suit, citing defamation of character.

Manson's 1998 album *Mechanical Animals* was banned from several chain stores in the US because the cover art was considered too unsettling for shoppers popping in to pick up shampoo and candy. The album design featured a shockingly altered Manson sporting a new set of breasts and other feminine-looking touches in addition to his trademark eyeliner and other heavy makeup.

NOT ONCE, BUT TWICE, THE G-STRING-CLAD PERFORMER ALLEGEDLY MOCK-HUMPED THE HEAD OF AN UNWITTING SECURITY GUARD FOR AN AUDIENCE'S AMUSEMENT

Manson was pushing the boundaries again in late 2000, and some US retailers covered up his *Holy Wood (In the Shadow of the Valley of Death)* CD, which featured a grotesque cover. On it, Manson—or half of Manson—appeared in a crucifixion pose, his lower jaw missing. The Goth antihero declared the ban a victory, claiming it proved his point about censorship, testing the limits of which was the apparent purpose for using the controversial artwork.

He was banned, unbanned, and banned again in too many North American cities to count. Most often, town leaders who opposed his arrival would have to eventually knuckle under due to loopholes in their own loose laws. In Italy, charges of public indecency were laid over the singer's signature butt-baring costumes.

His name routinely comes up at hearings and probes into teen suicides and killing sprees. Although no direct link has been established, his dark-lord-loving tunes are suspected of compelling several young men to end their lives. Manson complained to MTV Europe that he was tired of being blamed for "everything violent in the world." Public outrage toward the shock rocker caused him to abandon several US tour dates in the wake of the Columbine High School massacre. On April 20, 1999, two student outcasts went on a carefully planned rampage, killing ten fellow students and a teacher before turning their weapons on themselves. Some students claimed the killers were Manson devotees and may have been influenced by his sinister lyrics. Local authorities intervened and persuaded promoters to cancel a benefit concert Manson was set to headline in nearby Denver barely a week after the brutal murders.

SOME STUDENTS CLAIMED THE KILLERS WERE MANSON DEVOTEES AND MAY HAVE BEEN INFLUENCED BY HIS SINISTER LYRICS

The leather-clad musician has been implicated in the drug-related death of actor Keanu Reeves's ex-girlfriend Jennifer Syme. In her lawsuit against the singer, Syme's mother accuses Manson of supplying the twenty-nine-year-old with cocaine and other drugs at a party he hosted on April 1, 2001. The following morning, after riding with a friend back to Manson's home to pick up her SUV, she crashed into several other cars and died at the scene. The coke was found in her system. Manson expressed sadness over his friend's death but asserted that he responsibly fulfilled his duty by seeing that she was safely driven home. After that point she was essentially on her own. He calls the lawsuit "completely unfounded."

Marilyn Manson is a tremendous manipulator of media, and his dark lyrics nudge fans and foes alike into debates about the parameters of free speech. Does repeated listening to hate-filled lines like "Let's just kill everyone" and "We're just disposable teens" make an indelible impression on a young mind? The revolted jury is still out. ✪

MATTHEW
McCONAUGHEY

Plenty of actors play music on the side but only one (that we know of) is prolific in the genre of naked bongo drumming. Matthew McConaughey, the star of *A Time to Kill*, *Contact*, and *EDtv*, gave an impromptu performance for Texas police in the fall of 1999.

The southern heartthrob came to acclaim as a stoner in the 1993 flick *Dazed and Confused*, and on the day of his arrest at his home in Austin, Texas, he blurred the lines between art and life. Police were summoned when a neighbor complained of loud music coming from the actor's home at 3 A.M. Peering through a window, an officer saw a completely nude McConaughey dancing around his living room, beating on a set of bongos. A fully clothed onlooker was cheering and clapping in accompaniment. (He was later reported to be *Dazed* costar Cole Hauser.) Smelling marijuana, the officer entered, unannounced, interrupting the show. Both men were "very intoxicated" according to the police report, and a bowl of pot stems, seeds, and a pipe were in plain view.

When told to get dressed, McConaughey allegedly rushed the cop—a move that instantly cost him his freedom. Both men were cuffed, but only McConaughey was arrested. He spent the night in the local jail before posting a $1,000 bond. "I don't want to rent a place there, but it was a nice stay for a night," said Sandra Bullock's former squeeze the morning after.

A charge of drug possession was dropped due to lack of evidence, leaving a misdemeanor for resisting transport (he had to be forced into the squad car) and violating the local noise ordinance. McConaughey's lawyer cried foul over an illegal search and use of excessive force. The incident was finally settled when the actor paid a $50 fine for being too noisy. No one knows if McConaughey's sideline as one of the world's foremost naked bongo players is continuing, but if it is, he's doing a better job of keeping this particular talent out of the headlines. ✪

> **PEERING THROUGH A WINDOW, AN OFFICER SAW A COMPLETELY NUDE McCONAUGHEY DANCING AROUND HIS LIVING ROOM, BEATING ON A SET OF BONGOS**

JOHN McENROE

The London *Sun* newspaper summed it up pretty well: "He is the most vain, ill-tempered, petulant loudmouth that the game of tennis has ever known."

John McEnroe may have finished with the third most career singles titles on the pro tennis circuit, but he's in a league of his own when it comes to on-court antics. Rude, arrogant, and obnoxious, and displaying a level of self-control on par with a toddler, McEnroe is an admired but disliked, respected but unloved athlete. He earned the nickname Superbrat at the tender age of twenty and through his sixteen-year career, he dished out thousands of dollars in fines for abusive language toward court officials. His outbursts also cost him wins and notably got him disqualified from the Australian Open in 1990. In the game where love means nothing, sports journalists labeled him a crybaby for consistently prancing and pouting in full view of spectators when he didn't get his own way.

> RUDE, ARROGANT, AND OBNOXIOUS, AND DISPLAYING A LEVEL OF SELF-CONTROL ON PAR WITH A TODDLER, McENROE IS AN ADMIRED BUT DISLIKED, RESPECTED BUT UNLOVED ATHLETE

McEnroe's brutish behavior was so consistent and so outrageous that it threatened to overshadow his many accomplishments. No one can contest his domination of the game in the early 1980s when he won three Wimbledon and four US Open titles. He offers no apologies for his career-long cruel treatment of linesmen and umpires for their "bad calls" (read: calls not in his favor). McEnroe claimed to be able to "feel" when the ball was out, and knowing he was "right" made him crazy enough to act out on the court.

Only Jimmy Connors and Ivan Lendl won more singles tournaments than McEnroe's seventy-seven, but his bellyaching made him unpopular among fans and colleagues. Perhaps his bad attitude was ingrained early when he failed to sprout to the same height as many of his competitors, growing sideways instead. A teenage weight problem has a way of lingering in the mirror long after the fat has left the body, and McEnroe was a self-described "pudgy" adolescent. Born an air force kid in Wiesbaden, Germany, on February 16, 1959, his family moved back to New York before John was a year old. McEnroe qualified for Wimbledon at age eighteen, setting records as the youngest player and first-ever qualifier to reach the semifinals, where Jimmy Connors eventually shut him down. He turned pro at age twenty, beating Vitas Gerulaitis in his first US Open.

It wasn't long before McEnroe coined his familiar refrain, "You cannot be serious!" which he would shriek at officials for years to come. He wasn't the first to bring chronic whining and an explosive temper to the court—witness Ilie Nastase and Jimmy Connors before him—but McEnroe made it an art form. Despite the relentless coverage of his brash attitude, he somehow continued to focus and win accolades and tournaments. McEnroe shared his secret with an eighteen-year-old Boris Becker after the younger player pouted through an entire match. "Listen," he told Becker, "you've got to start winning something before you go pulling that." Three months later, Becker won Wimbledon.

Mac, as he is known to friends, scored points for style and originality, peppering court officials with such insults as "You're the pits of the world" and hurling curses rough enough to make a longshoreman blush. He claims his signature blowups became a song and dance, performed for an expectant crowd. The tirades became "like a cigarette addiction. It's not really what I'm feeling. I'm just doing it because it's the habit. I'd go out on the court and suddenly I'm doing something and I'd be like, 'Why am I doing this?'" He often appeared to enjoy being nose to nose with a linesman, tossing a racket, or clenching his fist. If it really was just an act, it continues to this day, and prompted opponent Johan Kriek to call for McEnroe's banishment from a tour—the 2000 Seniors' Tour. "If I'm the only one that has the guts to say he needs to be kicked off the tour, fine," said Kriek. "I work too hard to be treated like this. That guy McEnroe has got a screw loose."

> **MAC, AS HE IS KNOWN TO FRIENDS, SCORED POINTS FOR STYLE AND ORIGINALITY, PEPPERING COURT OFFICIALS WITH SUCH INSULTS AS "YOU'RE THE PITS OF THE WORLD" AND HURLING CURSES ROUGH ENOUGH TO MAKE A LONGSHOREMAN BLUSH**

His reputation spun off into a successful sideline of tennis commentary, which he wedged in between shrewdly chosen advertising deals as a pitchman with companies ranging from Nike to Rogaine. He even made a serious run for rock star status in the early 1990s, but to little avail. All told, Mac has amassed a huge personal fortune, several homes, and other trappings of the too-rich.

Despite his financial success, his personal life has been no more settled than his existence on the tennis court. The media scrutiny surrounding his first marriage to actress Tatum O'Neal resulted in a few reporters who were roughed up and photographers who were spat upon. Their volatile—and she says violent—union ended after a decade of drugs and torment. In his autobiography *You Cannot Be Serious*, McEnroe saved his most scathing remarks for Tatum and her well-known heroin addiction and subsequent attempts to get clean. (He was given full custody of their three children given her frequent stays in rehab.) O'Neal told ABC's Barbara Walters about several instances of Mac's alleged abuse, including his pushing her down a flight of stairs and nearly breaking her arm when she was nine months pregnant. She also claimed he took steroids to whip himself back into playing shape after the birth of their first child. O'Neal called her explosive ex "brutal, manipulative, a physical and sexual bully."

McEnroe later married singer Patty Smyth, whom he met during his short-lived musical career. In Smyth, Mac has met his soul mate. When a photographer tried to snap photos following their 1997 wedding, Patty reportedly decked him with her handbag. But the abuse isn't limited to tennis officials, reporters, and photographers. The eldest of McEnroe's six children has apparently asked his father to stop coming to his basketball games. It seems dad can't hold back from shouting at the refs.

The popularity of game show hosts who are as warm and cuddly as porcupines (*The Weakest Link*'s Anne Robinson, for example) made McEnroe a natural to host ABC's 2002 entry, *The Chair*. Contestants were strapped into a chair, monitored to ensure their heart rate remained calm, and then peppered with questions barked out by their hyper host. And there were surprises. On one memorable occasion, a live alligator was lowered over a contestant's head as he scrambled for answers to stay in the game while breathing deeply to control his pulse. It didn't look as if *The Chair* had legs—and it didn't. McEnroe took the news in typical fashion, acting out days later on the Seniors' tennis circuit, yelling at officials and even berating a fan. Who would expect anything less? ✪

GEORGE MICHAEL

With the benefit of several years of hindsight, George Michael now believes he got himself deliberately arrested in the lewd bathroom incident that finally dragged him out of the closet for all to see. But the singer of "I Want Your Sex" was tapping his foot to a different beat back in the spring of 1998.

It's not as if we were living in conservative times, when one's admission of homosexuality would mean the end of an illustrious career. That type of attitude kept Rock Hudson dating women for the cameras while he secretly went home to be with men. More than four decades later it would have been more than okay for an artist of George Michael's stature to admit he was gay. There was always some suspicion regarding his sexual orientation, but never a confirmation. Instead, he kept us guessing with videos full of writhing lovelies and ambiguous answers to questions about his sexuality.

> **MICHAEL OWNED UP TO HAVING BEEN EXCLUSIVELY GAY FOR TEN YEARS AND SHOCKINGLY ADMITTED THAT THE WILL ROGERS PARK INCIDENT WASN'T THE FIRST OF ITS KIND**

The guesswork was over after an undercover cop discovered the incognito singer in the public restroom at Will Rogers Park in Los Angeles. The officer contended Michael pulled down his pants and proceeded to fondle himself in full view. In the LAPD's books that's called lewd conduct, and the former Wham! frontman found himself under arrest and deeply humiliated. Anger surfaced first. Michael claimed the cop entrapped him and proceeded to post $500 for bail.

Just days after the arrest, the man behind hits like "I'm Your Man" and "One More Try" took control and appeared on CNN to beat the gossip hounds at their own game. Michael owned up to having been exclusively gay for ten years and shockingly admitted that the Will Rogers Park incident wasn't the first of its kind. During the previous displays, he had been lucky enough to avoid arrest.

In exchange for a guilty plea, Michael was fined $800, banned from the park, ordered to perform community service, and submitted to sexual counseling. The sentence was light; the maximum included up to six months' jail time. But in the incident's aftermath, there was one more niggling issue to deal with. The arresting officer filed a civil suit against the singer, claiming he had been slandered in a video filmed after the bathroom arrest. At issue was footage for the song "Outside," which featured a reenactment of the arrest and some kissing cops. A judge dismissed the $10 million lawsuit; it seems a public official can't claim emotional distress.

In a 2002 BBC interview, Michael admitted he consciously put himself in harm's way with his behavior. He claimed he exposed himself, literally, so he could be outed and refocus his out-of-control life. He was, he said, in deep grief over the deaths of his beloved mother and a longtime partner, and was still recovering from a long contract battle with Sony, his record label. Michael said he was looking for a way to honestly concentrate on himself—a proud, happy, gay pop singer.

Later that year, Michael courted controversy again with the release of his single and video for "Shoot the Dog," a politically charged song that takes jabs at Britain's close alliance with the US in the fight against terrorism. The attention-grabbing tune and animated video, lampooning the relationship between British Prime Minister Tony Blair and American President George W. Bush, were seen by some as a desperate act, given that Michael's previous single, "Freeek!," had failed to elicit much attention. The video depicts Blair and Bush as gay lovers and shows Blair, as a poodle, being petted by Bush.

Despite not being released in the US, Michael claimed the anti-American sentiment surrounding "Shoot the Dog" made him fear for his life during trips to the States to visit his home in Los Angeles, California, and his American lover and his family in Dallas, Texas. He denied that the song and satirical video were conceived as a publicity stunt, and he quickly did damage control to affirm that he was not an al Qaeda sympathizer, as had been claimed in a newspaper article. The singer maintained his intention was simply to spark debate about Britain's role in the war. "I knew I was going to walk into a wall of criticism because these are very reactionary times," Michael said. "But I felt I had to do this." ✪

ROBERT MITCHUM

Tough guy actor Robert Mitchum staged seriously comical feuds with his movie studios in reaction to a near-constant feeling of being shortchanged or disrespected. However, his biggest public faux pas occurred over an infraction that is much more common and far less serious today.

Mitchum was the kind of guy who never told a tale the same way twice; all of his yarns were fish stories. He was a talker, a grand storyteller, and a writer of stories, poetry, and songs. His reputation as a rugged everyman grew from a much-publicized eight-month stint in the US Army and celebrated roles as heroes and antiheroes in hit films like *The Story of GI Joe* and the original version of *Cape Fear*. (He had a cameo in the 1991 remake.) Called Bob by his closest friends, he didn't take his craft very seriously. His indifferent style of acting illuminated his feelings about the business. A former Mitchum assistant once explained why the actor's script was marked with a scrawled NAR beside his every line. The acronym stood for No Acting Required, Mitchum's own scathing commentary on the oft-awful material he found himself performing admittedly only for the paycheck.

RKO STUDIOS WENT INTO DAMAGE CONTROL MODE AND RELEASED A STATEMENT THAT DESCRIBED THEIR RUGGED STAR AS A "SICK MAN"

In the summer of 1948, Mitchum was shopping in earnest for a new home in the canyons of California. He and his family—wife Dorothy and their sons—needed bigger digs befitting a star of Mitchum's stature. Summoned to a home by a lithe and lovely blond who was in pursuit of the married but not unavailable star, Mitchum and the real estate agent arrived only to find themselves in police handcuffs minutes later. The duo faced a serious narcotics charge for smoking marijuana and Mitchum loudly lamented the certain end of his marriage and career. At the time, that fear wasn't too far-fetched. RKO Studios went into damage control mode and released a statement that described their rugged star as a "sick man." That characterization apparently angered Mitchum, and some say the sentence was actually crafted by his embarrassed but steadfast wife in cahoots with the studio's press agent.

The pampered movie star took up residence in a stark and barren prison bunk for a one-month stay, followed by two years' strict probation. It was a long sixty days in which the actor did hard labor, but he remained stoic and resolute throughout. Asked later if he felt he had been given fair treatment, Mitchum responded that a lighter sentence wouldn't have been a fair punishment in light of the day's very negative public opinion about drugs. RKO held his place in the film *The Big Steal* while Mitchum served his time, and his career was none the worse for his weed-prompted hiatus. The inmates of Wayside Honor Farm enjoyed Mitchum's legendary generosity for years to come. Given his empathy for the dullness of the inmates' lives behind bars, he donated several candy and soda vending machines after his release.

A practical joker and consistent rebel against authority, Bob Mitchum wasn't one to roll over if he felt he had been wronged. There was never enough pay, time off, or good lines in a movie script to satisfy his impossibly high standards. And he devised some very creative ways to make his feelings known to studio executives.

Mitchum was once very unhappy following the denial of his request for a new dressing room. Far from being just another star perk, his motive was practical. The harried actor was shooting three different movies on several separate RKO lots and locations, requiring him to hustle back and forth each day. Studio executives turned his request down flat. Soon after, the disgruntled actor proceeded to a central flower bed. Covered only by a towel slung around his waist, he carried a running garden hose and a bar of soap. He began showering in the open garden, attracting the attention of everyone within earshot. Finally, a studio honcho appeared in an office window and asked what the heck the troublesome star was up to. "Give me my dressing room, or I'll drop the towel!" Mitchum replied. Amid chants of "Drop the towel! Drop the towel!" the exasperated executive finally relented.

On another occasion, Mitchum and a friend returned to the studio lot after hours, claiming to have left a wallet behind. The daring, drunk duo relieved makeup rooms of wigs (they even took Lucille Ball's famous red tresses), cosmetics, and appliances, including several stand-alone hair dryers. The booty landed at the Mitchum house, where an unsuspecting and excited Dorothy Mitchum could hardly wait to try out her new dryer. In fact, that's where Dorothy was sitting—under her dryer, humming happily—when studio security showed up to repossess the goods. There was some discussion about criminal charges, but they were never filed.

PART WAY THROUGH COCKTAILS CHEZ LEMMON, THE MORTIFIED HOST RECEIVED A DELIVERY: AN UNUSUAL LARGE POTTED PLANT DECORATED WITH BALLOONS—OR, RATHER, CONDOMS BLOWN UP LIKE BALLOONS

One of Bob's bids to increase his pay involved the old, beat-up Chrysler he drove to work each day. When a superior remarked that it was time to get a new set of wheels and he didn't want to see Mitchum's clunker on the lot anymore, an insulted Mitchum exacted his revenge. The following day, with the Chrysler in the driveway of his home, the actor set out for the studio by bus. Between walking to a transit stop, transferring vehicles, and waiting for tardy buses, Mitchum didn't report for work until after noon. It was, he said, the price of leaving his eyesore of a car at home. Once again, the rebel got his way and the banished beater was suddenly acceptable again.

There were several other instances of standoffs, walkouts, and kerfuffles over costars, and they continued throughout Mitchum's long career. The hard-drinking actor touched off one notable screaming match with high-strung director Otto Preminger in 1974 while filming *Rosebud*. It was one of the legendary director's final pictures and he and his grumpy star did not see eye to eye. Following one particularly loud exchange of four-letter words, Mitchum was on his way home. The picture, eventually completed with Peter O'Toole in Mitchum's place, was a miserable flop.

Colleague and lifelong friend Jack Lemmon loved to tell the tale of the most embarrassing practical gag Mitchum ever played on him. Nearly divorced, Lemmon was dipping his toe back into the dating waters once again. While the two actors were on location together, Lemmon secured a first date with a young starlet and Mitchum caught wind of the rendezvous. Part way through cocktails chez Lemmon, the mortified host received a delivery: an unusual large potted plant decorated with balloons—or, rather, condoms blown up like balloons. Robert Mitchum had struck again.

After a career that included well over 100 films and having earned the status of revered legend, Robert Mitchum died of lung cancer in the summer of 1997, a few weeks shy of his eightieth birthday. He never won an Oscar, reportedly an alternately touchy and inconsequential fact of his life. And the echoes of his tall tales still make the rounds at Hollywood studios. ✪

JIM **MORRISON**

Some thirty years after his passing, the brief life and strange death of The Doors' charismatic, troubled lead singer Jim Morrison is still shrouded in myth and mystery. In just twenty-seven years, The Lizard King epitomized the rock and roll cliché: live fast, die young, and leave a beautiful corpse.

A shy, sensitive, prolific poet trapped inside the body of a sometimes-boorish chronic boozer—that was Jim Morrison. He wrote brilliant lyrics to hit songs like "Love Her Madly," "The End," and "Touch Me." His on-stage charisma, deep vocals, and movie star looks propelled The Doors to success in the late 1960s. An easily bored borderline genius, he also grew restless while tied down to a seven-record deal that forced him to face the nuts and bolts of the music business. After all, he was an *artist*. His role was to create, not to mess about with contracts and financial statements. His contempt for the business grew into contradictory feelings of love and loathing for the fans, the very people responsible for his tremendous success. His whiskey-soaked attitude spiraled downward and finally hit rock bottom during a show in Miami, Florida. What transpired that night essentially ruined what was to be the band's first full-length concert tour.

As Doors keyboardist and Jim's close friend Ray Manzarek tells it in his autobiography *Light My Fire*, Morrison had again been drinking too much. A porous soul, he was fresh from being mesmerized by performance artists who specialized in "confronting" their audiences. Jim decided rock and roll could use a little of that medicine and, without warning, he chose to debut his new approach in Miami. He yelled at the audience, ranted about their stupidity, and dared them to love him despite his comments. Then, to the rest of the band's surprise, Morrison began to slowly strip. The audience, now frenzied, cheered as he launched into a game of mock peek-a-boo with his private parts. Trouble was, he played the ruse too well and even the fans didn't know that they weren't seeing the real thing. Neither did Miami police, who were watching off-stage. They let Morrison be for fear of inciting a riot, but later arrested him for exposing himself in public and exhibiting drunkenness and lewd behavior. Five thousand dollars' bail and several convictions later, Morrison became one in a string of public figures with FBI files. He had left for a Jamaican vacation following the Miami show and created an international incident when the bureau filed a warrant for his arrest, allowing authorities to track him outside US borders.

> JUST A FEW MONTHS LATER, AFTER UTTERING THE PLAINTIVE QUESTION, "PAM, ARE YOU STILL THERE?" FROM HIS BATH, JIM MORRISON WAS DEAD

The conviction was appealed, but the damage was done. The rest of the tour dates dropped off one by one as word spread that in between tunes, The

Lizard King liked to take out The Lizard Prince. Soon after the Miami arrest, Morrison faced further charges for pinching a flight attendant's backside, a rather serious offence these days under a new law called "interference with a flight crew."

In the summer of 1971, Jim Morrison was disillusioned, burned out, and burdened by his troubles with the law. Reports claimed he was being pursued in more than a dozen paternity lawsuits. His closest friends, who desperately wanted him to give up drinking, had also just subjected him to an intervention. He left for a break of undetermined length to concentrate on his writing in Paris, France. His muse, Pam, was already there waiting for him. Just a few months later, after uttering the plaintive question, "Pam, are you still there?" from his bath, Jim Morrison was dead. Buried without benefit of an autopsy, those left behind will never truly know if the official determination of heart failure was what actually killed him.

Morrison's body is ostensibly buried in a Paris cemetery, where tens of thousands of fans continue to make an annual pilgrimage to mark the date of his death. Several years ago, a rumor surfaced that Morrison's plot lease was up and his remains would be shipped out of their final resting place. Not so, said cemetery managers at Père Lachaise, who insisted the shrine to The Doors' lead singer and rock and roll itself had a permanent place in Paris. The party atmosphere that perpetually surrounded Jim Morrison's tomb has died down in recent years now that, ironically, alcohol and music are banned from the site. ✪

EDDIE **MURPHY**

Is Eddie Murphy the kindest multimillionaire superstar in Hollywood? In May 1997, did he take to the mean streets like some sort of single-minded super-hero, trolling neighborhoods for unfortunate souls in need of assistance? Or did police intervention prevent him from making a very grave error that could have cost him his family and career?

As the actor tells it, he was out driving late one night, at nearly 5 A.M., on Santa Monica Boulevard. He was in search of a little light reading—some magazines to be specific—when he happened upon a sorry-looking specimen in need of a ride. The hitchhiker was a twenty-year-old transvestite prostitute named Atisone Seiuli. Now recall that Murphy is the same performer who, during his first few heady years of fame, was surrounded at all times by a half dozen bodyguards. However, the *Trading Places* star apparently had no safety concerns about letting this young stranger join him in his car—no muscle in sight.

Little did Murphy know, undercover police were patrolling the area. The particular stretch of road he was on is well known as a hangout for young gay hookers. It's even published as such in local guide books. Cops were soon on Eddie's tail and pulled the comedian and his passenger over. Seiuli was arrested on outstanding warrants and Murphy had some explaining to do. He claimed he was just trying to be nice. Because the self-professed humanitarian hadn't broken any laws, he wasn't placed under arrest.

THE HITCHHIKER WAS A TWENTY-YEAR-OLD TRANSVESTITE PROSTITUTE NAMED ATISONE SEIULI

The tabloids and several of the braver stand-up comedians had a field day with the incident and Murphy's supposed naïveté. One paper even headlined an interview with two transsexuals who claimed they had had relations with Murphy. The two also alleged that despite his beautiful wife and growing family, Murphy was a closeted homosexual.

The funnyman became furious and assembled a legal team to file a $5 million libel lawsuit against two tabloids. He accused them of knowingly printing false information. A third suit named a relative of Murphy's late-night passenger as a defendant who purportedly blabbed lies to a newspaper. The *Nutty Professor* star claimed the media scrutiny caused him to suffer "severe emotional and physical distress, requiring medical attention."

One lawsuit was settled out of court with terms kept private. Murphy dropped the second one, concluding the tabloid didn't act maliciously in its reporting. The jokes and the frenzy soon subsided and Murphy continued to star in family-oriented comedies like *Dr. Doolittle*. However, the embarrassment of daring to give one transvestite hooker a lift forever put an end to the brief appearance of Eddie Murphy in the role of Good Samaritan. ✪

JACK NICHOLSON

These days, road rage is, well, all the rage. It's just one more term in our seemingly endless supply of euphemisms for bad behavior, in this case referring to anger that boils over while one is behind the wheel of an automobile. Give the *As Good As It Gets* star credit for injecting some finesse into his bout with the condition by combining it with his favorite game: golf.

Nicholson narrowly escaped criminal prosecution for assault and vandalism after the notorious 1994 incident that began when a motorist allegedly cut off the actor in Los Angeles traffic. The common infraction must have occurred on a bad hair day for Jack, because he lost his trademark cool. According to published accounts, he pulled a golf club from his trunk, abandoned his vehicle at a red light, and began clubbing the other driver's Mercedes, smashing the hood and windshield. Reports claimed Nicholson used a 9 iron for the job, which is strange considering every good golfer knows a Mercedes calls for a driver. At any rate, one can only imagine the terrified, yet excited, reaction of the Mercedes's occupant: "If I live through this, cha-ching—it's payday!"

> HE PULLED A GOLF CLUB FROM HIS TRUNK, ABANDONED HIS VEHICLE AT A RED LIGHT, AND BEGAN CLUBBING THE OTHER DRIVER'S MERCEDES, SMASHING THE HOOD AND WINDSHIELD

The reluctant rebel from *Easy Rider* reached an out-of-court settlement with his clubee, who decided not to pursue criminal charges. The episode is now a permanent part of Hollywood lore known simply as "Nicholson's Golf Club Incident."

Four years later a more controlled Nicholson reacted calmly to a minor fender bender on those same streets of LA. The other driver, a twenty-three-year-old, and his twenty-year-old passenger sued the Oscar winner for damages after his Benz kissed the bumper of their BMW. Police determined fault lay with both parties. The BMW driver was speeding, and Jack made things worse by attempting an illegal left turn. Most surprising at the time, however, was the identification of Jack's passenger: an actress less than half his age, *The Practice* star Lara Flynn Boyle. The driving mishap dragged their hidden romance into the light of day and just weeks later, they made their first official appearance as a couple.

Far from damaging his image, these incidents have only enhanced Nicholson's reputation as a tough guy, a ladies' man, and one *serious* golfer. ✪

OASIS
(NOEL & LIAM GALLAGHER)

Never lacking for rock star arrogance and swagger, England's Noel and Liam Gallagher seem to have emerged virtually unscathed from years of public feuds and private fights. Once the biggest band in the world, Oasis has settled down into "respectable artist" territory while family life supercedes much of their music icon posturing of the past.

By design it was bound to be a tempestuous arrangement; big brother Noel wrote the songs and performed distinctive guitar licks while lead singer Liam, five years younger, absorbed all the glory out front. At the peak of their popularity in the mid-1990s, the brothers barely spoke except on matters concerning the band, and even those conversations would often escalate into shouting matches. There were no warm and fuzzy feelings between the Gallagher brothers.

Noel became king of stage walkoffs while Liam's frequent profanity-laced outbursts made him legendary beyond the music. Noel abandoned performances several times, citing different catalysts on each occasion, including unruly fans and inferior sound equipment. The brothers' creative and control differences came to a head in May 2000 when Noel abruptly left a tour on the eve of a concert in Paris. The band's cofounder was quickly—and only temporarily—replaced by another guitarist. Noel explained he needed time away from his brother, whom he claimed "talks too much." Later, Liam blamed his brother's first wife

> **BY DESIGN IT WAS BOUND TO BE A TEMPESTUOUS ARRANGEMENT; BIG BROTHER NOEL WROTE THE SONGS AND PERFORMED DISTINCTIVE GUITAR LICKS WHILE LEAD SINGER LIAM, FIVE YEARS YOUNGER, ABSORBED ALL THE GLORY OUT FRONT**

Meg Mathews for acting like a wedge in their relationship. "There were 50 people between me and him and we could not communicate," he told the London *Sun*. After Noel returned to the fold, Oasis became, according to Liam, "more of a band thing than it's ever been before."

The brothers' personal lives were often more interesting to the press than their uneven CD releases. Noel's divorce from Mathews and Liam's split with Patsy Kensit made headlines while music sales declined. The band peaked early with sales over ten million for each of *Definitely Maybe* and *What's the Story*

(*Morning Glory*); subsequent albums didn't fare as well with critics or fans. A lawsuit brought forth by a former drummer who claimed entitlement to a piece of the band's significant pie didn't help matters. The combined stress on both the public and private brothers finally boiled over.

Far from keeping the turbulence behind closed doors, the Gallagher boys almost delighted in waving their dirty laundry in front of the masses. In one example, Liam's controlled substance–fueled antics aboard a Cathay Pacific flight from Hong Kong to Australia resulted in the singer being slapped with a lifetime ban from the airline. Among other things, witnesses said Liam head-butted a fan and refused to calm down even after the captain emerged from the cockpit to restore order in the cabin. Much later Liam explained to the *Sun*, "I know how to behave but sometimes I can't be bothered because life is boring."

They also delighted in igniting public feuds with fellow Brit bands over everything from pop chart positions to public posturing. Notoriously, Noel called Blur's Damon Albarn a "fake" and labeled Radiohead as "miserable bastards." Noel claims the source of his disdain is both bands' hands-off stance toward fans and the media. He also emphasized that his feelings don't extend to the groups' artistry. "I actually like their music," he told the *Toronto Sun*. "I think that their attitude leaves a lot to be desired … being in a group should be a celebration."

> FAR FROM KEEPING THE TURBULENCE BEHIND CLOSED DOORS, THE GALLAGHER BOYS ALMOST DELIGHTED IN WAVING THEIR DIRTY LAUNDRY IN FRONT OF THE MASSES

As Oasis battles against changes in the music industry and the brothers live increasingly settled lives with steady partners and children of their own, it remains to be seen if they'll fulfill their ultimate goal. Boasts Liam, "We intend to continue until we have done the best album ever, and we don't feel that album is here yet." ✪

SINEAD O'CONNOR

From her cue ball coiffure to her outlandish protests, Irish singer Sinead O'Connor knew how to push people's buttons. She took on the heads of Catholicism and patriotism in poorly thought-out demonstrations, at great personal and professional cost.

O'Connor earned a platform for her opinions on the world stage following the release of her hugely successful 1991 album *I Do Not Want What I Haven't*

Got. At times she appeared to have a true sense of integrity, speaking publicly about political strife in her homeland and offering a depth of knowledge about world issues. At other times, however, her antics illuminated a shallow attempt to turn the spotlight on herself and audiences balked.

O'Connor capitalized on the success of songs like "Nothing Compares 2 U" and "The Emperor's New Clothes" with a concert tour that brought her to American soil. However, her many new fans quickly turned into foes. The misguided singer refused to perform if the US national anthem was played before an appearance in New Jersey. The audience did not take kindly to the snub; one thing all Americans agree on is the sanctity of "The Star Spangled Banner." The anthem incident was reportedly launched in protest of US politics, but its point was too vague to capture support. This was a woman in dire need of a good press agent.

> **IN THE LATE 1990S SHE ANNOUNCED SHE WAS A LESBIAN ONLY TO FOLLOW UP THAT DECLARATION A COUPLE OF YEARS LATER WITH NEWS THAT SHE HAD MARRIED A MAN IN DUBLIN**

In 1992, the singer shocked North Americans once again by ripping up a picture of beloved Pope John Paul II on *Saturday Night Live.* Again she offered no explanation for her actions and horrified viewers reached not only for their phones to complain to NBC, but also for their clickers to find another late-night show. That segment of *SNL* was edited and never rebroadcast, lest it reoffend forever in reruns.

O'Connor later apologized for upsetting millions of Catholics with the Pontiff photo incident, but it was too little too late. The public had already turned on her as witnessed by a sharp decline in record sales and overall disinterest in her as an artist. She explained her actions as born of frustration over a child abuse scandal involving the Irish Catholic Church that was covered up. "It wasn't an attack on the man," she claimed. But millions had already made up their minds that it was.

Her subsequent attempts to attract attention failed. For the most part, former fans kept their backs turned on O'Connor. In the late 1990s she announced she was a lesbian only to follow up that declaration a couple of years later with news that she had married a man in Dublin. In 1997, she fully embraced the church by becoming Mother Bernadette Mary, a priest for the Latin Tridentine Church, a Roman Catholic splinter group. She also made noises about recording fresh material under her new name. Look for it soon in a remainder bin near you. ✪

OZZY OSBOURNE

Life just isn't fair. Bite the head off of one measly bat and they'll brand you a bat-biter forever. In the case of legendary British rocker Ozzy Osbourne, that one headless bat has also spawned a lifetime's worth of urban legends.

Curiously, most of the notorious incidents from Osbourne's consistently exciting existence on this planet occurred in 1982. Ozzy had ridden his "Crazy Train" from Black Sabbath to a solo career just three years prior. In 1982, the unfortunate bat met its violent and untimely end during a now infamous bit of spontaneous theatrics during an Osbourne concert. But the headless bat had the last laugh; Ozzy was forced to undergo painful and lengthy rabies treatments as a precautionary measure against illness. Stories have since circulated involving Ozzy torturing puppies, mutilating doves, and performing other horrific acts of stage show violence against animals—all of which are untrue. It was one bat, one time—good night. After all, even rock and roll's prince of darkness tries hard not to repeat himself.

> **THE OZZMAN TOOK A TINKLE ON A WALL OF THE ALAMO MONUMENT IN TEXAS, REPORTEDLY WHILE WEARING A GREEN EVENING GOWN**

That same year, the Ozzman took a tinkle on a wall of the Alamo monument in Texas, reportedly while wearing a green evening gown. His wife, desperate to keep her wandering husband indoors at night, had hidden his clothes. No problem for Ozz—he simply wore hers. He was banned from the site for life. Several years later, full of regret, and newly recovered from his renowned drinking problem, Ozzy made a significant cash donation to the Daughters of the Republic of Texas as an apology.

Ozzy experienced another low in 1982, the circumstances of which are in full contention for the Darwin Awards Hall of Fame. The Darwins commemorate some of the stupidest ways our fellow humans have met their fate, and the death of Osbourne's guitarist and friend Randy Rhoads is certainly in the running. A brilliant axeman, Rhoads's licks helped define Ozzy's solo sound, but his influence was very short-lived. The twenty-five-year-old was killed in a small plane crash in Florida. He had persuaded the pilot to buzz the Osbourne tour bus for fun. However, they came in too close and the plane actually bounced off the bus roof before crashing. It was a devastating time for Ozzy; he not only lost a musician who influenced a generation of guitarists but also a very close pal.

Later in the decade, Ozzy was forced to defend his often-demonic lyrics under charges that they incited some young boys to commit suicide. It was an ironic situation for Ozzy to find himself in; according to the biography *Ozzy Unauthorized*, the rocker attempted to hang himself on a clothesline at age fourteen. His name was cleared of the accusations, but his life would never be the same. With the help of longtime wife and manager Sharon, Osbourne decided it was time to face down his biggest personal demon: alcoholism.

In perhaps the most surprising turnaround in rock and roll, Ozzy is now sober and a television darling with the success of the MTV reality show *The Osbournes*. His family's homes are actually wired for sight and sound so viewers can get a peek inside the unscripted (but heavily bleeped) real life of the adorable, bumbling rocker and his amusingly dysfunctional clan. And despite threats of retirement, he continues to make music that is still relevant. Ozzy Osbourne defeated seemingly insurmountable odds to become an international treasure. Long live the prince! ✪

SEAN PENN

He's a great actor, perhaps the best of his generation. But few describe Sean Penn as warm, friendly, or even nice. Between his disdain for his profession and his run-ins with photographers and movie industry types, the *I Am Sam* star has expended a lot of energy on bad behavior.

Many people believe Sean Penn's dark side emerged after he hooked up with Madonna in 1985, but it's not so. Long before meeting his first wife on the set of a music video, the twenty-four-year-old Brat Packer tossed a rock at photographers and paid a fine for the assault charge that ensued. Madonna just seemed to bring out the worst in him. The Material Girl and the temperamental star of *Fast Times at Ridgemont High* fell hard for each other and their combustible relationship became the focus of the media's attention at the time. Constant tracking by reporters and photographers gave volatile Penn plenty of opportunities to vent his seemingly endless anger. The couple's

> **THE TWENTY-FOUR-YEAR-OLD BRAT PACKER TOSSED A ROCK AT PHOTOGRAPHERS AND PAID A FINE FOR THE ASSAULT CHARGE THAT ENSUED**

cliffside wedding was drowned out by the whir of news helicopters overhead, prompting the enraged groom to scoot down to the beach and write a four-letter comment in the sand.

Their tempestuous marriage was marked by several scandalous moments, including a disastrous attempt by the couple to reinvent themselves as a Tracy-Hepburn duo for the 1980s. Their 1986 movie *Shanghai Surprise* flopped, nearly bankrupted ex-Beatle George Harrison's production company Handmade Films, and made a laughingstock of both stars. (Both of their film careers would recover nicely from the momentary embarrassment.) In 1987, Penn served a month behind bars for hitting a film extra and his altercations with shutterbugs continued. There is also an infamous and unsubstantiated story concerning his breakup with Madonna. It purports that Penn tied his wife to a chair and subjected her to several types of abuse before agreeing to a divorce. Neither the ex–Mrs. Penn or Sean have ever spoken about it, but the alleged legend lives on.

THE MATERIAL GIRL AND THE TEMPERAMENTAL STAR OF *FAST TIMES AT RIDGEMONT HIGH* FELL HARD FOR EACH OTHER AND THEIR COMBUSTIBLE RELATIONSHIP BECAME THE FOCUS OF THE MEDIA'S ATTENTION AT THE TIME

Penn's disdain for the movie industry is well known. Moguls and costars laud him as some sort of thespian genius, while he often responds with pure contempt for their lack of conscience, morals, taste—you name it. He continues to cash his paychecks, however.

Over the past decade his personal life has become more settled and he is presumably happier. Penn has been with actress Robin Wright since 1991. They married in 1996 and have two children. Instead of throwing stones, Penn has recently taken to putting pen to paper as his method of choice for venting anger. His poison-pen prose has attacked the likes of director Oliver Stone and 20th Century Fox head Rupert Murdoch. To the latter, Penn fired off a scathing letter after being refused Murdoch's private jet to fly his family to a movie premiere. He accused the media mogul's corporation and subsidiaries of "exploiting the pain and suffering of myself and my peers in their tabloids." Once again, his antics left baffled industry insiders shaking their heads in disbelief that someone so gifted could be so delusional. ✪

MATTHEW PERRY

In the stars-who-ought-not-drive file, we find *Friends* star Matthew Perry.

Millions of *Friends* fans dream of having Ross, Rachel, Phoebe, Monica, Joey, or Chandler drop by, but this unexpected visit went a bit too far. The streets of the Hollywood Hills are admittedly winding and steep, and Perry isn't the only star to have run off those narrow lanes (*see* Jason Priestley). However, TV's Chandler Bing differentiated his May 2000 accident from others by swerving to avoid an oncoming vehicle, losing control, and actually landing his Porsche on the porch of a house. The porch was totaled and the green Porsche had to be towed from the scene. No charges were laid and the attending officer merely helped facilitate the exchange of insurance information between Perry and the porch owner.

Alcohol and drugs were not factors in the Porsche-porch mishap, although Perry had recently been in rehab for a substance dependency. He had been reportedly addicted to painkillers and, as a result of the alleged drug abuse, suffered a painful pancreatic inflammation that landed him in hospital. Temporarily scared straight, the actor returned to the set of his sitcom twenty pounds lighter and vowing to live a cleaner life. (He would enter rehab again after signing a deal to become one of the wealthiest sitcom stars in history. He and his *Friends* costars reportedly agreed to earn $1 million each per episode.)

However, Perry's luck behind the wheel

> **TV'S CHANDLER BING DIFFERENTIATED HIS MAY 2000 ACCIDENT FROM OTHERS BY SWERVING TO AVOID AN ONCOMING VEHICLE, LOSING CONTROL, AND ACTUALLY LANDING HIS PORSCHE ON THE PORCH OF A HOUSE**

didn't improve with his health. Driving a silver BMW the year after he wrecked his Porsche, Perry was unfortunate enough to be T-boned by a little old lady in a 1989 Ford Escort. The crash was clearly the woman's fault, but no one was hurt and there were no arrests following the incident.

The actor's recurring troubles with drugs have interrupted his fledgling film career. They notably held up production for the movie *Serving Sara*, in which Perry costars with Elizabeth Hurley. Filming was shut down in February 2001 while the addicted star sought help once again for various dependencies.

And Perry's past troubles with drugs continue to haunt him. A seemingly credible rumor surfaced in 2001 that the actor was dying from an incurable liver condition, forcing his frantic publicist to issue a statement to the contrary. Between his fluctuating weight and occasional disappearing act, Matthew Perry will take his place in television history as the *Friends* friend who caused the most concern. ✪

DANA PLATO

Dana Plato's desperate bid to recreate the success of her youth did her as much harm as the variety of drugs she poured into her system. As the saddest component of the so-called *Diff'rent Strokes* curse (*see* Todd Bridges and Gary Coleman), Plato simply wasn't strong enough to withstand the force of fleeting fame and its taunting afterglow.

If not for her mother's intervention, Plato could have been a movie star right out of the gate. At the age of nine she won the now legendary Linda Blair role of the possessed child in the classic horror film *The Exorcist*. But at the time, Plato was very much a minor. Her guardian had veto power over career decisions and she exercised it, denying Dana the opportunity to act in the movie. Instead, Dana's mother agreed five years later to let her daughter star in the family sitcom *Diff'rent Strokes*, which centered on a lovable millionaire, his biological daughter (Plato), and his two adopted African-American sons (Bridges and Coleman). Along with a caring housekeeper, the TV family made up the most unconventional domestic situation in entertainment. Coleman, so cute in close-ups, was the breakout star and the rest of the cast rode his wave. Plato became a preteen pinup who literally grew up before the eyes of millions of viewers. The show was a certified hit for six years until it finally sputtered out in 1984.

> **IN 1991, PLATO APPEARED TO HIT ROCK BOTTOM WHEN SHE WAS ARRESTED FOR ROBBING A LAS VEGAS VIDEO STORE TO SCORE DRUG MONEY**

Plato, says fellow child star Johnny Whitaker (*Family Affair*), was vulnerable to unscrupulous entertainment industry leeches who convinced her she could repeat the success of *Strokes*. She was one of the few who peeled all for *Playboy* (1989) in a desperate bid for publicity, but the phone still didn't ring. In 1991, Plato appeared to hit rock bottom when she was arrested for robbing a Las Vegas video store to score drug money. She was bailed out of jail by sympathetic singer Wayne Newton. One year later, she was caught forging prescriptions for Valium, netting her five years' probation. To her credit, she didn't blame her drug addiction or scrapes with the law on having been a child star. "I would have crashed and burned no matter what," she said. The subsequent attention—albeit unwanted—refueled her hopes of kick-starting her dormant career. A few B movie roles (including the steamy *Different Strokes: The Story of Jack and Jill ... and Jill*) followed with no big break. Still, she remained optimistic.

Whitaker served as a sort of sponsor and confidant for the one-time star, and they talked nearly every day until her phone calls abruptly stopped. In her final interview on The Howard Stern Radio Show, which aired live the day before she died, Plato proclaimed herself to be happier than she'd ever been and again expressed hope for her career and her future.

In May 1999, the thirty-four-year-old actress and her fiancé Robert Menchaca were traveling the US in a newly purchased motor home. Parked outside his parents' home in Oklahoma for the night, Menchaca tried to wake Plato and found her body cold and unresponsive. Efforts to revive her—including those by Menchaca's mother, a nurse—failed. Toxicology tests showed Plato had overdosed on Valium and the painkiller Loritab, which had been prescribed following wisdom tooth extraction surgery weeks before. Although her death was first ruled accidental, the official coroner's conclusion was suicide. Plato left behind a teenage son and a bewildered audience of fans and curious listeners who had heard her nationwide interview the day before. Her TV brother Todd Bridges was reportedly devastated. Johnny Whitaker remembered her as "a beautiful girl," and laments that she "was really planning on getting everything together." ✪

ROMAN POLANSKI

In recent years the famed filmmaker's banishment, now two decades old, has been inching closer to an end. It's been so long since Polanski's transgression with a teenage girl that even his victim has forgiven him and wants authorities in the US to do the same.

Flush with fame and new money in the heady 1970s, the French-born, Polish-raised director of *Chinatown*, *Rosemary's Baby*, *Frantic*, and the Oscar-winning *Tess* was becoming one to watch on the Hollywood scene. However, an unspeakable tragedy changed his life, and his art, forever. Polanski's pregnant wife, actress Sharon Tate, was among the seven victims of a brutal killing spree by members of the Charles Manson "family."

In 1977, forty-two-year-old Polanski lured a thirteen-year-old girl to the Los Angeles home of his friend, actor Jack Nicholson (who was out of town), with the promise of featuring her photos in French *Vogue*. Polanski plied the teen with champagne and Quaaludes and seduced her. When the tryst was discovered (the girl's mother found partially nude pictures of her daughter and began asking questions), Nicholson and his live-in love at the time, actress Angelica Huston, both testified against their pal. Polanski pleaded guilty to unlawful sexual intercourse with a minor in exchange for having several other charges dropped. As the director and sometime actor later explained to *Esquire* magazine, the judge reneged on a deal that would have seen him serve ninety days. The charge carried a maximum sentence of fifty years in prison, so Polanski ran to Europe and eventually settled in Paris. He has never returned to US soil.

> **POLANSKI'S PREGNANT WIFE, ACTRESS SHARON TATE, WAS AMONG THE SEVEN VICTIMS OF A BRUTAL KILLING SPREE BY MEMBERS OF THE CHARLES MANSON "FAMILY"**

Polanski steadfastly refused to admit to his wrongdoing for more than fifteen years, claiming he was set up, the victim of a conspiracy. The man who once said, "When you are twelve, you no longer need the parents" now says his crime was "worse than Bill Clinton's."

Cautious negotiations for his safe return to the US have been stop-and-go. The Los Angeles judge who rescinded the plea bargain and vowed to arrest Polanski if he ever returned died in 1989. But so wary is the director still about subjecting himself to the long arm of American law, the publicity tour for his production of Broadway's *Death and the Maiden* was conducted afloat, in international waters, to avoid any chance of arrest.

Meantime, the thirteen-year-old girl Polanski seduced is now a thirty-something married mother of three who calls the 1977 incident "forced sex" and not actual rape. Samantha Geimer went public in 1997 to offer her support during negotiations to return Polanski to the US without a jail sentence. "I wish he would no longer be a fugitive," Geimer told TV's *Inside Edition*. For now Polanski remains a filmmaker in exile, relying on stars like Harrison Ford, Johnny Depp, and Hugh Grant to go to him as he continues to carefully wait and see what will unfold. ✪

PAULA POUNDSTONE

The year 2001 was a very unfunny one for comedienne Paula Poundstone.

Her troubles began in June, not far from her California home, when witnesses called police and reported that the comic appeared to be drunk behind the wheel. Four of her adopted and foster children were in the car with her on an outing for ice cream. The original criminal charges were shocking: they included child endangerment and lewd conduct involving a girl under fourteen. The latter accusation was dropped and the stand-up comic worked out a plea bargain on the former.

> **THE ORIGINAL CRIMINAL CHARGES WERE SHOCKING: THEY INCLUDED CHILD ENDANGERMENT AND LEWD CONDUCT INVOLVING A GIRL UNDER FOURTEEN**

"I created a dangerous situation for my children," offered Poundstone, then forty-one, in a mea culpa to the court. In return for a guilty plea she was spared jail time, but her life was altered significantly nonetheless. In addition to five years' probation, Poundstone was ordered to perform 200 hours of community service and to pay restitution to the children, including any future therapy costs. She was also prohibited from taking in any more children for the short or long term, and the foster kids in her care were removed from her home. She immediately checked into Promises, a live-in alcohol rehab center favored by the famous, for several months of treatment.

The funny lady did have to spend half a day behind bars, for violating the terms of her probation. When she was discovered taking a prescription medication not on the list of allowable drugs, she was cuffed and hauled off to jail. In sentencing her to the brief prison stint, the judge said he wanted Poundstone to realize the seriousness of her situation. She was fortunate the court didn't go for the allowable maximum: one month in the klink. Later, her six-month stay in rehab complete, the judge praised Poundstone for her recovery and gave her the green light to go home.

The formerly busy comic ended her hiatus from the club circuit in 2002. Poundstone expressed relief that audiences were willing to laugh along with her as she told jokes about her plight. Asked if she feared angering the judge by poking fun at herself and her situation, Poundstone said that after all she had been through, she didn't think she could make things any worse. ✪

JASON PRIESTLEY

A combination of notoriously treacherous Hollywood Hills streets and an alleged interloping deer proved too much to keep race-car driver, actor, and director Jason Priestley on the road. Of course, imbibing before driving didn't help matters.

In December 1999, the ex–*Beverly Hills 90210* star told police he swerved to spare the life of Bambi, causing his silver Porsche to topple several garbage cans and smash into a light standard before coming to rest by slamming into a parked car. Priestley's passenger, a twenty-seven-year-old male friend, suffered a broken arm in the accident, but refused to testify against his pal. While cops couldn't verify the deer tale, they did discover that Priestley, TV's former Brandon Walsh, had a blood alcohol level well above California's legal limit.

> **PRIESTLEY'S PASSENGER, A TWENTY-SEVEN-YEAR-OLD MALE FRIEND, SUFFERED A BROKEN ARM IN THE ACCIDENT, BUT REFUSED TO TESTIFY AGAINST HIS PAL**

Because he had no prior record, the resulting felony DUI charge was reduced after Priestley copped a plea. His punishment left the actor relying on the kindness of friends and hired drivers to get him around for one full year, as he surrendered his license in April 2000. He also won the chance to model a prison-issue orange jumpsuit while serving five days on a work-release program. The sentence also included three years' probation and three months in an alcohol rehab program, which the judge kindly delayed to allow Priestley to fulfill his thespian obligations.

The sometime documentary filmmaker (*Barenaked in America*) has taken his passion for speed off the city streets and channeled it into a sideline career in professional car and boat racing. After spending some time in the announcer's booth as an auto racing color commentator for the ABC network and displaying his driving talents as the celebrity component in several charity events, Priestley joyously signed on to the Kelly Team for the 2002 Indy Pro Series.

In April 2002 in Miami, a speedboating mishap resulted in broken bones for yet another Priestley passenger, while the pilot himself emerged unscathed. Priestley wasn't so lucky later in the year when his race car slid into a wall after hitting a slick spot during the final practice lap before an August race in Kentucky. Priestley took the near 115 mph impact headfirst and suffered a broken back, broken feet, a concussion, and facial cuts and bruising. He under went several hours of surgery followed by months of rehabilitation, and expects to make a full recovery. The actor said crack-ups are "all part of racing." Future copilots beware. ✪

PAUL REUBENS

There was a time when many people couldn't differentiate between the character of Pee-wee Herman and Paul Reubens, the performer who played him. Some didn't even know there *was* a Paul Reubens. So adept was he at morphing into the childlike goofball in the bow tie and shrunken suit, audiences can be forgiven for thinking Pee-wee was real.

Reubens spun his lovably irritating character into television gold for five years, hosting the Saturday morning children's show *Pee-wee's Playhouse*. That gig accompanied starring roles in the movies *Pee-wee's Big Adventure* and *Big Top Pee-wee*, and in countless other TV programs. However, the dual identities split forever

THE DUAL IDENTITIES SPLIT FOREVER IN 1991 WHEN REUBENS ALLEGEDLY ENJOYED AN ADVENTURE WITH HIS PEE-WEE IN A FLORIDA ADULT MOVIE THEATER

in 1991 when Reubens allegedly enjoyed an adventure with his pee-wee in a Florida adult movie theater. The beloved kiddie character died that day and Paul Reubens was thrust into the limelight all on his own.

Caught by detectives with his pants down following a screening of the X-rated flick *Nancy Nurse Turns up the Heat*, Reubens was charged with indecent exposure. He became the talk show joke *du jour*. As he later explained to *Vanity Fair* magazine, serial killer Jeffrey Dahmer was arrested at the same time, but the Pee-wee scandal overtook the hideous cannibal as the top news story. "It was just so bizarre," Reubens said. The court-imposed damage was minimal: he entered a guilty plea, paid his $50 fine, and performed community service. However, his reputation didn't fare nearly as well. The act on which he hung his career hat was forever history. CBS cancelled *Pee-wee's Playhouse*, believing parents would no longer approve of a man convicted of committing a lewd crime having influence over their wee ones. Pee-wee action figures were pulled from toy store shelves. Offers dried up and his career hit the skids.

Reubens's career suffered another blow when a 2001 raid on his Los Angeles home resulted in a misdemeanor charge of keeping child pornography. (In a related investigation, actor Jeffrey Jones, best known as the high school principal in Ferris Bueller's Day Off, was charged with hiring a teenage boy to pose for explicit photos.) Reubens's lawyer predicts an acquittal and claims the actor's extensive collection of vintage "art" does not include anything improper.

Despite the setbacks, Reubens managed to build up an acting résumé distinct from his one-note character of Pee-wee, though he has expressed an interest in reviving the playhouse player for another big screen adventure. Times have changed and the world has now seen far more shocking behavior from some in higher tiers of trust, including a reigning US president. Reubens thinks the time might be right for a Pee-wee comeback. In the meantime, he has made brief but memorable appearances in films like *Blow* and *Batman Returns*, and even hosted a short-lived game show called *You Don't Know Jack*. Reubens seems poised to continue to expose himself—professionally, that is.✪

LEANN **RIMES**

Feeling shortchanged by dear old daddy, the man who supported you, made sacrifices for you, and nurtured you into a megamillion-selling, record-breaking teenage country music diva? Well, missy, then you just amble on over to the courthouse, hire yourself a peck of lawyers, and sue him for being a lousy manager. Never mind that everyone will think he was also a lousy dad.

> **TROUBLE IS, YOU'VE DRAGGED HIS NAME THROUGH THE MUD**

Want to get married to a dancer you've known for less than a year and have the wedding look picture-perfect like the ones in bridal magazines? Well then, you need daddy to give you away. Trouble is, you've dragged his name through the mud, embarrassing him to the hilt. So just give your best "Aw, shucks," drop your lawsuit, and "allow" him to walk you down the aisle. All will be forgiven. After all, daddy's love is unconditional.

But for goodness sake, wait until you grow up a bit before you dare to reproduce. ✪

JOHN ROCKER

At some point every public figure learns that journalists really aren't friends or fans as much as they are simply people doing their jobs. They'll turn on the charm and flatter their subjects in hopes of getting a better quote. Whatever the celebrity says in an interview is grist for the writer's mill and if there's a juicy statement to work with, it will be ground to a fine powder and spread far afield. In December 1999, Atlanta Braves relief pitcher John Rocker offered up a veritable buffet of badly chosen declarations in an interview with *Sports Illustrated* magazine.

Consider Rocker's comments the antithesis to the good ol' New York City slogan, "I Love New York." He hated the Big Apple according to the tirade he launched on the city, claiming he'd retire before playing for a New York team.

AFP/CORBIS

John Rocker sticks his tongue out at New York Mets fans

The young hotshot hurler told the magazine, "The biggest thing I don't like about New York are [sic] the foreigners." The Archie Bunker of baseball continued ranting about people who don't speak English, wondering aloud about how "they got in this country." Rocker called taking the train in NYC "depressing," and ran down immigrants, single moms, HIV sufferers, and ex-cons to boot. The only people spared in his diatribe were other backward-thinking professional ball players from the Deep South.

The article unleashed a firestorm of criticism from New Yorkers, including the mayor. Even Christian leaders from Rocker's home state of Georgia weighed in on the issue. Some called his attitude racist while others said it was simply steeped in hate. Whatever it was, it put the twenty-five-year-old and his red neck on the hot seat. The Braves quickly issued a statement that distanced the organization from Rocker's comments. Some called for him to resign from the team. The league ordered him to undergo psychological testing to determine if there were deep roots to his alleged beliefs.

Rocker's quick, initial apology rang hollow in critics' ears, so he later issued a longer, more thorough statement of regret and attempted to explain himself. His "inappropriate comments" came, he said, after bad experiences with some fans in New York. One had spit on him while another hit him in the back with a thrown battery. Rocker claimed only New York fans taunted and tossed things at him on every visit. He admitted to ESPN that if he had read his own comments out of context, "I would have thought I was a complete jerk." But he was fresh off the fan assaults and looking for a forum in which to lash out. He hadn't anticipated the lashing's consequences would be so long lasting.

Rocker reiterated his apology prior to a Mets-Braves game at Shea Stadium six months after the trouble first began. Over the boos and heckles of fans, and under the watchful eye of hundreds of extra police officers, Rocker took

A massive security detail awaits John Rocker's arrival at Shea Stadium on June 29, 2000

to the field. A special cover was made to protect the Braves bullpen and an officer was suited up in a team uniform in order to blend in and keep close tabs on the most wanted man in baseball. Snipers watched the game from overhead and Shea even slowed down beer sales in hopes of preventing a drunken riot. Rocker dodged bottles and plastic balls, and pitched the Braves to a 6-4 win. He succeeded in doing what he pleaded with fans and reporters to do: bring the focus of baseball back to the game itself.

His satisfied grin was short-lived, however, as the Braves dealt him to Cleveland, who quickly passed him on to Texas. During his short, frustrating stint as an ineffectual closer with the Cleveland Indians, he once again treated the press to several displays of his immaturity. Photos of Rocker angrily pitching his glove into the dugout after being pulled from a game and accounts of his tossing water at fans kept his name on the lips of sports talk show hosts and his reputation in a negative light. ✪

DENNIS **RODMAN**

Basketball-*cum*-wrestling star Dennis Rodman's life as a celebrity has been a nearly continuous string of publicity stunts. His nickname is The Worm, but he's been more of a snake on the court and in the eye of the camera lens.

The bleached blond sometime actor (*Double Team*) has kissed and proudly told about some of his famous former paramours. Following a fling with Madonna, he made the classless move of publicly debunking the myth of the Material Girl's sexual adventurousness. He has also been quick to marry and nearly as quick to divorce. His first marriage, to a model, lasted less than three months. His second wedding ceremony was staged as a publicity stunt to promote his autobiography. After hinting in several 1996 interviews that he was about to be betrothed to "a beautiful, intelligent woman," Rodman arrived at a book signing wearing full wedding regalia—only it was the bride's. Onlookers gawked in disbelief as Rodman, in white dress and veil, claimed he wanted to "marry the people of the world." His third attempt, a 1998 marriage to ex–Baywatch babe and *Playboy* pinup Carmen Electra, was merely nine days old before the first talk of an annulment surfaced. The relationship ultimately lasted only a few more months, but not before the couple was cited for a quarrel in a Miami hotel that left them both scratched and bruised.

> AFTER HINTING IN SEVERAL 1996 INTERVIEWS THAT HE WAS ABOUT TO BE BETROTHED TO "A BEAUTIFUL, INTELLIGENT WOMAN," RODMAN ARRIVED AT A BOOK SIGNING WEARING FULL WEDDING REGALIA— ONLY IT WAS THE BRIDE'S

The Worm's sweet gift for sinking basketballs turned sour due to his constant sulking and diva-like behavior. His professional basketball career was capped in the spring of 1999 after one too many late arrivals for practice with the LA Lakers, with whom he'd been playing for two months. The final straw was Rodman's tardy and groggy appearance after he returned from a week's stay in Las Vegas; he actually arrived at practice without his shoes and socks. The Lakers cut him loose (but paid his million-dollar contract), citing his lack of leadership and failure to produce on the court. Rodman complained to reporters that his former team used him as the fall guy for their losing year.

A long list of accusations against Rodman includes criminal and civil actions, some of which are proven, and some not. He has been charged with driving drunk and being drunk in public. He has been sued for purportedly grabbing the butt of a waitress and accused of raping a woman. There was also an instance of obstructing restaurant inspectors at his LA eatery. His Newport Beach, California, home is one of the area's most popular for drop-ins by local police investigating noise complaints. The Worm's arrests and indictments happen with such regularity that they're no longer big news. There is only one thing left for Rodman to do that would surprise the media and his fans: drop quietly out of sight. ✪

PETE ROSE

A lifelong passion for baseball led Pete Rose into the sport's record books. A penchant for gambling keeps him from taking his place in its Hall of Fame.

A teammate once said that Rose played like every game was the seventh in the World Series. The Cincinnati-born ball player, nicknamed Charlie Hustle, was a fan favorite with his hometown team and went on to earn three batting titles. When he left the Reds for Philly in 1978, he signed the richest contract of the time: $800,000 a year. Rose returned home in the mid-1980s to take the helm of his beloved Reds.

It was during this time that he allegedly used bookies to place bets on professional sports, including baseball, often losing big sums of money. Rose admitted to gambling on several sports, but denied baseball was among them. However, his pattern of betting continued through the summer months when baseball was the only professional sport in season. A 1989 probe claims to have turned up more than fifty bets by Rose on the Reds, each for a minimum of $10,000. Gambling on your own team is considered one of the sport's most serious infractions, as it promotes a perception that the group's integrity has been undermined. But there was no evidence that Rose threw any games or interfered with their natural outcome. Still, the disgraced legend was banned from the league he loved so much, and subsequent requests for reinstatement have been either ignored or denied.

ROSE ADMITTED TO GAMBLING ON SEVERAL SPORTS, BUT DENIED BASEBALL WAS AMONG THEM

Even if Rose were welcomed back into the baseball fold, Hall of Fame rules dictate that he would need approval from 75 percent of the Baseball Writers' Association of America in order to be inducted. Rose has a lot of support from the sporting community and his fans, but his name will always be associated with some of the very darkest days in the history of America's national pastime. ✪

ROSEANNE

Big, brash, ballsy, and proud, Roseanne broke comedic ground as an in-your-face female comedian. For Roseanne, no topic was taboo. Unfortunately, her Domestic Goddess character's impact on television was all too often eclipsed by her prominence in the tabloids.

Roseanne Barr Pentland Arnold Thomas changed the face of television forever. *Roseanne*, which hit the airwaves to critical acclaim in 1988 and lasted nine years, was the first truly female-centric sitcom: there was no doubt that Roseanne's character Rosie was the head of her household. The Conner family was as far removed from most TV homes as it could possibly get. Characters on *Roseanne* worked in blue-collar jobs, fought hard with each other, endured financial problems, suffered losses of life and of dreams, and made mistakes that weren't all fixed by the end of the half hour.

LONDON FEATURES INTL.

Tom Arnold reveals a keepsake of his marriage to Roseanne Barr, a memento that he would one day come to regret

Off-screen, Roseanne was fighting hard for the creative control she had on-screen. In the show's early days she battled—and beat—cocreator Matt Williams in a tug-of-war played out as much in the press as on the *Roseanne* set. Anyone who got in the way of Roseanne's vision for the show was soon steamrolled and replaced. Besides the cast, there was only one supporting player who enjoyed job security and that was her eventual second husband and fellow stand-up comic Tom Arnold. Hired on as a writer, Arnold eventually wormed his way in front of the camera to become a recurring player. The lunatics were running the asylum and in their personal lives, Barr and Arnold became an unstoppable force in bad taste. They fondled each other in public, smooched like school kids, and were known to gleefully moon a crowd if the mood struck them. They grabbed a few million inches of newsprint by announcing they had planned a three-way marriage with Tom's twenty-four-year-old assistant Kim Silva. There was something about their chemistry that temporarily paralyzed the brain cells that control good judgment.

The couple created a sitcom for Tom, *The Jackie Thomas Show*, which lasted only one sad season. Upon its cancellation by CBS, Roseanne threatened to move her program to another network until it was pointed out that she didn't have the power to do so. Rosie and Tom's frenetic passion fizzled after four years and a nasty divorce followed a flare-up centered on Tom's relationship with his assistant in 1994. He and Silva were rumored to be having an affair, something he denies although he does say their relationship was "intimate." All Tom and Roseanne had left was a lifetime's worth of video footage to be embarrassed about. But one truly memorable public display orchestrated by the delusional duo stands out even among such a vast array of missteps.

> **THE LUNATICS WERE RUNNING THE ASYLUM AND IN THEIR PERSONAL LIVES, BARR AND ARNOLD BECAME AN UNSTOPPABLE FORCE IN BAD TASTE**

Roseanne obliged when she was invited to open a San Diego Padres baseball game in the summer of 1990 by singing the American national anthem. As she explained in her autobiography *My Lives*, she's no great vocalist. The crowd at San Diego Stadium would call that an understatement. She claims she was filled with dread from the song's start, realizing she began too sharp and wouldn't make it through without croaking out the high notes. And in a seemingly mocking, haphazard fashion that's exactly what she did. She punctuated the performance with a move she had hoped would help her fit in with the players on the field: she spat on the ground and grabbed her crotch.

She may as well have burned an American flag right out in center field. The crowd was livid and booed its disapproval. The nationwide media coverage was relentless, forcing her to assert her patriotism. Still, the hoopla didn't put a dent in *Roseanne*'s ratings; if anything, it helped the show.

Roseanne went on to marry and divorce her bodyguard Ben Thomas and host a short-lived, self-titled talk show. Since it went off the air, she has mostly stayed out of the public eye. If history is a guide, the respite will be brief. No doubt Roseanne will find another way to reinvent herself and burst back into our living rooms. ✪

DIANA ROSS

Call her Miss Ross and touch her at your own peril, even if it's in the line of duty.

Motown legend Diana Ross gave a bit of what she says she got to a customs officer at London's Heathrow Airport. Returning to New York from a video shoot in September 1999, the body-suited Ross, bound by a wide belt with a large silver buckle, says she was manhandled by a female security officer after setting off the metal detectors. Ross contends the woman let her fingers do the walking on several inches of her forbidden feminine territory, including her buttocks and breasts — twice. The singer told ABC's Diane Sawyer that she questioned the necessity of the intimate probe and was told, "It's my job." An attempt to complain to airline staff fell on deaf ears so a frantic and tearful Miss Ross launched a similar but, she says, less intrusive physical search of her searcher — a sort of tit for tat. What's ironic is that just two weeks prior, Ross surprised onlookers by reaching out and jiggling the exposed left breast (save for a purple pastie) of rap artist L'il Kim at the MTV Music Awards. Ross apparently prefers the role of feeler to feelee.

> ROSS SURPRISED ONLOOKERS BY REACHING OUT AND JIGGLING THE EXPOSED LEFT BREAST (SAVE FOR A PURPLE PASTIE) OF RAP ARTIST L'IL KIM AT THE MTV MUSIC AWARDS

Witnesses at the airport claim the songbird "went mad" after being subjected to nothing more than a standard pat-down. Heathrow issued a statement claiming Ross overreacted, and sixty million people annually go through the same frisking procedure with few complaints. Ross told Sawyer that she was sorry for getting so upset, but she stood by her gripe about the grope.

The ex-Supreme was hauled off the plane in humiliating fashion in front of other passengers, including the Royal Family of Brunei. Police detained and questioned her for several hours. Ross says she has never felt so afraid in her life, and cried throughout the ordeal. She was cautioned but not charged after offering her version of the alleged assault, and she caught the last Concord home. The incident remains on her record and could be used against her in the event of a similar episode in the future. In August 2002, the songstress checked herself into rehab for treatment of undisclosed "personal issues," and she was later nabbed for D.U.I. Ross has also urged Heathrow to follow the lead of other international airports and employ the use of handheld metal detecting wands rather than continuing to rely on the human touch. ✪

MICKEY ROURKE

Mickey Rourke's ex-wife, model Carre Otis, says her foremost wish is that the actor would stay out of her life. It's no wonder: their long and stormy relationship ended with allegations that the *Rumblefish* star battered his beautiful bride.

The New York–born Rourke built his big screen persona by playing the sexy bad boy in films like *91/2 Weeks*, *Body Heat*, and *Wild Orchid* (Otis costarred in the latter). Universally recognized as a bomb, 1990's *Wild Orchid* nonetheless attracted more than its share of attention when it was revealed that its stars were apparently having real sex on the screen instead of the simulated variety. Rourke grew increasingly uncomfortable with the trappings of fame and eventually ducked out of Hollywood. At the age of forty, he abandoned acting for professional boxing.

> UNIVERSALLY RECOGNIZED AS A BOMB, 1990'S *WILD ORCHID* NONETHELESS ATTRACTED MORE THAN ITS SHARE OF ATTENTION WHEN IT WAS REVEALED THAT ITS STARS WERE APPARENTLY HAVING REAL SEX ON THE SCREEN INSTEAD OF THE SIMULATED VARIETY

Otis and Rourke's on-again, off-again relationship was crystallized when they wed in 1992. Carre's star fell as her weight bloated beyond catwalk standards, allegedly due to drug and alcohol abuse. Rumors that Rourke was a wife-beater came to light two years later when police arrested the actor for allegedly hitting and kicking Otis. Charges were dropped after she refused to cooperate with prosecutors. Rourke even shot her in the arm — accidentally — while cleaning his gun. They soon split up, reunited, and split again. Today Otis is clean and healthy, and a busy plus-size model.

Rourke's hiatus from acting didn't last very long, but his more recent credits don't measure up to performances in earlier gems like *Diner* and *A Prayer for the Dying*. Although he's mostly keeping a low profile, Rourke did make the gossip sheets in 1999 for walking off the set one day into shooting the indie flick *Luck of the Draw*. Reports claimed the director refused to honor Rourke's request that his dog Bo Jack appear in a scene, and the actor quit the picture in protest. Of course, the official reason for the incident came under the all-encompassing, face-saving umbrella of "creative differences." ✪

WINONA **RYDER**

Producers of the big screen comedy *Mr. Deeds* were reportedly very angry with their star for not pleading guilty to a shoplifting charge, which would have quickly put the whole mess to rest. Instead, Ryder pled innocent to charges stemming from her starring role in a Saks Fifth Avenue security video, which allegedly caught her clipping security tags off several expensive, designer clothing items. Her pixie face was even kept off the *Deeds* movie poster for fear that potential audiences would only conjure up the court case. Whoever said there's no such thing as bad publicity hasn't met Ms. Ryder.

The situation had all the exciting and tragic elements of a movie script. It's alleged that Ryder went on a $6,000 shopping spree in December 2001 at a Beverly Hills Saks and left without paying for her luxury articles. Bail was set at $20,000 despite Ryder's lawyer's complaint that the new district attorney was simply hell-bent on making an example of any celebrity and used Winona, who became a victim of bad timing.

> **RYDER PLED INNOCENT TO CHARGES STEMMING FROM HER STARRING ROLE IN A SAKS FIFTH AVENUE SECURITY VIDEO, WHICH ALLEGEDLY CAUGHT HER CLIPPING SECURITY TAGS OFF SEVERAL EXPENSIVE, DESIGNER CLOTHING ITEMS**

Just getting into the courtroom past the crush of media was a drama for the two-time Oscar nominee. As she arrived for one of the pretrial hearings, Ryder suffered a broken arm after wrestling her way through supporters sporting "Free Winona" T-shirts, only to be struck by a wayward camera that came in a little too tight for a close-up. The court case was set back while doctors set her fractured limb. Then, the ultimate humiliation: a Saks security guard testified he thought the quirky actress was a homeless person when he first spied her on the in-store monitors. He claims the *Reality Bites* star clipped off security tags from the tops, hair bows, and other goodies, and then proceeded past cashiers and out of the store. It's also alleged that Ryder was carrying a painkiller without a prescription. Convictions on all charges—grand theft, burglary, vandalism, and unlawful possession of a drug—carry a near-four-year prison term.

Then prosecutors leaked a bombshell: it wasn't the first time Ryder had been accused of getting a five finger discount. Although she was never charged, *Newsweek* magazine claimed the district attorney's office knew of another shoplifting incident involving the *Girl, Interrupted* star. Though that revelation appeared to give the prosecution some leverage, a rumored plea bargain never came to pass. Ultimately Ryder was convicted but spared the humiliation of being forced to wear a drab prison uniform. After two days of deliberations, the jury found her guilty on the felony grand theft and vandalism charges and she was sentenced to a court-recommended two-year probation term with community service and court-approved counseling tacked on.

During the trial, Ryder, whose waning acting career has recently been on an upswing, didn't appear to be taking the charges very seriously. She risked the wrath of the court by taking comical shots at her plight when she hosted the 2001–02 season finale of *Saturday Night Live*. The onetime quintessential Gen-X girl cemented her reputation as a bit of a ditzy broad during the episode.

Some psychologists say shoplifting offers a quick thrill for those who live thrill-free lives. Most retail thieves can well afford the items they steal. Shoplifting can be a reaction to a stressful situation and incidence of the condition increases dramatically over the holiday season. Some folks think they're doing nothing wrong while others feel a sense of entitlement to whatever they desire. Still others crave the attention getting caught will bring. True kleptomania—the compulsion to steal—is rare. It remains to be seen which category Ms. Ryder falls into. ✪

STEVEN **SEAGAL**

Extra, Extra: "Steven Seagal's Reputation Under Siege"; "Accuser Says Seagal Not Above the Law"; "Ex-Partner Out for Justice from Seagal."

Clever media types love to spin the titles of a star's films to scream out accusations against them. And with the topsy-turvy life of actor, singer, and Buddhist tulku Steven Seagal, they've had lots of opportunities to make headline origami.

The martial arts expert and action hero has often found himself in court throughout his career. A divorce from wife Kelly LeBrock here, a lawsuit over a movie deal gone awry there—typical Hollywood stuff for the most part. But it was his two attempts at reinventing himself that sparked the biggest legal fires for the pony-tailed star to extinguish.

Magazine articles had long painted Seagal as a loser with the ladies. *Penthouse*, for one, quoted a half dozen female staffers from the set of the movie *Out for Justice* who claimed the boss used the casting couch to his advantage and reached out to touch their breasts during interviews. One of the women said Seagal made a habit of brushing up against nearly every female who entered his radar screen. The piece purported to be taking the wraps off a long-standing Hollywood secret concerning the star's boorish behavior.

Patricia Nicholas, a rock producer with whom Seagal had some sessions, claimed the wannabe country warbler (check out his crooning on the *Fire Down Below* soundtrack) was fixated on her breasts for the duration of a failed attempt to record some of his music. Nicholas, who took legal action, attested Seagal mounted a hate campaign against her after she refused his advances. The Los Angeles Superior Court sided with Nicholas, but decided not to impose a damage award. During the trial, Seagal testified he was being "shaken down" by the plaintiff, who vowed to continue her legal battle until the *Marked for Death* star is hurt in his most sensitive spot—his wallet.

> **REPORTS SURFACED THAT SEAGAL WAS THE UNNAMED MOVIE MOGUL TARGETED BY AN EXTORTION PLOT**

A longtime devotee of Buddhism, Seagal was elevated to tulku, a reincarnated lama, by the Supreme Head of the Nyingma School of Tibetan Buddhism. *Time* magazine alleged the actor bought the honor by donating generously to the school. Seagal's spokesperson countered *Time*'s claim and explained that the disciple was designated a "sacred vessel" based entirely on personal merit. It's a very rare honor; there are only a handful of others deemed worthy of tulku status by the school.

One of the aging action star's oldest colleagues says the divine lama gave a little too much over to his beliefs, including control of his career. Julius R. Nasso, the co-owner of Seagal's production company and the producer of several flicks including 1987's *Above the Law*, is suing his old partner for $60 million, claiming breech of contract. Nasso says Seagal had agreed to star in four more movies in collaboration with their company, but backed out after a Buddhist adviser named Mukara allegedly demanded that he cut ties with his business partners or lose his status as lama. Nasso further alleges that Seagal followed Mukara's directive to sever ties with his own children. The four-movie deal was apparently inked around the same time Seagal was given the title of tulku and Nasso says he forked over millions for book rights and production costs only to have Seagal suddenly pull the plug. In response, the actor said he simply decided, on his own, to dissolve the partnership and it is in fact *Nasso* who owes *him* money. He also expressed disbelief that his religion would be attacked in such a public manner.

Meanwhile, in New York City, the plot thickened. Reports surfaced that Seagal was the unnamed movie mogul targeted by an extortion plot allegedly involving Nasso. Seagal's ex-partner and more than a dozen members of New York's Gambino Crime Family were corralled, including Peter Gotti, brother of the late John "The Teflon Don" Gotti. The gaggle of Gambinos was charged with a shopping list of suspected infractions including extortion, witness tampering, and money laundering. Prosecutors claim Nasso is a Gambino Family associate, involved with the other indicted men in a plot to extort hundreds of thousands of dollars from "an individual in the film industry." In light of the Nasso lawsuit and Mafia accusations, possible scenarios for the genesis of the Seagal-Nasso working relationship are nefarious at worst and naïve at best.

> **SEAGAL'S EX-PARTNER AND MORE THAN A DOZEN MEMBERS OF NEW YORK'S GAMBINO CRIME FAMILY WERE CORRALLED, INCLUDING PETER GOTTI**

And just how does this heroic holy man handle the apparent conflict between his serene and compassionate existence as a lama and the regular butt-kickings he gives to all comers in his movies? The soft-talking star justifies the cinematic violence he perpetrates by pointing out it's always against evil thugs and only in defense of something or someone worthwhile. In his personal life, however, Seagal continues find himself on the defensive in situations where thuggery just won't cut it. ✪

TUPAC **SHAKUR**

The apple doesn't fall far from the tree. Shakur, the son of suspected Black Panther party members, was a thoughtful, intelligent gangsta rapper and actor who was determined to make it as a performer despite having grown up on a street tough in Harlem. But in a hail of bullets in the fall of 1996, so much promise was snuffed out at age twenty-five.

American rappers of the early 1990s took themselves and their creative energy very seriously. Even though their music was moving from the clubs to lucrative contracts signed in office towers made of steel and glass, their roots continued to show. To the labels they brought with them the gang mentality they had learned on the streets, which ended up splitting the country's rap artists into two warring factions: East Coast and West Coast. It was that senseless legacy that is thought to have led to Shakur's murder, which officially remains unsolved, although there's plenty of suspicion and speculation about who may have pulled the gun's trigger.

Tupac simultaneously sprang into music stores and onto movie screens in 1992. His debut CD, *2Pacalypse Now*, was number one on the charts just as his first starring role in the film *Juice* was hitting theaters. His musical roots were in the hood, but his heart lay in more sensitive territory. Tupac's lyrics belied his introspective nature, centering as they did on cop killing and violence. Still, he peppered his multiplatinum CDs with heartfelt odes to his mom or a girlfriend. He also lived what he rapped, serving prison sentences for assault (on a director who refused to cast him in a movie) and sexual assault (on a female fan). He also took five bullets during a robbery attempt at Death Row, his record label. The crime remains unsolved because of his refusal to cooperate with the investigation. It was another hallmark of a life lived by the code of the streets: don't rat on your brothers.

> **THE CADDY PULLED NEXT TO KNIGHT'S CAR AND RIDDLED IT WITH BULLETS; SHAKUR WAS HIT SEVERAL TIMES, INCLUDING TWICE IN THE CHEST**

Following the September 7, 1996, boxing match between Mike Tyson and Bruce Seldon at a Las Vegas hotel (which should have been the most violent episode of the night), Shakur rode to a nightclub with Death Row founder Marion "Suge" Knight. The music mogul's BMW was stopped at a red light when a white Cadillac approached their ten-car convoy. The Caddy pulled next to Knight's car and riddled it with bullets; Shakur was hit several times, including twice in the chest. Knight, less seriously wounded, floored the car and took off. He eventually attracted the attention of police, who called paramedics. Shakur's situation was touch-and-go from the beginning; he even endured surgery to remove his right lung. After initially being in a coma, Shakur did regain consciousness, but was kept heavily sedated. His condition later stabilized and then quickly worsened. Tupac succumbed to his injuries six days after the drive-by shooting.

Police complained that despite the presence of professional bodyguards and several of the late rapper's friends, they received little cooperation in their investigation of the shooting. Knight claimed he heard everything that transpired that night, but "saw nothing." Accusations flew between the rapping camps from both coasts, but the talk didn't evolve into anything concrete. A recent report based on a two-year probe by the *Los Angeles Times* claims larger-than-life rapper Notorious BIG offered gang members $1 million and allowed the shooter to use his own Glock pistol to cap his long-running feud with

THE TRUTH BEHIND SHAKUR'S SLAYING WILL LIKELY NEVER BE KNOWN FOR CERTAIN

Tupac. In Randall Sullivan's book *LAbyrinth*, a former LAPD detective fingers Death Row CEO Suge Knight for allegedly setting up the murder because Tupac was preparing to leave Death Row and Knight owed him a huge sum of money. Two of the major players in both scenarios have since joined Tupac next to the great boom box in the sky. Orlando Anderson, a Crips gang member long thought to have been Shakur's murderer, was killed two years later in an unrelated incident. Biggie died in a rain of bullets after leaving a California party in 1997. The truth behind Shakur's slaying will likely never be known for certain.

Several lawsuits for various alleged infractions have arisen from Tupac's ashes, including trademark infringement, wrongful death, and a claim from his estate that Death Row was cheating the artist out of royalties. Despite selling some sixty million albums and snagging plum acting roles in movies like *Juice* and *Poetic Justice*, Shakur apparently died $5 million in debt.

In death, Tupac Shakur has become a symbol for gang violence. Some fans even claim he's still alive. His attempts to live on the right side of the law were fleeting and his guiding philosophy was permanently fixed on his own skin; across his stomach were the tattooed words *Thug Life.* ✪

CHARLIE SHEEN

He's a good actor, but a very bad boy. There are a bunch of credits you won't find included on Charlie Sheen's professional résumé: party animal, born-again Christian, alleged assaulter, repeat rehaber, and hooker hirer.

The son of Martin Sheen and brother of actors Emilio and Ramon Estevez (while Estevez is the family surname, Charlie has chosen to use his father's stage name as well as give his real name, Carlos, an American makeover), Charlie is the family rebel. A fast-living, hard-partying young man for whom everything came relatively easily, Charlie has had a special knack for getting into trouble.

Following more than a decade of nearly nonstop revelry in the mid-1990s, the *Platoon* and *Wall Street* star claimed he was taking his life on a 180-degree turn. He demanded he be called Charles to reflect his newfound serious attitude, and he claimed to have embraced religion. Booze and drugs were things of the past, he asserted. He married a good girl, model Donna Peele, but divorced her a year later. While echoes of his public denouncement of his former lifestyle still hung in the air, Sheen was rushed to a Los Angeles hospital, suffering from a drug overdose. Besides threatening his health, the OD was a probation violation and earned Sheen a twelve-month extension. The original probation sentence stemmed from a conviction for splitting open the lip of former girlfriend, adult film star Brittany Ashland. Charlie's father actually telephoned the judge in charge of his son's case in a self-described "act of love" to inform the magistrate of the overdose. Dad was at the end of his rope. Family interventions dating back to 1990 hadn't made a difference. The Sheens were very afraid that their youngest boy would end up dead.

> **THERE ARE A BUNCH OF CREDITS YOU WON'T FIND INCLUDED ON CHARLIE SHEEN'S PROFESSIONAL RÉSUMÉ: PARTY ANIMAL, BORN-AGAIN CHRISTIAN, ALLEGED ASSAULTER, REPEAT REHABER, AND HOOKER HIRER**

Charlie's name became tantamount to any ordinary john when it was revealed that he was a regular customer of Hollywood Madam Heidi Fleiss. His sales receipts for her "escort service" topped $50,000. Although many famous names were offered up as possible customers for Heidi's hookers, Sheen's was one of the select few that was openly confirmed. The actor agreed he had no trouble attracting nonprofessional dates, but said he grew weary of the media's scrutiny of his love life. He told ABC's *20/20*, "I discovered this amazing way to not have to go out there and meet somebody." Fleiss did time for her crimes. Sheen's sentence for being her customer will last a lifetime.

After proving that he had stayed sober for an uninterrupted stretch, the *Spin City* star's probation term was eventually cut by an approving judge. This time, the clean lifestyle seems to be sticking. When Charlie Sheen's name is mentioned in the press these days, it's more likely in conjunction with news about a career move or his seemingly permanent relationship with actress Denise Richards. ✪

MARTIN SHEEN

The star of TV's *The West Wing* is decidedly left-wing in his real-life role of activist. Like his son Charlie, Martin has seen the inside of a jail cell, but for very different reasons.

A health crisis on the set of 1979's *Apocalypse Now* was a catalyst for change in Sheen's life. The actor suffered a heart attack and thereafter vowed to do good in the world for his family and on behalf of causes he believed in. For a devout Catholic and a staunch Liberal, those causes are many. He campaigns for animal rights and for social safety issues. During a 1995 Greenpeace protest on the Magdalene Islands, he was nearly clubbed to death by angry seal hunters. He protests against the arms race, poverty, and abortion. He is a pacifist. Now in his sixties, Sheen has built up enough clout in Hollywood to afford him the luxury of negotiating time off from portraying President Josiah Bartlett to attend rallies and protests. He once said, "I love my country enough to risk its wrath."

> **DURING A 1995 GREENPEACE PROTEST ON THE MAGDALENE ISLANDS, HE WAS NEARLY CLUBBED TO DEATH BY ANGRY SEAL HUNTERS**

Demonstrators must salivate at the thought of someone as famous as Sheen joining their ranks. His presence guarantees television coverage and widens common knowledge about any cause. He was arrested in 1998 along with hundreds of others at an army school in Georgia that housed recruits linked to murders in El Salvador. No actual charges were laid. Prosecutors didn't blink when Sheen was arrested three years later for protesting the star wars defense system on a California air force base. The actor's attorneys worked out a deal with prosecutors so the shooting season of *The West Wing* wouldn't be delayed: a guilty plea in exchange for a $500 fine and a lifetime ban from the base. Sheen's request that the fine be given to charity was denied. "The government has enough of my money," he had reasoned.

That Thanksgiving, Sheen offered a free soy-based turkey substitute to 450 homeless shelters across the US. As part of an initiative by People for the Ethical Treatment of Animals (PETA) to keep turkeys off dinner tables, Sheen wrote letters to the shelters, pleading with them to consider the needs of homeless vegetarians. More than fifty of them took Sheen up on his offer of mock turkey.

Does the man face a conflict at work, playing a character very much in favor of nuclear arms while he personally prefers to turn the other cheek? His attitude on the issue is simple: it's just acting. And a little bit of the real Martin Sheen creeps into *The West Wing* story line from time to time. President Bartlett once pardoned a turkey. ✪

O. J. SIMPSON

Cold-blooded murderer or unfortunate former hero? Choose one. Or, if you're the American criminal and civil justice systems, choose one each.

Football star and occasional actor O. J. Simpson unwillingly became the hottest thing on North American television in 1995. He stood accused in the brutal 1994 knife slayings of his ex-wife Nicole Brown and her friend Ron Goldman. It was alleged that Simpson killed Nicole in a fit of jealous rage, and Ron was in the wrong place at the wrong time and made the fatal mistake of attempting to defend her. The crime scene, the backyard of Nicole's Los Angeles home, was a horrifying, bloody mess, illuminating the murderer's savagery and the desperate struggle mounted by the victims. The only eyewitness, Brown's pet Akita named Kato, wasn't talking. The so-called Trial of the Century was long, sensational, and poorly presented. The proceedings were tainted by accusations of racism and more focus was put on the prosecutor's hairstyles than on the actual evidence, of which there was plenty. DNA samples and damning testimony of Simpson's sometimes-cruel treatment of his wife notwithstanding, the accused was acquitted.

THE VICTIMS' DEVASTATED FAMILIES LAUNCHED A CIVIL LAWSUIT AGAINST SIMPSON FOR WRONGFUL DEATH—AND WON

Later, the victims' devastated families launched a civil lawsuit against Simpson for wrongful death—and won. How a suspect can be found not responsible in criminal court but liable in a civil action is one of the peculiarities of living in the land of the free. Simpson cried poor, but was put on the hook for $33.5 million in damages to the Browns and the Goldmans.

It appeared to Simpson's detractors that his volatile temper overtook him again in December 2000. A motorist claimed The Juice chased him in a Lincoln Navigator after he honked when the former footballer ran through a stop sign in Miami. The man said Simpson forced him off the road and, while yelling at him, reached into his car and angrily pulled his glasses off his face. In a bit of judicial déjà vu, the jury was not persuaded and set Simpson free. Had he been convicted, O. J. faced up to sixteen years in prison.

Today, millions of people still believe Orenthal James Simpson got away with two murders. He has always maintained innocence and vowed at the trial's end never to give up the search for evidence leading to the real killer. While nothing has turned up yet, Simpson continues his dedicated quest almost daily, cleverly disguised as an avid player on some of the finest golf courses in the United States. ✪

FRANK **SINATRA**

An ambitious, vain lad from Hoboken, New Jersey, who amassed virtually as many superhuman nicknames as number one hits, Frankie Sinatra was blessed with a pleasant baritone and charisma to spare. Add a heaping helping of good luck and shrewd marketing moves implemented with expert timing, and the result was one of the most enduring performers of our time. But the Chairman of the Board's six-decade musical legacy is clouded by mystery and innuendo; allegations of Mob connections and other nefarious business dealings haunted the singer his whole life and linger even after his death.

Frankie's career and personal transgressions were plentiful, so in this collection, we'll look only at the best of the worst.

The young singer's original goal was to oust top crooner Bing Crosby from the pop charts. He eventually succeeded and became the biggest music star on the continent. Frank branched out into movies and even won an Oscar for 1953's *From Here to Eternity*. But success didn't arrive without some crafty maneuvers along the way. During his early concert appearances, girls swooned and fainted only because they were recruited and paid for their trouble. Frank and his manipulative team worked the angles, rooting out any approach that would get their rising star's name into the newspaper. Hiring fake groupies, giving out freebies, providing fabricated biographical details—Frank was willing to do whatever it took to get to the top.

> **ALLEGATIONS OF MOB CONNECTIONS AND OTHER NEFARIOUS BUSINESS DEALINGS HAUNTED THE SINGER HIS WHOLE LIFE AND LINGER EVEN AFTER HIS DEATH**

Surely enough he became the "in" musical thing among teens, causing a frenzy akin to a solo Backstreet Boy. Girls wanted to kiss him while guys thought he oozed cool. Some of the critics didn't get it, however, and Frank was the type of guy who read all of his reviews, taking the bad ones to heart. In 1947, Sinatra gleefully punched out columnist Lee Mortimer, whom he blamed for "needling" him in print for more than two years. Mortimer called the cops and Frank found himself singing the tune of jailbird until he made bail. Mortimer claimed someone threatened his life for having reported Frank's fisticuffs, inferring Mafia hit men were behind the sinister warnings. But he stuck to his guns and Sinatra was ordered to pay him $9,000 in restitution along with court fees. Sinatra was also forced to issue a public apology.

EACH TIME HE WAS ASKED, SINATRA DENIED HAVING ANYTHING MORE THAN AN ACQUAINTANCE WITH THE MAFIOSI

Sinatra launched public feuds with gossip columnists Rona Barrett, Rex Reed, and Liz Smith, once telling an audience that the scribes and their ilk "are probably the lowest form of journalists." Once he developed a loathing for someone, he was loath to let go. Ol' Frankie held on to a grudge like a drowning man clings to a life raft.

Frankie was a huge hit with the ladies. A spurned girlfriend was so distraught over being dumped by the budding crooner that she had him arrested on an archaic morals charge. He married young and reproduced early. His first wife, Nancy, suffered through several of her husband's affairs. In 1949, after newspapers caught wind of Frank's dalliance with actress Ava Gardner, Nancy held a press conference and stoically announced to the world that she'd wait patiently for her husband to return home. After all, he always did. It was the juiciest scandal of the day: there was Frank, the villain for abandoning his family; Ava, the homewrecker; and Nancy, the supportive yet humiliated spouse and doting mother. But the scandalous relationship with Ava was a boon to Frank's sagging singing career—he was suddenly a hot property again. Their liaison was a real-life soap opera, full of infidelities on both sides and Frank's fake suicide attempts involving gun shots, wrist slashings, and a headfirst foray into a gas oven. The daring duo once landed behind bars in Indio, California, after shooting up streetlights and storefronts in the desert with their matching .38s. In Kitty Kelley's Sinatra tell-all *His Way*, she reports that Frank's press agent was summoned to pay off witnesses, the most troublesome of which was the local man whose stomach was grazed by one of the reckless couple's stray bullets. Frank and Ava finally married in 1951 and tortured each other emotionally before eventually seeking a 1957 Mexican divorce.

Among his other conquests was Marilyn Monroe, whom he reportedly considered marrying. He is alleged to have begun an affair with actress Lauren Bacall near the end of her husband Humphrey Bogart's battle with cancer (never mind that Bogart was one of Frank's old friends). Mia Farrow briefly became his third bride when she was a twenty-one-year-old starlet (a year younger than Frank Jr.!) and he was pushing fifty and desperate to inject some youthfulness into his persona.

> THEIR LIAISON WAS A REAL-LIFE SOAP OPERA, FULL OF INFIDELITIES ON BOTH SIDES AND FRANK'S FAKE SUICIDE ATTEMPTS INVOLVING GUN SHOTS, WRIST SLASHINGS, AND A HEADFIRST FORAY INTO A GAS OVEN

But Frank didn't collect just beautiful ladies. He also had a weakness for the rich and powerful. He boasted about counting the Kennedys among his friends.

When the Chairman of the Board testified before the Nevada Gaming Control Board on the sticky subject of organized crime, his irritation was obvious. Mob men seek out performers, Sinatra explained, because they're perpetually starstruck. He, the object of their idolatry, was merely polite; he shook a few hands and welcomed any and all guests into his hotel—end of story, he claimed. Frank was attempting to expand his investments in Las Vegas casinos (he already owned a share in The Sands) and the hearings were called to probe a visit he had received from famed Mafia man Sam Giancana. The song and dance man had apparently hosted the renowned Mobster at The Sands. While the lengthy probe continued, President John F. Kennedy was reported to have commented on the case while visiting Vegas. "Aren't you all being a little harsh on Frank out here?" he asked Governor Frank Sawyer. But the commission had taped conversations in its possession in which notorious Mobsters repeatedly referred to the singer. Each time he was asked, Sinatra denied having anything more than an acquaintance with the Mafiosi. Despite support from high places, Frank's gaming license was revoked and he was ordered out of the Nevada gambling business. God forbid anything immoral should have happened in Sin City.

Sinatra's priorities were upended in 1963 when his aspiring singer-son Frank Jr. was kidnapped at gunpoint. It was headline news, the biggest kidnapping case in the US since 1932, when the Lindbergh baby was stolen. The FBI was called in and Frank authorized that any amount of money be used—a million dollars or more, if needed—to get his son back alive. The kidnappers had a more modest demand: just $240,000. The trio was caught the day after the complicated drop-off. Frank Jr. was returned unharmed and most of the money was recovered. As a show of gratitude, Sinatra sent $2,000 gold watches to each of the agents on the case and to FBI director J. Edgar Hoover. A TV station in London reported the kidnapping plot was devised as a tasteless publicity stunt. That claim drew Sinatra's wrath and a libel lawsuit, which he won, though he donated the award to charity.

A rift later developed between Sinatra and his namesake when three women filed paternity suits against the younger Frank. Each time Frank Sr. hired lawyers to fight the accusations, while privately berating his busy lad for tarnishing the family name. Under his father's watchful eye, Frank Jr. reportedly paid child support to each of the young mothers.

In the early 1980s, Frank's movie career was essentially over and he was anxious to diversify his interests. He made another run for a gaming license, rallying his famous friends to his defense. Gregory Peck and Kirk Douglas appeared in person to support Frank, while Bob Hope sent a sworn affidavit. Sinatra's testimony focused on his lack of knowledge about the Mafia and he explained away photos of himself grinning alongside known Mobsters as run-of-the-mill fan snapshots. Frank's bid to get back into the gambling game was approved.

SINATRA'S PRIORITIES WERE UPENDED IN 1963 WHEN HIS ASPIRING SINGER-SON FRANK JR. WAS KIDNAPPED AT GUNPOINT

Sinatra attempted retirement in virtually every decade of his career. In 1973 he pronounced that the blood-sucking press was driving him off the concert stage, but he eventually returned and headlined tours with old pals like Dean Martin and Sammy Davis Jr., to great acclaim. When he and Dino quit their final tour together, ostensibly because of his own poor health, Frank stopped speaking to his old friend. Martin succumbed to emphysema in 1995. Sinatra continued to record, updating his sound by teaming with current popular singers like U2's Bono and k.d. lang for a series of hugely popular *Duets* CDs.

Frank finally found marital bliss with Barbara Marx, ex-wife of comic Zeppo, whom he wed in 1976 and was with until his death in May 1998. Suspicions about Mob ties and notoriety for angry outbursts are as much part of his legacy as any of his dozens of hit records or Hollywood movies. Some say his lack of tolerance for criticism was born on the streets of New Jersey when as a lad he learned to defend himself with his fists against racial slurs. Others claim Old Blue Eyes was simply an egocentric chump with a huge chip on his shoulder who, despite all of his riches, still believed he hadn't been given his due. ✪

CHRISTIAN SLATER

He was scared straight by a short stint in jail. That may be the only reason actor Christian Slater is alive today. Some of his contemporaries—River Phoenix and Chris Farley come to mind—who loaded up on as much booze and as many drugs as Slater did weren't lucky enough to live to tell the tale.

Current photos of the *Heathers* star depict a devoted family man, content with his wife and growing brood. Just a few years ago, the young actor had very little in common with the man he is today. A notorious partyer and alleged philanderer (despite having a long-term girlfriend), Slater knew how to find a good time.

> **HE WAS SCARED STRAIGHT BY A SHORT STINT IN JAIL**

His cataclysmic meltdown occurred at a friend's party. Slater, on a bender of several days' duration, expanded his delusional horizons by supplementing booze with cocaine. To say he lost it would be putting it rather mildly. The *Very Bad Things* thespian belted his girlfriend in the face, trained his chompers on the stomach of an acquaintance, and lunged at police while attempting to grab an officer's gun. He was subdued only after one of the cops put him in a choke-hold until he passed out. Slapped with a slew of charges including battery, resisting arrest, and various drug offences, Slater was also sued by an officer he whacked in the melee. Next stop: rehab. There, the troubled actor met with his personal demons face to face for several months. That stay was followed by regular attendance at AA meetings. His dedication to the 12-step program was well known due to a media frenzy surrounding his every move—the "anonymous" part of AA was taken right out of the equation.

Slater's lawyers hoped his time served in rehab would count against any jail sentence, but a stern judge dashed those wishes. In addition to a fine, mandatory AIDS education (because of the biting incident), and treatment for batterers, Slater was shipped off for ninety days in the pokey, followed by yet another ninety in rehab. The judge agreed to a few days' delay on the sentence's start to allow the actor to be feted at the premiere of his movie *Rain*.

Slater was a "model prisoner" for two months in a light security center. He had a television, wore his own clothes, and ate his choice of food. Still, the daily routine was far removed from his movie star life: he cleaned toilets, washed police cars, and mopped floors. And it was a powerful experience, enough to reform the former party boy into a clean-living, doting husband to his wife and loving dad to their son and daughter. Sometimes stars get lucky enough to live out a real-life happy ending. ✪

ANNA NICOLE SMITH

Playboy's 1993 Playmate of the Year has been rescheduling a multimillion-dollar celebratory shopping spree for more than seven years.

The 1993 Playboy Playmate of the Year

Born Vicki Lynn Hogan in Mexia, Texas, Smith came to fame as a buxom model in glossy ads for Guess jeans and an eye-popping *Playboy* centerfold. She has also served as the eye candy in movies like *Naked Gun 33 1/3: The Final Insult.* But early on, the young divorced mother made her living as a topless dancer. Despite Smith's obvious assets, club owners felt her full figure was less of a draw than the sinewy forms of her colleagues, and relegated her to the less desirable shifts. That was when an aging customer became her guardian angel.

In 1991, eighty-six-year-old oil billionaire J. Howard Marshall took her away from the bump and grind and provided for her every whim; he paid for dance lessons, trips, necessities, and frivolities for Smith and her son Daniel. The couple embarked on wedded weirdness two years later. While she jetted off to see and be seen in Hollywood, he was tucked into bed nightly at 7 P.M. back in Houston. After just fourteen months as fossil and wife, her antique angel was dead. Smith promptly invested herself in a long-term fight with Marshall's youngest son Pierce, initially for half of her husband's $1.6 billion fortune. A court eventually settled on $475 million, but that ruling was overturned. A judge pegged her entitlement at $88.5 million, a figure also now under appeal. If she ever gets her hands on the millions she was promised, she has big, albeit vague, plans: "I'll do something that would make my husband proud."

The blond bombshell claims to have had a medical textbook's worth of health problems since the death of her supportive spouse. A thirty-day stay in the Betty Ford Center—"a terrible place"—helped her kick an addiction to painkillers and alcohol.

Smith has vowed to continue fighting until she receives what her husband promised her: a big, fat wad of cash. So far, she hasn't seen one cent. "He wanted to make me happy," she claims. Pierce, meanwhile, has his heels dug in and refers to Smith not as Step Mom, but as Miss Cleavage. Marshall's eldest son Howard III was disinherited altogether.

Anna Nicole Smith leaves the courthouse in January of 2002

After several years of doing sporadic work while keeping herself available for court appearances, Smith found a regular gig in 2002 on the E! network, home of *The Ozzy Osbourne Show*. *The Anna Nicole Smith Show* was apparently being planned long before the Osbournes were unleashed on an unsuspecting viewing public; it follows the plus-size model on her daily routine. Asked by CNN's Larry King if she would ever marry a geriatric again, she replied, "If he treats me nice." ✪

SNOOP **DOGG**

He beat a murder rap and spun a waning music career into a burgeoning sideline as a supporting movie star. Snoop Dogg's street smarts have served him well on the dog-eat-dog boulevard of broken dreams.

Calvin Broadus was saddled with the nickname Snoop because of his resemblance to Snoopy, the beloved Peanuts character. A long history with drugs, including a conviction for cocaine possession, seemed to be all but erased as Snoop's debut album *Doggystyle* entered the music charts at number one. But his soaring career as a gangsta rapper was put on pause in the summer of 1993. As Snoop drove on a Los Angeles street, his bodyguard McKinley Lee, in the car with him, shot and killed a twenty-year-old alleged rival gang member riding in a vehicle next to them. Both Snoop and Lee were charged with first-degree murder. The indictment was added to the musician's rap sheet, which includes a charge for illegally carrying a semiautomatic weapon. The murder case would eat up the next two years of the two men's lives and by the time it wrapped, gangsta rap fans had moved on and Snoop's genre was essentially DOA.

Snoop and Lee were both acquitted of murder, but the jury deadlocked on the lesser charge of manslaughter. At trial's end, the previously tight-lipped Snoop told all to MTV. He claimed that Lee's shot prevented the dead man from pulling a gun and putting a bullet in his own Snoop-shaped brain. The rapper admitted he wasn't "all the way happy" about the trial's outcome, considering a young man was still dead. He probably still wasn't overjoyed when he wrote a check for an undisclosed amount to the victim's family to settle their wrongful death lawsuit against him, even though their original claim of $25 million dollars isn't believed to have been met. The family claimed Snoop's acquittal was a result of his celebrity and not the facts.

> **AS SNOOP DROVE ON A LOS ANGELES STREET, HIS BODYGUARD McKINLEY LEE, IN THE CAR WITH HIM, SHOT AND KILLED A TWENTY-YEAR-OLD ALLEGED RIVAL GANG MEMBER RIDING IN A VEHICLE NEXT TO THEM**

Snoop's latest scrapes with the law have been comparatively minor. The Dogg loves his weed. Police have found small amounts of marijuana on his person, in his tour bus, and in his car. Annoying little appearances before a judge have been followed by token fines.

With his rap career fading fast, Snoop is reinventing himself by showing off his acting chops with memorable roles in films like *Baby Boy* and *Training Day*. Staying on the virtual straight and narrow is keeping this Dogg out of the doghouse. ✪

SUZANNE SOMERS

The bubbly blond from *Three's Company* was once guilty of buying into her own press.

Her sitcom, blamed for creating a new genre known as Jiggle TV, debuted in 1977 to critical groans but huge ratings. Somers and costars Joyce Dewitt and John Ritter played roommates in this modern version of the classic farce. The show made instant stars of its leads, but Somers was a standout. Her effervescent Chrissie Snow spun Somers into an instant pinup and "it" girl. Her new luxurious lifestyle was a far cry from her previous struggle to merely survive. As an underemployed single mom, she was once so desperate to feed her son that she wrote bad checks in order to buy food, a scheme that landed her in jail. Good notices for a brief but memorable turn as the blond in the T-bird in the film *American Graffiti* led to Somers being cast in *Three's Company*, where her popularity quickly eclipsed her castmates'.

As the show reached peak ratings in 1980, Somers and husband Alan Hamel hired a Hollywood shark to manage her blossoming career. This superagent decided the time was right to demand more money (the actress was reportedly making $30,000 per episode). She had just won a People's Choice award and had been sitting atop the ratings game for a three-year stretch. During contract renegotiations, she allegedly hit producers for a raise to $150,000. (She later said the six-figure amount was used as a negotiating tactic: aim high and settle lower.) There were no multimillion-dollar *Friends* contracts in those days; Somers's demand was a precedent-setting and outlandish move, and it was not met with humor. The actress was instantly demoted, allowed to appear in only one minute of screen time per subsequent episode before she was fired altogether. The situation drove a wedge between the three musketeers of comedy television, with Dewitt and Ritter on one side and Somers alone on the other. Her costars didn't even speak to her during the taping of their last episode together. The devastated and bewildered actress was quickly replaced by one slender, blond, jiggly roommate after another.

SHE ALSO BECAME AN ADVOCATE FOR THOSE WHO SUFFERED CHILDHOOD ABUSE AT THE HANDS OF AN ALCOHOLIC, AS SHE DID WITH HER OWN FATHER

Somers's career was in a tailspin for some time following her expulsion from the sitcom, but it rebounded with a hit Las Vegas revue, another sitcom (*Step by Step*), several book deals (including a volume of poetry), and spokesmodel status for Thighmaster and Buttmaster. She also became an advocate for those who suffered childhood abuse at the hands of an alcoholic, as she did with her own father. Somers is currently battling a foe far more threatening than any network producer. Suffering from breast cancer, she has defied doctors' advice and injects herself daily with an alternative therapy called Iscador. By speaking out about her treatment and sharing her optimism for her prognosis, Suzanne Somers is now a much more serious type of poster girl. ✪

BRITNEY **SPEARS**

When Britney Spears sings "I'm Not That Innocent," she does it honestly. Nonetheless, the world's most famous virgin hangs on desperately to that persona despite its obvious antiquity.

Spears is one of America's hottest exports. She jettisoned to the front of the teen queen pack with the album *Baby One More Time* and her navel-baring videos. Unlike, say, Marilyn Manson, Spears is keeping many parents onside with their kids' musical preferences. Despite gyrating her nearly naked body around the stage like an exotic dancer, she continues to merit their approval through a repeated assertion that fulfills a parental ideal: she's a virgin and wants to remain so until she marries. Ideals are called as such because they're virtually

> **DESPITE GYRATING HER NEARLY NAKED BODY AROUND THE STAGE LIKE AN EXOTIC DANCER, SHE CONTINUES TO MERIT THEIR APPROVAL THROUGH A REPEATED ASSERTION THAT FULFILLS A PARENTAL IDEAL: SHE'S A VIRGIN AND WANTS TO REMAIN SO UNTIL SHE MARRIES**

unattainable, but Spears hung her hat on the virginity claim and has stood firm. However, her longtime secret romance with N'Sync heartthrob and former fellow Mousketeer and *Star Search* loser Justin Timberlake finally burst out from under its wraps. Soon, little chinks began to form in Spears's chastity belt.

Rival pop sensation Pink saw through the ruse. She told an interviewer she'd like to sleep with Timberlake and mocked Britney's virginity claims. Once word boomeranged to Britney, it hatched a good old-fashioned feud. The World Entertainment News Network reported Spears checked into the posh, $2,000 per night St. Martin's Lane Hotel in London, England, only to be greeted in the lobby with posters of her adversary. In a rare public display of diva-ism, Spears ignored the hotel manager's pleas and stomped out, choosing the even more expensive Imperial Suite at the Mandarin Oriental. In a fit of pique, Pink dealt the final volley by sending a bouquet of lilies to Britney's suite. Spears is allergic to that particular flower.

Several tabloids printed articles about Britney's mom's fierce protectiveness, namely that she apparently sent a bodyguard along on her daughter's dates with Timberlake. Those same tabs claimed to uncover evidence that

Britney and Justin were actually living together, even missing scheduled appearances to frolic in hotel rooms instead. The couple made headlines when they briefly broke up, allegedly because a pregnancy scare caused Spears to freak out and demand a wedding proposal from a panicky Timberlake.

The London *Sun* claimed to finally have proof that the "I'm Not a Girl, Not Yet a Woman" singer had vaulted into adult territory. It quoted an unnamed passenger on a flight from Atlanta to Los Angeles who had the good fortune to sit next to a very chatty Timberlake. The *Sun* claims the curly-haired popster told his seatmate that everyone thinks his cheeky ex-sweetie is a virgin, but she lost that status a while ago, adding, "And I should know."

Spears's saccharine image was already tarnished upon the circulation of a tape recorded backstage at Brazil's Rock in Rio Festival when Spears didn't realize her microphone was on. It revealed a Britney never before heard in public, spewing from a ribald vocabulary that would make a longshoreman blush. "Don't tell me they're just, like, letting the audience just f——ing stand out there like that," she ranted. "Oh my God, okay. Okay, let's hurry, y'all, seriously. This is retarded!"

Her film debut, in which she played someone other than herself, was the coming-of-age-on-the-road flick *Crossroads*. As light as a piece of cotton candy and nearly as sweet, the film nearly featured the public premiere of Britney's bare breasts. However, that experimental scene was left on the cutting room floor to preserve the movie's teen-friendly PG-13 rating and its star's highly buffed image as a good little girl who simply likes to pretend she's all grown up. We know better. ✪

DARRYL STRAWBERRY

Ask the landlord of any apartment complex and they'll tell you that renters aren't as responsible as owners. Renters ignore problems, leave messes, and simply don't care if they wreck the place because fixing it is ultimately someone else's predicament. Darryl Strawberry treats his body as if he's renting it.

The former major league baseball player has been hell-bent on self-destruction. Despite recent claims that he's prepared to pay his debt to society in full, Strawberry continues to put himself back in the debit column with frequent parole violations for partying.

Strawberry was convicted in 1999 of drug offences and alleged solicitation involving a prostitute. Since then he's broken the terms of his parole a half dozen times, once escaping a treatment facility and then leading authorities on a cross-Florida trip as he binged on various substances. On another occasion, he got hopped up on a combination of crack cocaine and the antianxiety medication Xanax. Major League Baseball issued a suspension and newspapers readied his obituary. In addition to his

> **IN 2002, THE EIGHT-TIME ALL-STAR WAS BACK BEFORE A JUDGE, ACCUSED OF HAVING SEX WITH A FELLOW REHAB RESIDENT AND TRADING ITEMS FOR CIGARETTES**

various addictions, he developed colon and stomach cancer, and endured the removal of one kidney and debilitating chemotherapy treatments.

In 2002, the eight-time All-Star was back before a judge, accused of having sex with a fellow rehab resident and trading items for cigarettes. No more suspended sentences or touchy-feely therapy centers for Strawberry; this time the judge played hardball with an eighteen-month jail sentence. Inexplicably, Strawberry's wife has continued to support her wayward spouse by appearing at his frequent court dates and remaining steadfastly stoic.

A return to baseball as a player is now out of the question for the forty-something three-time World Series champ. New York Yankees honcho George Steinbrenner has said he'd like to have Strawberry back with the team in a coaching capacity. For now Strawberry receives ongoing cancer and drug treatment in prison, where he's clad in a bright orange jumpsuit. It's a fashion statement that's far removed from the prestige of a professional ball player's uniform. ✪

BILLY BOB
THORNTON

In his opening monologue for a 2001–02 season episode of NBC's *Saturday Night Live*, Oscar winner Billy Bob Thornton owned up to an awareness of the obvious: people think he's weird.

Various reports have claimed the moviemaking triple threat—actor, screenwriter, and director—is a hyperactive package of oddities that eats only orange food, becomes strangely nervous while watching old movies, and has a paralyzing phobia that prevents him from being in the company of antique furniture. The good ol' boy from Arkansas admits to a vast collection of intermittent quirks, but the orange food diet is not among them. "I'd be dead if I only ate orange food," he told *Premiere* magazine. "There's carrots, oranges and papaya and pumpkin—that's it." But he's not completely unfamiliar with unusual meal plans. He did go on an all-potato diet in the early 1980s, which nearly cost him his life due to heart failure brought on by malnutrition. While slimming down for a movie role in 1998, Thornton says he "got anorexic" by losing 59 pounds off his six-foot frame, dropping to a scarily svelte 138 pounds. "Frankly, for a while there," he told the *LA Daily News* of his inability to eat, "I think I had a little mental problem."

> **THE ACTOR HAD NO CHOICE BUT TO ADMIT TO EVERY NOW AND AGAIN BORROWING A LITTLE SOMETHING FROM JOLIE'S LINGERIE DRAWER**

Thornton's eccentricity also extends to fashion. He confessed to occasionally slipping into the slinky underthings of his fifth wife, actress Angelina Jolie. That fact was uncovered when a fellow gym member noticed Thornton's lacy skivvies peeking out from under his sweatpants as he worked out. The actor had no choice but to admit to every now and again borrowing a little something from Jolie's lingerie drawer.

Referring to it as his "first love," Billy Bob was into music, specifically rock and roll, long before Hollywood came knocking. He has since been afforded the opportunity to take a break from films and return to his roots, releasing an album of quavering semi-country tunes and launching a concert tour. But beware potential groupies. Jolie publicly declared that if she caught Thornton cheating on her, she'd beat him up. It's likely the fantastically fit *Tomb Raider* star would also have saved a punch or two for his partner.

The wiry, tattooed thespian was already on wife number four, *Playboy* model Pietra Cherniak, as he hit it big in 1996. He had become what seemed like an overnight star by playing a mentally challenged man in his own independent film *Sling Blade*. Pietra and her ample cleavage were barely on the Hollywood scene for a year before she took the couple's two young sons and fled her marriage, alleging Thornton was physically abusive. The couple filed mutual restraining orders and while Pietra gave scads of scandalous interviews about how her husband allegedly treated her poorly (before their divorce agreement placed a gag order on her), Thornton remained mostly silent. She even claimed he sent her home early from an Oscar party so he could be alone with actress Laura Dern. Despite repeated denials of an affair, Thornton and Dern quickly set up house upon the end of Thornton's marriage to Pietra. He credits Dern, whom he now calls a "great girl," for helping him quit drinking.

Dern and Thornton cohabited for three years—until shortly after Billy Bob met Angelina, cast as his spouse in the movie *Pushing Tin*. Although he returned home when the film wrapped, Dern says he soon pulled a disappearing act to be with Jolie. "While I was away making a movie, my boyfriend got married and I never heard from him again," she said. Jolie and Thornton wed quickly and simply, both wearing jeans, in a May 2000 Las Vegas ceremony that cost $189. Although they've dried up, the newlywed couple's initial public declarations of love and passion were nearly overwhelming to a jaded public collectively crying out, "Enough already!" "Sex for us is almost too much," said Billy Bob. "I was watching her sleep and I had to restrain myself from literally squeezing her to death. You know when you love someone so much you could almost kill them?" We sure do. It's called murder and it's a very bad thing. Around their necks they both wore silver lockets containing small amounts of each other's blood as an unconventional and creepy symbol of their sacred devotion.

JOLIE AND THORNTON WED QUICKLY AND SIMPLY, BOTH WEARING JEANS, IN A MAY 2000 LAS VEGAS CEREMONY THAT COST $189

Regardless of how it appeared, the charismatic and kooky couple claimed to have an ordinary, normal marriage. A frustrated Thornton told CNN he wished people would "stop focusing on the electric chair in the basement that we don't have."

They gave us plenty to focus on in the summer of 2002 when pictures of a solo Jolie surfaced in the tabs, along with shots of their newly adopted baby boy from Cambodia, named Maddox. Whether it was the eccentricities, a sudden dousing of their "eternal" flame, or the pressure of being new parents, Jolie and Thornton finally admitted they had split in early 2002 and moved into different Los Angeles hotels. The separation came as Thornton went out on a concert tour, leaving Jolie at home with their new son. Jolie soon filed for divorce, making her a two-time divorcée. As Thornton signs off on his fifth divorce, it is clear there ought to be a law against him ever mouthing and mocking those sacred vows again. ✪

JOHN TRAVOLTA

Never underestimate the awesome power of the movie star. If his ego is rubbed the right way, like a mind-bending entertainment superhero he'll attract a green light and millions in financing. But it's a delicate balance. If he becomes unhappy, he can also sink a project like a stone. It's become part of Hollywood folklore that John Travolta orchestrated the now legendary demise of a highly anticipated movie.

Everyone's favorite sweathog was on a roll. After his career flatlined for a stretch post–*Welcome Back, Kotter* and –*Saturday Night Fever*, the comeback kid boomeranged in a big way as Chili Palmer, the Miami loan shark-turned-movie producer in 1995's *Get Shorty*. That ensemble comedy's success catapulted Travolta back into leading man status and he quickly inked a reported $17 million deal to star for Roman Polanski in *The Double*. That film was never made and Polanski now considers it a dead issue. Those are the undisputed facts. What serves as the filling in that gossip sandwich is a little more difficult to pin down for certain.

John Travolta in a scene from Battlefield Earth

Pampered Travolta and his temperamental director clashed very early on, during rehearsals. The actor later admitted Polanski told him he was "bad" and constantly berated him about his poor performance. Conversely, sources from the set claimed Travolta bristled at the notion of being expected to take direction from his director. The star quickly had his fill of the conflict and fashioned a family excuse to flee Paris and fly home. He claimed his son Jett had an ear infection that required devoted daddy's attention. Once he was back on US soil and his son's health had apparently improved, Travolta simply held out and refused to return to work if things didn't change. He offered the studio $3.5 million of his own money to have Polanski removed from the project, but was turned down.

Desperate to save their $60 million venture, producers quickly replaced Travolta with Steve Martin while launching a breech of contract lawsuit against their original star. With Travolta off the film and everything in disarray, costar Isabelle Adjani also took flight. Facing the loss of those marquee names and their assurance of success, everyone else also quickly lost interest.

Travolta finally spoke to *Paris Match* about his reasons for bursting the project's balloon. He said the script had changed and the final draft was for a movie that he didn't sign up for. The new version even included a nude scene. Travolta pointed out to *E!* that he had never appeared on film in the buff and he had no plans to start "now that I'm fat." The lawsuit and the star's countersuit were settled out of court, with terms kept confidential. *The Double* is no longer on the books as a "live" project. Curiously, Travolta later chose to devote a year of his life to making the Scientology stinkburger *Battlefield Earth*. Go figure. ✪

DONALD TRUMP

His first wife, Ivana—bleached, beehived, and sporting an expensive sense of entitlement—called him The Donald. As the extravagant 1980s drew to a close, The Donald tired of his thirteen-year-old marriage to the former model and took up with a younger version. He unwittingly orchestrated one of the most explosive and legendary first meetings between a wife and a mistress on the celebrity-filled ski hills of Aspen, Colorado.

Trump, Ivana, and their three children were holed up in Aspen for their annual family ski vacation. Unbeknownst to Ivana, The Donald had also squired away his new love, former Georgia beauty pageant winner Marla Maples, at the same resort. While his clan was otherwise engaged with the moguls, Donald could dart off for a tryst with the other woman. By this time, rumors of Donald and Marla had already evolved from a whisper to a scream, but Ivana, always the stoic socialite, was still trying to save face and her crumbling marriage.

Marla soon tired of being confined to her chalet. She was a see-and-be-seen kind of girl. Why should Donald have all the fun? So the fledgling actress the tabloids had come to call the Georgia Peach dressed up in her ski bunny best and headed for the hills. Most accounts of the infamous incident claimed it was Ivana who spotted Marla first and in den mother fashion, furiously snow-plowed over to her rival. The nasty confrontation included screaming by both parties, with Donald's ringing ears caught in the middle. He was a panicked referee in a fight that had no rules. Within full earshot of fascinated fellow skiers, the shrieking dialogue went something like, "Leave my husband alone!" countered with, "We're in love!" Somehow the catfight was contained without bloodshed. Donald and Ivana separated two months later, and so began a bitter thirteen-month battle over her financial settlement. Mrs. Trump reportedly ended up with between twenty-five and fifty million of The Donald's dollars.

Maples and Trump were on-again, off-again for a few years. They eventually married after the birth of their daughter in 1993, then separated in 1997. Reports alleged there was another woman involved in the breakup, model Carla Bruni, who also contributed to the demise of the Mick Jagger-Jerry Hall union. Another account claimed the happy Trump home never recovered from Marla's midmarriage, beachside tryst with a muscular bodyguard. Like Donald's first divorce, the split with Marla was bitter. Maples contested the terms of their prenuptial agreement, which limited her share of his billions to single-digit millions. Trump said it was "pretty tacky" that she later auctioned off the 7.5-carat diamond engagement ring he had given her.

> **HE UNWITTINGLY ORCHESTRATED ONE OF THE MOST EXPLOSIVE AND LEGENDARY FIRST MEETINGS BETWEEN A WIFE AND A MISTRESS ON THE CELEBRITY-FILLED SKI HILLS OF ASPEN, COLORADO**

Still single, The Donald hasn't lost his eye for beautiful women. As owner of the Miss USA Pageant, he's assured of getting up close and personal with each year's new crop of American beauties. ✪

IKE TURNER

On his website, Ike Turner arrogantly and incorrectly titles himself the Father of Rock and Roll. True, he has been inducted into the Rock and Roll Hall of Fame. It's also true that he performed on some rock classics. In the 1960s, he delivered his great discovery—Tina Turner—to the world. According to her bestselling autobiography I, Tina, Ike literally beat that talent out of her. Acting as a conduit for Tina's blaring voice and sexy moves was indeed Ike's most positive contribution to music.

In I, Tina, the author, née Anna Mae Bullock, recalled her reaction at age sixteen when she first saw Ike Turner close-up: "God, he's ugly." But the piano player for bluesman Sonny Boy Williamson was also charismatic and full of big ideas. It wasn't long before Tina was sleeping with him and agreeing to become his umpteenth wife while they dreamed of singing stardom.

The dream quickly became a nightmare. Ike and Tina's marriage wasn't deemed legal because the groom hadn't bothered to divorce his previous wife. (Some accounts put his current betrothal total at thirteen.) Their stars rose through the 1960s and early 1970s with a string of hits including "Nutbush City Limits" and "Proud Mary," but success didn't calm Ike's nasty temper. The emotional abuse he heaped on Tina and the breakneck tour schedule he insisted they keep were exhausting for her. The physical assaults he allegedly subjected her to stretched from "run-of-the-mill" punches and slaps to burns from lit cigarettes to broken bones. Through it all, Ike flaunted his frequent liaisons with other women, torturing Tina by telling her she didn't compare to them. A sex addict before the term was invented, Ike claims to have had his first sexual experience at age six. From that moment, he never looked back.

As Ike & Tina Turner & the Ikettes reached their zenith on the pop charts, Tina contemplated suicide as her only way out. Instead, she wisely chose to leave Ike with only the clothes on her back and thirty-six cents to her name. Ike chased her with menacing lawyers, but Tina stayed one step ahead. She let her husband keep everything from their lives together in exchange for dropping the lawsuits. She got a truly fresh start. Tina survived the leanest times imaginable to eventually launch an explosive solo career.

> **A SEX ADDICT BEFORE THE TERM WAS INVENTED, IKE CLAIMS TO HAVE HAD HIS FIRST SEXUAL EXPERIENCE AT AGE SIX**

"I'm not the dude you see in the movie," Ike told an interviewer about Tina's biopic *What's Love Got to Do with It*, "not even close." The hit flick of 1993 painted Ike as a perfect loser in life, love, and business. There's a Titanic-sized chasm between Tina's and Ike's versions of events concerning their relationship. However, his drug convictions (cocaine was his substance of choice) and jail sentences put a sizeable dent in his credibility.

Many years after their divorce, her scars healed and her emotions in check, Tina spoke of the sinusitis that plagued her, a result of having had her "face bashed in" during her marriage. Following surgery to correct the condition, "I ended up with ... another nose," she said. And a fine nose it is.

Now retired, Tina remains one of the world's most beloved stars, who enjoyed a tremendous career revival in the 1980s with songs like "What's Love Got to Do with It" and "Better Be Good to Me." We've heard precious little from Ike, although he continues to record. Tina spun heartbreak into happiness, living an idyllic life with a longtime love in a posh hideaway in the south of France. Ike continues to claim that he's being denied his rightful place by those who chronicle rock's evolution. In 1991, Ike and Tina Turner were inducted together into the Rock and Roll Hall of Fame. Although Ike appears alongside his former wife and partner in music history, it's easy to assess which half of the duo actually had the lioness's share of the talent. ✪

MIKE **TYSON**

Ear-biting, temper-losing, leg-gnawing, child-eating ... wait, that last one hasn't moved beyond a threat—we hope. Mike Tyson's many scuffles in and out of the ring prove that he is indeed all bite.

Attempts to push Tyson out of boxing for good have failed. He's been a blight on the sport as well as one of its biggest stars. Tyson's unpredictable and unforgivable antics on both sides of the squared circle have attracted fans like witnesses to a devastating roadside accident. But they've also left a dull finish of shame on the man himself and those who have supported him.

Except for his bank account balance, the former boxing champ's fortunes have taken a nosedive in recent years. The compact and (some say) crazy fighter discovered his talent for landing jabs when he was twelve while serving time in a correction facility for armed robbery. The realization saved him from the street gang that was leading him ever deeper into a life of crime. He tried unsuccessfully to make the 1984 US Olympic team and decided to turn pro instead. Undefeated in his first year at the age of twenty, he became the youngest athlete ever to hold the heavyweight champ title. Iron Mike grew into the most exciting thing to get into the ring

> ON A NATIONAL TELEVISION APPEARANCE, TYSON GENTLY STROKED HIS WIFE'S NECK WHILE SHE CALMLY DESCRIBED THEIR LIFE TOGETHER AS "A LIVING HELL"

since Muhammad Ali, although he wasn't nearly The Champ's equal when it came to classy behavior. As his notoriety rose, so did the wealth and persona of his louder-than-life former manager Don King, whose straight-up hairstyle makes him appear permanently, cartoonishly frightened. King's client was a top draw on pay-per-view, raking in tens of millions. If Mike Tyson wanted to fight—anyone, anytime—scads of fans coughed up $29.95 to witness the spectacle from the comfort of their own La-Z-Boy chairs.

But the thrill ride started to derail more than a decade ago. Some say it began with a whirlwind 1988 marriage to actress Robin Givens and their headline-making divorce barely a year later. On a national television appearance, Tyson gently stroked his wife's neck while she calmly described their life together as "a living hell." When they split, Tyson leveled gold-digging allegations against the young starlet and her mother, while Givens offered accounts of alleged beatings and infidelities by her boxer husband. Givens made a major show of refusing alimony, but promptly launched a $125 million libel lawsuit against Tyson, who had allegedly called his ex-mother-in-law "the slime of the slime" in a newspaper interview. Robin settled the suit for a reported $2.5 million.

The marriage served as a hard lesson for Tyson, who was on a desperate search for someone to call family following abandonment by his father and the deaths of his mother and both of his original trainers. In 1992 he was imprisoned, serving half of a six-year sentence for raping a Miss Black America contestant. (An investigation following another rape claim at Tyson's Las Vegas home many years later was closed without charges, due to insufficient evidence.)

Friends said the penitentiary changed Iron Mike. He converted to Islam, read *Malcolm X*, and his badass attitude underwent a revolution. But the "new" Mike Tyson was merely a temporary replacement, which he proved when he got back into the ring. Tyson went on to earn hundreds of millions more in high-profile bouts, the most famous being a 1997 melee with Evander Holyfield during which Tyson actually bit off and spit out part of his opponent's ear. Holyfield claimed he became a meal only because of Tyson's sheer desperation once he realized he was clearly losing the match. The Nevada State Boxing Commission, not amused by Tyson's act of cannibalism, fined him $3 million and banned him from fighting for one year.

> **THE ESPN SPORTS NETWORK QUOTED TYSON TAUNTING UPCOMING OPPONENT LENNOX LEWIS BY SHOUTING, "I WANT YOUR HEART! I WANT TO EAT YOUR CHILDREN!"**

Horrified to find himself in arrears to the IRS for $13 million upon his return to the ring, Tyson blamed Don King for allegedly siphoning off more dough than he was entitled to. The dynamic duo of pro fighting disentangled in a split as bitter and overrun with lawyers as the nastiest divorce.

Tyson simply couldn't keep a cap on his anger. A 1999 road rage incident landed him briefly back behind bars. The following year, a thirty-eight-second fight against Lou Savarese ended with Tyson belting the referee. The ESPN sports network quoted Tyson taunting upcoming opponent Lennox Lewis by shouting, "I want your heart! I want to eat your children!" Ears just weren't enough to satisfy him anymore.

Iron Mike was at it again during a January 2002 news conference to announce the April date and Las Vegas location for the Tyson-Lewis matchup. He came at Lewis, throwing a punch at a bodyguard and biting his rival's left leg. Tyson launched an obscenity-laced tirade at a reporter who shouted, "Put him in a straightjacket!" The boxer later claimed that both camps had agreed to stage the phony fracas to hype the fight, except word somehow hadn't made it to Lewis's entourage. The State of Nevada was fed up and denied Tyson the right to fight in Las Vegas. The search for a new site found Memphis, Tennessee, agreeable to June 8, though organizers outlined strict conditions for the event. However, Tyson's posturing and boasting didn't translate into the ring. He lost to Lewis in humiliating fashion and meekly requested a rematch. The prefight prancing egomaniac was reduced to a limping loser after being knocked out in the eighth round. To top off the experience, the celebrity-filled audience wasn't even a sellout. The match did, however, set a record for the biggest haul ever for a pay-per-view event, at $103 million.

His second wife has divorced him and although he'll continue to fight, he'll never again be a contender for the title. With his dreams of once again wearing the championship belt no longer alive, a new facial tattoo, and his family life in shambles, it remains to be seen if money alone can buy happiness for Mike Tyson. ✪

ROGER **WATERS**

It may have been the only time in the history of rock and roll that a spitball spawned the idea for a concept album. Then again, we *are* talking about rock and roll, so one can't be entirely sure. But it was only after Pink Floyd cofounder and songwriter Roger Waters's gnawing inner turmoil was unleashed on a fan that he conceived the enduring classic *The Wall*.

Loads of rock stars dread performing in huge stadiums. Intimacy is lost in the echoes. The sound is often tinny and thin as it travels through so much extra space. In a cavernous coliseum, the human connection that compels musicians to create their art is broken. In the late 1970s, Britain's premiere art rockers were touring the world, buoyed by the insane international success of the album *Dark Side of the Moon* and supporting their new creation, *Animals*. As Waters tells it, the invisible bond between band and audience in their previous, smaller club dates was "magical." There was no such satisfaction for

Waters on the arena tour. By the time Pink Floyd touched down at Montreal's Olympic Stadium and played for a crowd of eighty thousand plus, his frustration was nearing a boil.

Waters says he realized he was bottoming out as a grinning young fan clamored toward him, scaling the fence designed to keep the masses away from the masters. Suddenly enraged, Waters spit at him. His aim was true. The loogie landed squarely on the face of the startled Floydite. It was a turning point for the axeman, as his imagination flooded with sinister thoughts of lobbing bombs into an unsuspecting, adoring crowd and reveling in their delicious, momentary surprise. Later he conceived the concept of constructing a huge wall, a literal and physical manifestation of the overwhelming detached feeling he routinely experienced while singing and playing on stage in huge, sold-out venues. Its symbolism also extended to blocking off the nasty or difficult parts of one's life, brick by brick, until they are easily ignored. Naturally, the wall eventually has to come down.

> **MORE THAN TWENTY YEARS AFTER ITS RELEASE, THE WALL REMAINS AMONG THE TOP FIVE BEST-SELLING ALBUMS IN THE WORLD. AND IT ALL BEGAN WITH A BAD GIG AND A BALL OF SPIT**

Bandmate Richard Wright attests that Waters's attack of conscience didn't completely deflate his rock star ego. Frustrated by the keyboardist's admitted lack of contribution to the project, Waters tossed him out of the band. However, Wright hadn't yet recorded all of his tracks for the new album's songs when he was unceremoniously turfed. Tempers eventually cooled and Wright returned to the fold.

The privilege of achieving rock stardom was suddenly an empty shell for Roger Waters, who literally walked away from the band—hard-won royalty agreements in his back pocket, of course. Still, more than twenty years after its release, The Wall remains among the top five best-selling albums in the world. And it all began with a bad gig and a ball of spit. ✪

OSCAR WILDE

Talk about ancient history. Literary great Oscar Wilde did hard time more than a century ago for behavior that barely bears notice anymore.

Born in 1854, Wilde was the passionate, prolific, Oxford-educated child of a surgeon and a poet. In the late 1800s, he was Britain's leading playwright and favorite writing son. But for Wilde, notoriety came before fame.

As a sharply dressed man-about-town whose signature costume included a plush green velvet coat and a fresh sunflower peeking out from a button-hole, Wilde didn't lack for self-confidence. While entering the US for a year-long tour, he is reported to have replied cheekily to a customs officer in New York City who asked if he was bringing anything into the county: "I have nothing to declare except my genius." He was a sweet and doting husband to a beautiful fan named Constance, who bore him two sons. But a seduction and a subsequent affair with a randy family friend awakened the playwright's

A SUBSEQUENT AFFAIR WITH A RANDY FAMILY FRIEND AWAKENED THE PLAYWRIGHT'S SUPPRESSED LONGINGS FOR THE COMPANY OF SAME-SEX PARTNERS — AN ACT THAT WAS ILLEGAL AT THE TIME

suppressed longings for the company of same-sex partners—an act that was illegal at the time. He later fell in love with a materialistic and adventurous young man named Lord Alfred Douglas, nicknamed Bosie, the son of the eighth Marquess of Queensberry.

It was during the heady first years of their relationship that Wilde found tremendous inspiration and wrote most of his best-loved works. He abandoned his family and in order to please his lover, joined him in employing the sexual favors of "rent boys." The Marquess, angered over the "immoral acts" involving his son and the writer, wrote Wilde a scathing, accusatory letter. Bosie seized upon Oscar's shock and anger to enact his own revenge on a father he already hated. He steadily eroded Oscar's better judgment and persuaded his lover to sue for libel. It was a worrisome gamble, as Wilde's homosexuality—still against the law—would be revealed in open court in the process. The first jury failed to reach a verdict. The second sided with the defendant, and the case turned about on Wilde's character after several of the young prostitutes testified to his many indiscretions.

Convicted of gross indecency, Wilde was sentenced to two years of hard labor in a squalid prison. Amid disgusting conditions, including a lack of plumbing and barely edible gruel as his only food, he was frequently ill. The toll disease took on his body during those twenty-four long months contributed to his eventual demise. Released in 1897, he never returned to his former spirited self. His once flamboyant personality was shattered. Wilde's wife persuaded him to bid Bosie a permanent adieu, which he attempted for her sake. After her death, Wilde once again set off to be with his soul mate, although their reunion lasted only a few short weeks. Most other friends and supporters abandoned him in disgust. Broke and relying on the kindness of strangers for sustenance and shelter, the humiliated and ailing writer hid from scorn by adopting the pseudonym Sebastian Melmoth. In 1900 he succumbed to meningitis and died nearly penniless in a cheap Paris hotel.

Wilde's works have weathered the decades well. *The Importance of Being Earnest* and *An Ideal Husband* are now major motion pictures. Several films have chronicled his life, including *Wilde*, starring Stephen Fry in the title role. Tightly wound Victorian mores are at least partly to blame for the downfall of Oscar Wilde. But so is a manipulative romantic relationship, which is as likely to occur today as it was more than 100 years ago. ✪

SEAN YOUNG

In the late 1980s she appeared in sultry personas on-screen in movies like *No Way Out*. Off-screen she became known as the ex-girlfriend from hell. Legend has it that she and actor James Woods had an intense but brief on-set affair while shooting the druggie flick *The Boost*, in which they played spouses. When the fling ended badly, Woods alleged Young's new role was that of a stalker.

Woods proudly carries a reputation for being one of Hollywood's most generously endowed stars. He has employed his greatest asset in romances with beautiful actresses, including Heather Graham and Nicolette Sheridan. After shooting on *The Boost* wrapped, Woods disentangled himself from Young and headed home to his steady. He wasn't about to disturb his domestic bliss for a bit of on-the-job tomfoolery. But Young was having none of Woods's wham-bam-thank-you-ma'am attitude.

Strange things began to happen around the Woods household. Dismembered dolls appeared on the doorstep. Harassing phone calls came in the dead of night. Photos of mutilated animals appeared in the mailbox. Woods added two and two and came up with Young. His accusations made for fine tabloid fodder, as did his lawsuit against her. She chose to respond in the court of public opinion, making the chat show rounds to state her innocence. Miraculously, the dolls stopped showing up, as did the photos and phone calls. Woods married and then quickly divorced his girlfriend. Emotions subsided and the lawsuit was dropped. Young married an actor she has just recently divorced.

Splitting up with her husband apparently sparked a cleaning spree in Young's life. In 2002, she used her own website to sell off some of her personal things, including her copy of a script for *The Boost* and her own baby blanket, among other items. One article that drew a little too much interest was her on-set diary from *The Boost*, in which she offered a detailed account of her first meeting with Woods. She revealed she was so anxious when the day came that "I grabbed my teddy bear because I felt very nervous and scared." The diary goes on to explain how the duo hit it off when they discovered their mutual dislike for director Oliver Stone. Young writes, "He [Woods] said that he and Oliver had to be physically restrained from one another on the set of *Salvador*." As soon as word reached the media, the diary was pulled from the sale.

> **IN THE LATE 1980S SHE APPEARED IN SULTRY PERSONAS ON-SCREEN IN MOVIES LIKE *NO WAY OUT*. OFF-SCREEN SHE BECAME KNOWN AS THE EX-GIRLFRIEND FROM HELL**

Young developed a reputation for being difficult to work with, and movie offers thinned out. Determined to be cast as Catwoman in 1992's *Batman Returns*, she appeared—unannounced—at the Warner Bros. studio in full cat regalia to lobby for an audition. Instead, she was escorted off the lot. But this cat had one more life. The actress made a scheduled appearance on Joan Rivers's short-lived late-night talk show wearing a black mask and literally begged for the part. The stunts didn't work and Michelle Pfeiffer was awarded the role of the fantastic feline.

In the decade or so since her last outrageous exploit, Sean Young has mellowed, become a mom, and faded into the endless sea of competent midrange actresses. They are the ones who have adequate talent for getting steady work but not the right stuff for threatening Julia Roberts's box office clout or Meryl Streep's lofty place in cinematic history. ✪

(DIS)HONORABLE
MENTIONS

What follows is a peek into the lives of a few stars who came just slightly off their hinges. Though their behavior wasn't bad enough to warrant entry into the tantrum-throwers' Hall of Fame, each still merits a mention for the explosive, if temporary, furor they inspired.

Ben Affleck

Pearl Harbor star Ben Affleck insulted British fans (and nonfans for that matter) during an interview with Channel 4's *Big Breakfast* show. While attending the film's glitzy May 2001 premier in Hawaii, Affleck said he thought the US should steer clear of the Monarchy because he didn't want "alcoholic ninety-year-olds running the country." The Oscar winner went on to describe British women as "quite loose" and "women of easy virtue," but was quick to add that *Pearl Harbor* costar Kate Beckinsale was an "exception." Ironically, just three months after the interview, Affleck checked himself into the Promises rehab facility in Malibu, California, to receive treatment for "alcohol abuse."

Stephen Bing

Movie producer Steve Bing (*Get Carter*) impregnated and then humiliated supermodel and actress Elizabeth Hurley, claiming someone else fathered her son Damian. DNA tests proved otherwise, supporting Hurley's claim that their relationship was exclusive—at least on her end. Bing also cried foul over accusations that he was the father of a little girl with Lisa Bonder Kerkorkian, ex-wife of MGM studio mogul Kirk Kerkorkian. Bing launched a billion-dollar lawsuit after his DNA was allegedly tested without his consent. When it was proven that he was the father and Kerkorkian was sterile, Bing withdrew the lawsuit.

Tommy Lee Jones

Men in Black II star Tommy Lee Jones hates T-shirts and clothing labels. During an interview and photo shoot to promote the film with *Entertainment Weekly* magazine, Jones reportedly acted "horrifically," even after his publicist did a sweep of the room to make sure the offending Ts and labels were removed. The publicist warned that if things weren't just so, "he'll walk off the set." The interviewer was allegedly overheard telling colleagues, "I wish I had the balls to air the outtakes, to prove what a bastard he is." Jones apparently goes ballistic if he comes into contact with the items because "labels freak him out."

Toby Keith

Country singer Toby Keith missed the point when he was invited—and then uninvited—to open a Fourth of July celebration on the ABC network. Keith insisted on playing his September 11 reaction song "Courtesy of the Red, White and Blue (The Angry American)," which producers nixed because of the lyric, "You'll be sorry you messed with the US of A / Cuz we'll put a boot in your ass. / It's the American way." Keith railed against show host, news anchor Peter Jennings, speculating to CNN that Jennings's Canadian roots were at the core of his objections to the song, which Keith said reflected the anger Americans were feeling. Producers countered that their show was meant to be a celebration of American music; Keith's musical rant against terrorism simply didn't fit the theme or set the tone they were aiming for. The program went on without him.

Jennifer Lopez

She may sing that "Love Don't Cost a Thing," but keeping singer and actress Jennifer Lopez happy is a very pricey endeavor. The "personal requests" in her contract rider call for some very specific items to be stocked in her dressing room and hotel suite, including sheets with a certain thread count, full-length mirrors in every room, and lit candles. She even asks that an expensive fragrance be sprayed into her path as she walks. The star of *The Wedding Planner* insists on as many as ten hotel suites to accommodate her entourage of sixty, even if they all haven't traveled with her. Lopez loves to be surrounded by white. She requires dressing rooms replete with white lilies and roses, white drapes, white couches, and accents of white silk, muslin, and lace. A CD player and a VCR must be at her disposal (what, no DVD?) and while on location, her forty-foot trailer (minimum) must be stocked with Evian water at room temperature and Snapple Raspberry Iced Tea. Lopez says she's worth the trouble because she "works harder" than anybody else.

Michael Ovitz

At one time he was one of the most powerful men in Hollywood. Michael Ovitz, the former head of the CAA Talent Agency in Los Angeles told *Vanity Fair* magazine his fall from the top was at the hands of a group of Hollywood players known as the Gay Mafia. Ovitz claims the merry mob was ostensibly led by Dreamworks cofounder David Geffen, and it systematically conspired to ruin him. Ovitz later apologized for the disparaging remarks about homosexuals in *Variety*, but it was too late: "Gay Mafia" is now a permanent part of our lexicon.

Julia Roberts

Actress Julia Roberts is arguably the most powerful woman in Hollywood, and she wielded that clout in her personal life when marrying cameraman Danny Moder became her goal. Moder, then wed for four years to makeup artist Vera, was having difficulty extricating himself from his marriage; Vera was reluctant to let go. Roberts decided to shame the first Mrs. Moder into releasing her hold. The Oscar-winning actress had a T-shirt with the quip "A Low Vera" created and then ensured she was photographed wearing it. The scene was a scarily similar to Goliath stomping on David—a totally unfair fight. Roberts also reportedly shelled out tens of thousands of dollars to pay Vera to divorce Danny. With the ink barely dry on the divorce decree, Moder and Roberts wed on Independence Day, July 4, 2002.

BIBLIOGRAPHY

Most of the source material for this book was compiled from various issues, editions, and postings in the following pool of publications, television shows, and websites:

Chronicle (Augusta)	*People*
Entertainment Weekly	*Premiere*
Esquire	*Sports Illustrated*
Inside Edition	*Sun* (London)
Los Angeles Times	*Time*
Mirror (London)	*Toronto Sun*
National Enquirer	*Vanity Fair*
New York Post	*Variety*
News of the World	www.ananova.com
Newsweek	www.eonline.com
Penthouse	www.foxnews.com

Alternately, the references listed below were the sole source of information for certain celebrities and incidents:

Allen, Tim. *Don't Stand Too Close to a Naked Man*. New York: Hyperion, 1994.

Arnold, Roseanne. *My Lives*. New York: Random House Audio Books, 1994. Cassette.

Carey, Drew. *Dirty Jokes and Beer*. New York: Hyperion, 1997.

Crawford, Christina. *Mommie Dearest*. New York: William Morrow, 1978.

Crawford, Sue. *Ozzy Unauthorized*. London: Michael O'Mara Books, 2002.

Ezterhas, Joe. *American Rhapsody*. New York: Alfred A. Knopf, 2000.

Giuliano, Geoffrey. *Sinatra: A Tribute.* New York: Bantam Doubleday Dell Audio Publishing, 1998. Cassette.

Jackson, LaToya and Patricia Romanowski. *Growing Up in the Jackson Family.* New York: E. P. Dutton, 1990.

Kelley, Kitty. *His Way: The Unauthorized Biography of Frank Sinatra.* New York: Bantam, 1986.

Linson, Art. *What Just Happened?: Bitter Hollywood Tales from the Front Line.* New York: Bloomsbury, 2002.

Wilson, Earl. *Sinatra: An Unauthorized Biography.* New York: Macmillan, 1976.

ABOUT THE AUTHOR

Lisa Brandt is a veteran broadcaster, celebrity interviewer, and entertainment writer. She has contributed to several magazines and writes a biweekly newspaper column, "The Public Detective." She lives in Burlington, Ontario.